2nd Conference of the Asia-Pacific Chapter of the Association for Computational Linguistics and the 12th International Joint Conference on Natural Language Processing (AACL-IJCNLP 2022)

System Demonstrations

Online
20-23 November 2022

ISBN: 978-1-7138-6311-3

Printed from e-media with permission by:

Curran Associates, Inc.
57 Morehouse Lane
Red Hook, NY 12571

Some format issues inherent in the e-media version may also appear in this print version.

Printed with permission by Curran Associates, Inc. (2023)

Association for Computational Linguistics
209 N. Eighth Street
Stroudsburg, Pennsylvania 18360

Phone: 1-570-476-8006
Fax: 1-570-476-0860

acl@aclweb.org

Additional copies of this publication are available from:

Curran Associates, Inc.
57 Morehouse Lane
Red Hook, NY 12571 USA
Phone: 845-758-0400
Fax: 845-758-2633
Email: curran@proceedings.com
Web: www.proceedings.com

AACL-IJCNLP 2022

The 2nd Conference of the Asia-Pacific Chapter of the Association for Computational Linguistics & the 12th International Joint Conference on Natural Language Processing

Proceedings of System Demonstrations

November 20 - 23, 2022

Introduction

Welcome to the proceedings of the system demonstrations session. This volume contains the papers of the system demonstrations presented at the 2nd Conference of the Asia-Pacific Chapter of the Association for Computational Linguistics and the 12th International Joint Conference on Natural Language Processing (AACL-IJCNLP) on November 20 - 23, 2022.

The AACL-IJCNLP 2022 demonstrations track invited submissions ranging from early research prototypes to mature production-ready systems. We received 17 submissions this year (an increase of 30% over the previous edition of the conference), of which 10 were selected for inclusion in the program (acceptance rate of 58.8%) after review by at least two members of the programme committee.

We would like to express our gratitude to the members of the programme committee. The candidate papers were selected by the demo chairs based on the feedback received by reviewers. Demonstration papers will be presented at the conference during the two poster sessions.

Maria Liakata
Wray Buntine
AACL-IJCNLP 2022 Demo Chairs

Demonstration Co-Chairs

Maria Liakata, Queen Mary University of London, UK
Wray Buntine, Vin University, Hanoi, Vietnam

Table of Contents

Conference Program

VScript: Controllable Script Generation with Visual Presentation
Ziwei Ji, Yan Xu, I-Tsun Cheng, Samuel Cahyawijaya, Rita Frieske, Etsuko Ishii, Min Zeng, Andrea Madotto and Pascale Fung

TexPrax: A Messaging Application for Ethical, Real-time Data Collection and Annotation
Lorenz Stangier, Ji-Ung Lee, Yuxi Wang, Marvin Müller, Nicholas Frick, Joachim Metternich and Iryna Gurevych

PicTalky: Augmentative and Alternative Communication for Language Developmental Disabilities
Chanjun Park, Yoonna Jang, Seolhwa Lee, Jaehyung Seo, Kisu Yang and Heuiseok Lim

UKP-SQuARE v2: Explainability and Adversarial Attacks for Trustworthy QA
Rachneet Sachdeva, Haritz Puerto, Tim Baumgärtner, Sewin Tariverdian, Hao Zhang, Kexin Wang, Hossain Shaikh Saadi, Leonardo F. R. Ribeiro and Iryna Gurevych

TaxFree: a Visualization Tool for Candidate-free Taxonomy Enrichment
Irina Nikishina, Ivan Andrianov, Alsu Vakhitova and Alexander Panchenko

F-coref: Fast, Accurate and Easy to Use Coreference Resolution
Shon Otmazgin, Arie Cattan and Yoav Goldberg

PIEKM: ML-based Procedural Information Extraction and Knowledge Management System for Materials Science Literature
Huichen Yang

BiomedCurator: Data Curation for Biomedical Literature
Mohammad Golam Sohrab, Khoa N.A. Duong, Ikeda Masami, Goran Topić, Yayoi Natsume-Kitatani, Masakata Kuroda, Mari Nogami Itoh and Hiroya Takamura

Text Characterization Toolkit (TCT)
Daniel Simig, Tianlu Wang, Verna Dankers, Peter Henderson, Khuyagbaatar Batsuren, Dieuwke Hupkes and Mona Diab

Meeting Decision Tracker: Making Meeting Minutes with De-Contextualized Utterances
Shumpei Inoue, Hy Nguyen, Hoang Pham, Tsungwei Liu and Minh-Tien Nguyen

VScript: Controllable Script Generation with Visual Presentation

Ziwei Ji, Yan Xu, I-Tsun Cheng, Samuel Cahyawijaya, Rita Frieske, Etsuko Ishii, Min Zeng, Andrea Madotto, Pascale Fung
Center for Artificial Intelligence Research (CAiRE)
Hong Kong University of Science and Technology
zjiad@connect.ust.hk, pascale@ece.ust.hk

Abstract

In order to offer a customized script tool and inspire professional scriptwriters, we present **VScript**. It is a controllable pipeline that generates complete scripts, including dialogues and scene descriptions, as well as presents visually using video retrieval. With an interactive interface, our system allows users to select genres and input starting words that control the theme and development of the generated script. We adopt a hierarchical structure, which first generates the plot, then the script and its visual presentation. A novel approach is also introduced to plot-guided dialogue generation by treating it as an inverse dialogue summarization. The experiment results show that our approach outperforms the baselines on both automatic and human evaluations, especially in genre control.

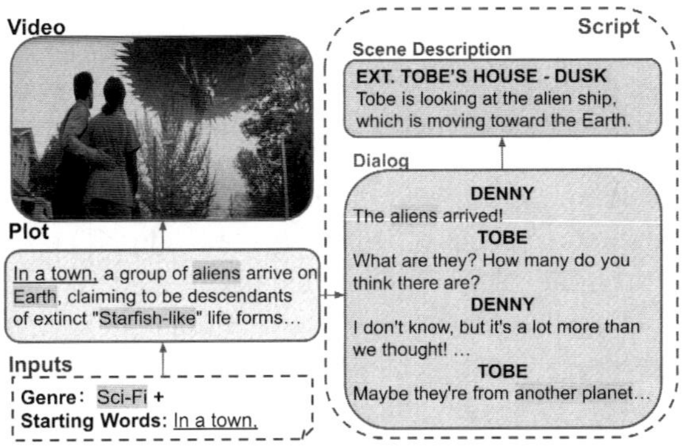

Figure 1: An example of the generated script (right) with its visual presentation (top left) from **VScript**. Given the inputs, i.e., genre and starting words, a plot is generated, which guides the generation of a script consisting of a scene description and a dialogue. The words highlighted in pink show the belongingness to the given genre (`Sci-Fi`). Additionally, the video vividly presents the script.

1 Introduction

Artificial intelligence (AI) introduces significant changes in the creation of artworks, such as stylistic painting (Kotovenko et al., 2019), poem writing (Hu and Sun, 2020), music composition (Dong et al., 2018), and converting the perception of creativity. In particular, AI can assist in streamlining the art-making process and give humans fresh inspirations (Anantrasirichai and Bull, 2021), and one plausible application is scriptwriting. As a specific literary form, the script is indispensable in cinematography and theater (Owens and Millerson, 2012; Walker et al., 2012). To enable the collaboration between scriptwriter and AI, an automatic script generation system must equip with three aspects. First, the system must generate a complete script consisting of chronological scene descriptions and dialogues. Second, the system should provide controllability, e.g., customize script genre or storyline (Cavazza and Young, 2017). Third, as a creative work, the generated script is required to have rich and diverse content.

While Zhu et al. (2020) propose a narrative-guided script generation task, they only focus on retrieving dialogue utterances and omit scene description, an essential component of a script describing the environment and characters. Other works (Chen et al., 2019; Bensaid et al., 2021) take inspiration from storyboarding and utilize a series of images to demonstrate stories. Nevertheless, no prior work presents scripts by leveraging video, a more informative and attractive medium. In addition, prior works lack the ability to control certain elements, such as genre. Controllable generation systems (Keskar et al., 2019; Dathathri et al., 2019; Madotto et al., 2020) can help to allow the customization of scripts based on user preferences.

In this paper, we present **VScript**, a controllable script generation system that includes all essential components of a script. We adopt a hierarchical structure for our framework by implementing high-level planning (Fan et al., 2018) and following the guidelines of video-making processes (Owens and Millerson, 2012). As shown in Figure 2, **VScript** is composed by **Script Generation** and **Visual Presentation** modules. The examples of correspond-

Proceedings of the 2nd Conference of the Asia-Pacific Chapter of the Association for Computational Linguistics and the 12th International Joint Conference on Natural Language Processing: System Demonstrations, pages 1–8
November 20–23, 2022.

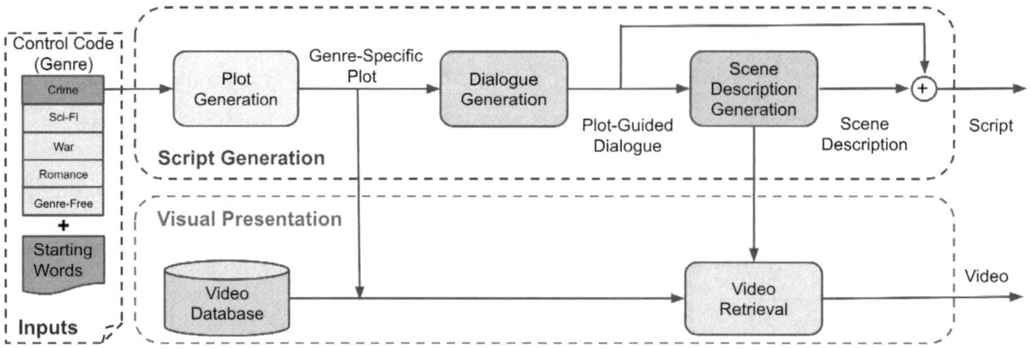

Figure 2: **VScript** consists of two modules, i.e., **Script Generation** and **Visual Presentation**. Given the genre and starting words, the Script Generation module generates a genre-specific plot, dialogues, and scene descriptions. The Visual Presentation module searches for a relevant visualization from a large video database.

ing components are in Figure 1. **Script Generation** module consists of three sub-modules: 1) plot generation, 2) dialogue generation, and 3) scene description generation. Firstly, the system generates a genre-specific plot as an outline of the script. To avoid generating aimless scripts, the system allows users to provide some brief initial information, i.e., genre and the beginning of the plot, for a high degree of control over the script on the genre and story trend. Secondly, we conduct a zero-shot plot-guided dialogue generation by framing the problem as an inverse task of abstractive dialogue summarization. Finally, we generate scene descriptions based on the dialogues to produce complete scripts. **Visual Presentation** module vividly demonstrates the script by retrieving videos from an automatically constructed video database. It can serve as a rough visual draft to improve users' engagement and help scriptwriters rapidly iterate ideas.

To our best knowledge, we are the first to tackle the controllable script generation task, which controls a script's genre and storyline. We also introduce a practical approach for plot-guided dialogue generation by treating the task as inverse dialogue summarization, which improves the diversity of the generated dialogue while maintaining relevancy to the plot. In addition, we explore effective methods to produce an eloquent real-time visual presentation from the generated script. According to the evaluation results, our scripts are controllable and preferred by humans. Thus, **VScript** can serve as a tool for users to produce scripts with their preferences and for scriptwriters to optimize the writing process. We think **VScript** has the potential to promote AI-human collaboration in script generation. Limitations and Ethical Considerations are discussed in Appendix A and B.

2 Related Work

Story Generation In recent years, methods for story generation have focused on using neural networks and have shown promising results. Martin et al. (2018) decompose a story as a sequence of events and apply sequence modelling to generate the story. Fan et al. (2018) employ a hierarchical story generation by generating a premise and transforming it into a passage. Plan-and-Write (Yao et al., 2019) extracts a storyline composed of keywords and generates a story based on the storyline. Rashkin et al. (2019) generate a narrative using a set of phrases that describe key characters and events in a story. Lovenia et al. (2022) generate a story using a genre and an image as its context.

Controllable Text Generation Model Conditional deep generative models are effective in improving the controllability of the models. CTRL (Keskar et al., 2019) is a class-conditional language model (CC-LM) pre-trained on 50 domains with different control codes. Plug and Play Language Models (PPLM) Dathathri et al. (2019) combine pre-trained language models and attribute classifiers to steer generation. GeDi (Krause et al., 2020) incorporates CC-LM as a discriminator to control generation towards the desired attribute.

3 Methodology

As shown in Figure 2, our framework can be decomposed into two modules: script generation and visual presentation. We will describe these two modules in detail in the following sections.

3.1 Script Generation

A plot, or so-called outline, is a vital component required for professional script writing, which specifies a series of headings showing the main themes that need to be discussed (Owens and Millerson, 2012). Following this concept, we first generate a genre-specific plot to hierarchically guide the dialogue and scene description generation. We condition the dialogue on the plot and the scene description on dialogue instead of the other way around since dialogues between characters change dynamically to reflect the progression of the plot, while scene descriptions mainly provide detailed information about where and how the dialogue takes place. In this work, we select four classic and popular genres for the plot generation, i.e., `Crime`, `Sci-Fi`, `War`, and `Romance`.

3.1.1 Genre-Specific Plot Generation

Inspired by CTRL (Keskar et al., 2019), we first train a class-conditional language model (CC-LM) for plot generation by adopting control codes which are a set of predefined genres. Then, by training different types of text with different control codes concatenated in the front, the model can learn the correlation between the types and the control codes so that the different control codes can guide the generation process of the language model. We fine-tune GPT2-large (Radford et al., 2019) on CMU Movie Summary Corpus[1], which contains 42,306 movie plots from Wikipedia and the corresponding metadata, such as genre. In our work, the genres of movies are treated as control codes. Each control code guides the generation of episodes of the desired type. See Appendix C for more details.

Plot Rescoring To ensure the consistency of the generated plots and the target genre, we further train a multi-class genre classifier that can predict the probabilities of a plot belonging to each genre. Then, we generate N plots with the same genre and starting words via Top-K sampling. Finally, we select the plot with the highest probability among all the generated N plots.

3.1.2 Plot-Guided Dialogue Generation

The dialogue in the script is required to be casual, natural, and in line with the plot. However, to our knowledge, there is no open-source dataset for plot-to-dialogue generation, and building it would require intensive human labour. Thus, we treat this task as an inversed abstractive dialogue summarization, where the model is trained to generate the whole dialogue based on the dialogue summary. The model learns to generate the entire dialogue in one fell swoop, which is different from conventional dialogue models generating dialogues turn-by-turn. Two dialogue summarization corpora, SAMSum (Gliwa et al., 2019) and DialogSum Corpus (Chen et al., 2021), are combined as the training set. A GPT2-large model is trained on the inversed version of it. During the inference time, we assume that each sentence in the plot can be expanded into a single scene, which can be decomposed into the scene description and the dialogue. We leverage our fine-tuned model to generate dialogues for each plot sentence.

3.1.3 Scene Description Generation

A scene description includes the scene header, i.e., location and time, and the scene context. In order to infer such scene descriptions from each dialogue, we fine-tune the GPT2-large on a paired scene-dialogue corpus. During preprocessing on Film Corpus 2.0[2], we pair each scene description with its corresponding dialogue to construct the dataset for dialogue-to-scene generation. Finally, we concatenate the scene description and the corresponding dialogues to form a scene. A script is formed by concatenating multiple scenes.

3.2 Visual Presentation

In addition to the generated script, we provide a visual presentation, which can serve as a rough visual draft for the users. We retrieve a video clip whose caption describes similar actions or events to the generated script. Note that we only utilize the visual contents of the retrieved video and ignore the auditory information. This disregard is intended to enhance retrieval quality, as the conversational content and visual appearance of a video are often inconsistent. For example, a video shows two women sitting face to face at a café, looking bright and peaceful, while their conversation is about fierce interstellar wars. In this section, we explain our video database construction process and the retrieval method.

Video Database Construction We construct a video database including news broadcasts, documentaries, and movie recaps from social media and only preserve the video if 1) it has captions; 2) there is a voice-over to introduce and describe what is happening; 3) most of the frames have rich content. Post-processing and filtering are further conducted

[1] http://www.cs.cmu.edu/~ark/personas/

[2] https://nlds.soe.ucsc.edu/fc2

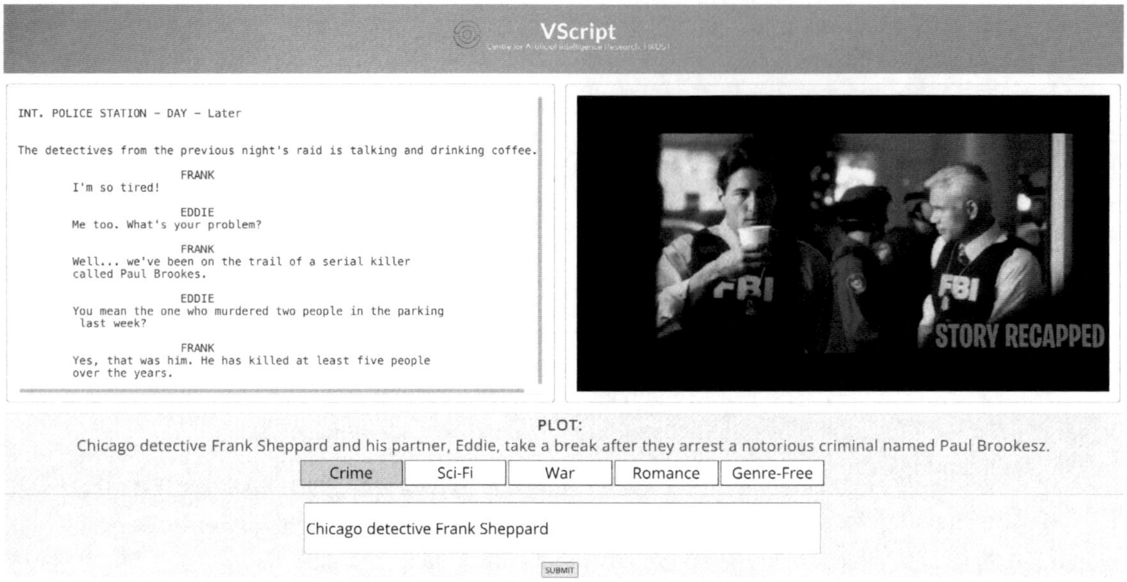

Figure 3: The **VScript**'s user interface. There are three main areas: script area (top left), video area (top right), and interaction area (bottom centre). For example, a user chooses "`Crime`", and input "`Chicago detective Frank Sheppard`". Then, the generated script and its visual presentation are displayed separately.

to ensure the quality of the videos. The characters (including number and gender), time (day/night) and locations in the videos are detected for video retrieval. In addition, we classify the video captions by a zero-shot text classifier [3] to split this database based on genres. For more details, see Appendix D. Since our method is zero-shot and independent of the video contents, users can replace the video database with any preferred videos.

Video Retrieval To match the video clips with the generated scripts, we use plots as queries for video retrieval since there may be trivial and lengthy dialogues in scripts that affect the coherence among the retrieved video clips. For each plot sentence, we retrieve video clips from the video database by calculating the cosine similarity between the sentence embedding of the plot and the corresponding caption with the pre-trained DistilRoBERTa-based model [4]. We also use the videos' pre-detected gender and location information to filter out some improper candidates and select the best matching video clip.

4 Interactive User Interface

An example of the interaction between users and **VScript** is illustrated in Figure 3. The user interface comprises three parts: the script area (top left), the video area (top right), and the interaction area (bottom centre). First, users select the script genre among `Crime`, `Sci-Fi`, `War`, `Romance`, and `Genre-Free`. Second, users type the starting words into the input box and submit. Finally, the generated script will be displayed in the script area and its visual presentation in the video area. Users can interrupt at any time and choose the genre or input some words to steer the script's development.

5 Experiments

5.1 Baselines

Plot Generation We fine-tune **GPT2**-large on CMU Movie Summary Corpus and a **CC-LM** using GPT2-large backbone on the same corpus without the genre-classifier.

Plot-Guided Dialogue Generation We fine-tune **DialoGPT**-large (Zhang et al., 2020) on the inversed SAMSum and DialogSum Corpus, where the model generates dialogue turn-by-turn iteratively. We fine-tune GPT2-large on the inversed SAMSum and DialogSum Corpus, where the model generates dialogue turn-by-turn (**GPT2 T**).

Overall Script Generation In contrast to our proposed pipeline, we fine-tune GPT2-large directly on the scripts from the Film Corpus 1.0[5] in an end-to-end manner without plot (**GPT2_E**).

[3] `https://huggingface.co/facebook/bart-large-mnli`

[4] `https://github.com/UKPLab/sentence-transformers`

[5] `https://nlds.soe.ucsc.edu/fc`

Model	PPL	Genre-ACC(%)
GPT2	20.43	-
CC-LM	21.98	63.50
CC-LM+Classifier (Ours)	21.98	95.50

Table 1: Automatic Evaluation for Plot Generation.

Model	BLEU	Sent Sim	Repeat (%)	Dist-n (n=1,2,3)
DialoGPT	13.35	54.18	20.25	1.7/13.6/42.69
GPT2 T	13.37	55.34	18.73	1.73/14.29/43.89
GPT2 (Ours)	16.4	58.97	9.68	3.19/22.4/53.32

Table 2: Automatic Evaluation for Plot-Guided Dialogue Generation.

Model	Dist-n (n=1,2,3)	Repeat (%)
GPT2_E	8.42/36.19/68.46	12.52
Ours	5.47/35.81/73.3	4.35

Table 3: Automatic Evaluation for Scripts.

Video Retrieval To verify our video retrieval, we use **VideoCLIP** (Xu et al., 2021), a pre-trained model for zero-shot video and text understanding.

5.2 Evaluation

5.2.1 Automatic Evaluation

Genre-Specific Plot Generation We score perplexity (**PPL**) of texts generated from our model and baseline (GPT2-large) by another model for fluency evaluation. We use the GPT-Neo-1.3B model since it is large enough to represent the real sentence distribution. We also calculate **Genre-ACC**, the accuracy of genre control, with the NLI-based zero-shot text classifier. As shown in Table 1, our method can control genre more effectively with only a slight reduction in fluency.

Plot-Guided Dialogue Generation We evaluate models on the test set of SAMSum and DialogSum. We use **BLEU** to compare the generated dialogue with the gold-standard human reference. We also calculate **Sentence Similarity**, which is defined as the cosine similarity between sentence embeddings [6] of plot and dialogue. In addition, we calculate **Distinct-n** to measure the diversity of generated texts, and **Repeat**, the average percentage of the unigrams that occur in the previous 8 tokens (Welleck et al., 2019), to measure the level of repetition. As shown in Table 2, generating the entire dialogue directly rather than turn-by-turn makes the plot-guided dialogues more similar to the gold references and higher semantic similarity with the plot. Both the generated dialogues and the scripts from our model (in Table 3) show higher diversity and lower repetition over the baselines.

Ours vs GPT2-E	Win(%)	Loss(%)	Tie(%)
Preference	54.00	27.33	18.67
Genre Control	95.33	4.00	0.67

Table 4: Human Evaluation for Scripts.

Ours vs VideoCLIP	Win(%)	Loss(%)	Tie(%)
Relevance	27.33	13.33	59.33

Table 5: Human Evaluation for Video Retrieval.

5.2.2 Human Evaluation

We conduct human evaluations further to assess the quality of **VScript** using Amazon Mechanical Turk. We randomly select 50 samples per model, and three annotators then evaluate each sample to rule out potential bias. We conduct A/B testing against the baseline GPT2_E to assess generated scripts on **Preference** and **Genre Control**. For **Preference**, we ask the annotators to choose which script is the better one from three aspects [7]: 1) format, whether the text meets the standard of film scripts; 2) fluency, whether the writing is smooth and grammatically correct; and 3) consistency, whether the content is logically consistent. For **Genre Control**, we ask the annotators to choose which script better belongs to a given genre. In both tests, the annotators are given four choices: {neither, both, sample A, or sample B}. As shown in Table 4 [8], human judges prefer the scripts generated by **VScript**, which is inline with the automatic evaluation. For video retrieval, we conduct A/B testing against VideoCLIP to evaluate the **Relevance**. The **Relevance** between the script and video retrieved by **VScript** is slightly higher than the baseline, as in Table 5 [8].

6 Conclusion

We propose the first controllable script generation framework **VScript** that can generate scripts of specific genres and follow the plots. Our framework adopts a hierarchical structure, which generates the plot, then the script and its visual presentation. We adopt inversed abstractive summarization for dialogue generation. Based on our experiments, **VScript** outperforms the baselines, and its effectiveness in genre control is proven.

[6] https://huggingface.co/sentence-transformers/paraphrase-distilroberta-base-v2

[7] Please refer to Appendix G for the results of each aspect.

[8] The result is statistically significant with $p < 0.05$.

References

Nantheera Anantrasirichai and David Bull. 2021. Artificial intelligence in the creative industries: a review. *Artificial Intelligence Review*, pages 1–68.

Eden Bensaid, Mauro Martino, Benjamin Hoover, and Hendrik Strobelt. 2021. Fairytailor: A multimodal generative framework for storytelling. *arXiv preprint arXiv:2108.04324*.

Marc Cavazza and R Michael Young. 2017. Introduction to interactive storytelling. *Handbook of digital games and entertainment technologies*.

Shizhe Chen, Bei Liu, Jianlong Fu, Ruihua Song, Qin Jin, Pingping Lin, Xiaoyu Qi, Chunting Wang, and Jin Zhou. 2019. Neural storyboard artist: Visualizing stories with coherent image sequences. In *Proceedings of the 27th ACM International Conference on Multimedia*, pages 2236–2244.

Yulong Chen, Yang Liu, Liang Chen, and Yue Zhang. 2021. Dialogsum: A real-life scenario dialogue summarization dataset. In *Findings of the Association for Computational Linguistics: ACL-IJCNLP 2021*.

Sumanth Dathathri, Andrea Madotto, Janice Lan, Jane Hung, Eric Frank, Piero Molino, et al. 2019. Plug and play language models: A simple approach to controlled text generation. In *ICLR*.

Hao-Wen Dong, Wen-Yi Hsiao, Li-Chia Yang, and Yi-Hsuan Yang. 2018. Musegan: Multi-track sequential generative adversarial networks for symbolic music generation and accompaniment. In *AAAI*.

Angela Fan, Mike Lewis, and Yann Dauphin. 2018. Hierarchical neural story generation. In *ACL*.

Bogdan Gliwa, Iwona Mochol, Maciej Biesek, and Aleksander Wawer. 2019. Samsum corpus: A human-annotated dialogue dataset for abstractive summarization. *EMNLP-IJCNLP 2019*, page 70.

Jinyi Hu and Maosong Sun. 2020. Generating major types of chinese classical poetry in a uniformed framework. In *Proceedings of the 12th Language Resources and Evaluation Conference*.

Oana Ignat, Santiago Castro, Hanwen Miao, Weiji Li, and Rada Mihalcea. 2021. Whyact: Identifying action reasons in lifestyle vlogs. In *EMNLP-IJCNLP*.

Nitish Shirish Keskar, Bryan McCann, Lav R Varshney, Caiming Xiong, and Richard Socher. 2019. Ctrl: A conditional transformer language model for controllable generation. *arXiv preprint arXiv:1909.05858*.

Dmytro Kotovenko, Artsiom Sanakoyeu, Pingchuan Ma, Sabine Lang, and Bjorn Ommer. 2019. A content transformation block for image style transfer. In *Proceedings of the IEEE Conference on Computer Vision and Pattern Recognition*, pages 10032–10041.

Ben Krause, Akhilesh Deepak Gotmare, Bryan McCann, Nitish Shirish Keskar, Shafiq Joty, Richard Socher, and Nazneen Fatema Rajani. 2020. Gedi: Generative discriminator guided sequence generation. *arXiv preprint arXiv:2009.06367*.

Holy Lovenia, Bryan Wilie, Romain Barraud, Samuel Cahyawijaya, Willy Chung, and Pascale Fung. 2022. Every picture tells a story: Image-grounded controllable stylistic story generation. *arXiv preprint arXiv:2209.01638*.

Andrea Madotto, Etsuko Ishii, Zhaojiang Lin, Sumanth Dathathri, and Pascale Fung. 2020. Plug-and-play conversational models. In *Findings of EMNLP 2020*.

Lara Martin, Prithviraj Ammanabrolu, Xinyu Wang, William Hancock, Shruti Singh, Brent Harrison, and Mark Riedl. 2018. Event representations for automated story generation with deep neural nets. In *AAAI*.

Nedjma Ousidhoum, Xinran Zhao, Tianqing Fang, Yangqiu Song, and Dit-Yan Yeung. 2021. Probing toxic content in large pre-trained language models. In *ACL-IJCNLP 2021*.

Jim Owens and Gerald Millerson. 2012. *Video production handbook*. Routledge.

Alec Radford, Jeffrey Wu, Rewon Child, David Luan, Dario Amodei, et al. 2019. Language models are unsupervised multitask learners. *OpenAI blog*.

Hannah Rashkin, Eric Michael Smith, Margaret Li, and Y-Lan Boureau. 2019. Towards empathetic open-domain conversation models: A new benchmark and dataset. In *ACL*.

Marilyn A Walker, Grace I Lin, Jennifer Sawyer, et al. 2012. An annotated corpus of film dialogue for learning and characterizing character style. In *LREC*.

Sean Welleck, Ilia Kulikov, Stephen Roller, Emily Dinan, Kyunghyun Cho, et al. 2019. Neural text generation with unlikelihood training. In *ICLR*.

Hu Xu, Gargi Ghosh, Po-Yao Huang, Dmytro Okhonko, Armen Aghajanyan, Florian Metze, Luke Zettlemoyer, and Christoph Feichtenhofer. 2021. Videoclip: Contrastive pre-training for zero-shot video-text understanding. In *EMNLP-IJCNLP*.

Lili Yao, Nanyun Peng, Ralph Weischedel, Kevin Knight, Dongyan Zhao, and Rui Yan. 2019. Plan-and-write: Towards better automatic storytelling. In *AAAI*.

Wenpeng Yin, Jamaal Hay, and Dan Roth. 2019. Benchmarking zero-shot text classification: Datasets, evaluation and entailment approach. In *EMNLP-IJCNLP*.

Yizhe Zhang, Siqi Sun, Michel Galley, Yen-Chun Chen, Chris Brockett, Xiang Gao, Jianfeng Gao, Jingjing Liu, and Bill Dolan. 2020. Dialogpt: Large-scale generative pre-training for conversational response generation. In *ACL (demo)*.

Yutao Zhu, Ruihua Song, Zhicheng Dou, Jian-Yun Nie, and Jin Zhou. 2020. Scriptwriter: Narrative-guided script generation. In *ACL 2020*, pages 8647–8657.

A Limitations

The performance of video retrieval is limited to some extent by the quality of the sentence embedding, face detection, and place detection via off-the-shelf tools. The effect of visual presentation depends heavily on the quality and quantity of the video database. More exploration in video retrieval or video generation can also improve the matching quality between a script and its visual presentation. In addition, we would explore a more fine-grained control, such as specific settings, character personalities, or event details for future work.

B Ethical Considerations

Copyright We collect publicly available YouTube videos using the official YouTube API and follow the typical processing procedures (Ignat et al., 2021). We use the muted video footage and are neutral to the opinions expressed therein. We will not release the database and are accountable for violating other parties' rights or terms of service.

Toxic Content VScript leverages large language models, which raise awareness of carrying biases and toxic content (Ousidhoum et al., 2021). Therefore, we create lists of banned words that block them from the generated script to filter the possible curse words, racial slurs and sexually explicit contents. Since our videos are retrieved from publicly accessible media, which could include bloody and erotic content, we also filter these video clips based on the descriptions and captions.

C Genre-Specific Plot Generation

As shown in Figure 4, the genres of movies are treated as control codes. Each control code guides the generation of episodes of the desired type. The generation probability distribution can be decomposed as follows:

$$p(x|c^g) = \prod_{t=1}^{T} p(x_t|x_{<t}, c^g) \quad (1)$$

$\mathbf{C} = \{c^1, ..., c^g, ..., c^G\}$ denotes the control code, where c^g means the control code for g-th genre (G genres in total).

The CC-LM is trained on a set of plots $\{x^1_{1:T^1}, ..., x^n_{1:T^n}, ..., x^N_{1:T^N}\}$, where each plot $x^n_{1:T^n}$ corresponds with the control code $c^x \in \mathbf{C}$. The training loss is denoted as:

$$L = -\sum_{n=1}^{N}\sum_{t=1}^{T^n} \log p_\theta(x^n_t|x^n_{<t}, c^x) \quad (2)$$

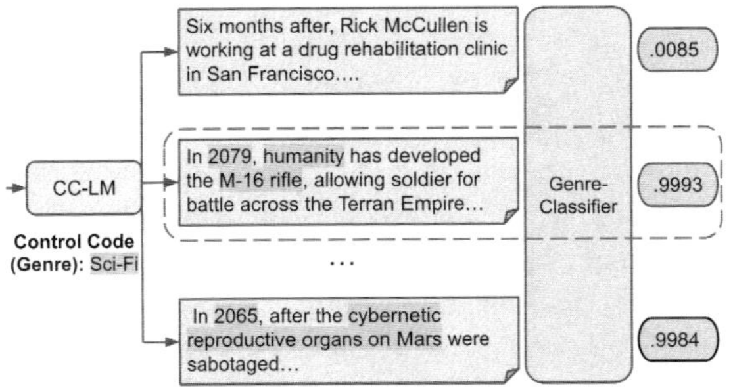

Figure 4: The process of plot generation. The CC-LM generates several candidates, and then the Genre-Classifier scores and ranks them to select the one that most belongs to the expected genre.

Plot Rescoring To verify the genres of the generated plots, we train a multi-class genre classifier ϕ to predict the probability of the generated plot belonging to a specific genre g. By leveraging Top-K sampling, we generate $N(N = 10)$ plots $\{X_1, ..., X_n, ...X_N\}$ with the genre and the starting words. Finally, we select the plot X^*_g with the highest probability over all the generated plots, which is defined as:

$$X^*_g = \arg\max_{n \in \mathbf{N}} p_\phi(\mathbf{y} = y_g|X_n) \quad (3)$$

where $\mathbf{y} = \{y_1, ..., y_g, ...y_G\}$ denotes the genre classes of the generated plot and y_g is the class corresponding to genre g.

D Video Database Construction

Firstly, we obtain videos and corresponding captions about news broadcasts and movie recaps from YouTube via the official API. Since some captions are generated automatically word by word, there is no punctuation, and they are not spliced into sentences. We use DeepSegment[9] to sentence-tokenize these captions. To ensure the richness of the video image content and improve the quality of video clips, the frames only consisting of hosts or speakers are filtered automatically. We use RetinaFace-R50 from InsightFace [10] to detect face. If there is only one face in the centre of the picture whose size is within an appropriate range, and it does not move

[9]https://github.com/notAI-tech/deepsegment

[10]https://github.com/deepinsight/insightface

for several frames, we will judge it as a speaker and delete these frames. We also use InsightFace to detect the gender of characters in the videos per second. We use DenseNet-161 from Places365 [11] to recognize the location of scene in the video. Furthermore, in order to match the time in scene description, we train a Vision Transformer (ViT) [12]-based day/night image classifier on Aachen Day-Night Dataset [13], AMOS Day-Night Dataset [14], and [15]. Finally, we classify the video captions by NLI-based Zero Shot Text Classifier (Yin et al., 2019) to split this corpus based on genres. Since our method is zero-shot and independent of the video contents, users can update or replace the video database on their wish.

E Background Music

In order to render the atmosphere, we also use different styles and moods of music for different genres of the script. For example, the music for crime is rapid and intense, while that for romance is relaxing and soothing.

F Experimental Settings

F.1 Plot Generation

For CC-LM, we fine-tune GPT2-large with control codes (prefixes): "`This is a crime/romance/sci-fi/war plot.`". We use the training hyperparameters: the learning rate is 3e-5, AdamW optimizer, and WarmupDecayLR scheduler and generate plots using top-k (k=4) sampling. For Genre-Classifier, we fine-tune BART-large with the same training hyperparameters: the learning rate is 3e-5, AdamW optimizer, and WarmupDecayLR scheduler. For the GPT2 baseline, we fine-tune the model with the same hyperparameter setting as GPT2-large models in our pipeline.

F.2 Plot-Guided Dialogue Generation

The model in this stage of our pipeline has the same training and generation hyperparameters as the GPT2-large model in Appendix F.1. For the DialogGPT baseline, we fine-tune the model with a learning rate (5e-5), and the other hyperparameters are the same as GPT2-large models in our pipeline. For GPT2 Turn-by-Turn (GPT2 T) baseline, we use the same hyperparameter setting as the GPT2-large models in our pipeline.

[11] `https://github.com/CSAILVision/places365`

[12] `https://huggingface.co/google/vit-base-patch16-224-in21k`

[13] `https://www.visuallocalization.net/`

[14] `https://www.kaggle.com/datasets/stevemark/daynight-dataset`

[15] `https://github.com/kushagra2jindal/DayNightClassificationModel`

Model	Format (%)	Fluency	Consistency
GPT2-E	93(0.26)	2.92(0.45)	2.85(0.45)
VScript	**95(0.22)**	**3.06(0.42)**	**3.00(0.50)**

Table 6: Additional human evaluation for scripts.

F.3 Scene Description Generation

The model in this stage of our pipeline has the same hyperparameters as GPT2-large model in Appendix F.1.

F.4 Overall Script Generation

For GPT2_E baseline, we use the same hyperparameter set with the GPT2-large model in Appendix F.1.

G Additional Human Evaluation

In addition, we also evaluate the quality of each generated script for a more comprehensive study, compared with GPT2-E model. As mentioned in Section 5.2.2, we breakdown the **Preference** metric into three aspects: **Format**, **Fluency**, and **Consistency**. **Format** measures whether our generation meets the standard of the script, which is defined as a text that contains a scene header, and dialogue (including monologue). For this metric, we conduct True/False binary evaluation. **Fluency** reflects whether the writing is smooth and non-repetitive, without grammatical and spelling mistakes. **Consistency** emphasizes whether the content is logically consistent. For Fluency and Consistency, we leverage a 4-point Likert Scale, where 1 indicates non-fluent/inconsistent and 4 indicates a very fluent/consistent text. For each model, we randomly sample 50 generated scripts from each model. And each script is evaluated by three annotators. An individual t-test is conducted for significance validation of the human evaluation results. As shown in Table 6 [16], while achieving script formulation, our system has slightly higher fluency than the baseline model, indicating that fluency is not compromised. Our framework is also more consistent and logical, with considerably higher consistency than GPT2-E.

[16] The result is statistically significant with $p < 0.05$.

TexPrax: A Messaging Application for Ethical, Real-time Data Collection and Annotation

Lorenz Stangier[*†] and **Ji-Ung Lee**[*†] and **Yuxi Wang**[‡] and **Marvin Müller**[‡]
Nicholas Frick[‡] and **Joachim Metternich**[‡] and **Iryna Gurevych**[†]
Ubiquitous Knowledge Processing (UKP) Lab[†]
Institute of Production Management, Technology and Machine Tools (PTW)[‡]
Department of Computer Science and Hessian Center for AI (hessian.AI)[†]
Department of Engineering[‡]
Technical University of Darmstadt

Abstract

Collecting and annotating task-oriented dialog data is difficult, especially for highly specific domains that require expert knowledge. At the same time, informal communication channels such as instant messengers are increasingly being used at work. This has led to a lot of work-relevant information that is disseminated through those channels and needs to be post-processed manually by the employees. To alleviate this problem, we present TexPrax, a messaging system to collect and annotate *problems*, *causes*, and *solutions* that occur in work-related chats. TexPrax uses a chatbot to directly engage the employees to provide lightweight annotations on their conversation and ease their documentation work. To comply with data privacy and security regulations, we use an end-to-end message encryption and give our users full control over their data which has various advantages over conventional annotation tools. We evaluate TexPrax in a user-study with German factory employees who ask their colleagues for solutions on problems that arise during their daily work. Overall, we collect 202 task-oriented German dialogues containing 1,027 sentences with sentence-level expert annotations. Our data analysis also reveals that real-world conversations frequently contain instances with code-switching, varying abbreviations for the same entity, and dialects which NLP systems should be able to handle.[1]

1 Introduction

The lack of annotated data—especially in languages other than English—is one of the key open challenges in task-oriented dialogue processing (Razumovskaia et al., 2022). This becomes even more challenging for very task-specific application domains with only a small number of experts that are sufficiently qualified to generate dialogue data or provide annotations (Sambasivan et al., 2021). At the same time, using informal communication channels such as instant messengers at work has become increasingly popular (Rajendran et al., 2019; Newman and Ford, 2021). Although this can accelerate troubleshooting, most of the knowledge that is communicated informally may be lost without an additional error tracking process; which in turn increases documenting work for employees (Müller et al., 2021a). Whereas this could be alleviated by NLP-based assistance systems—that for instance automatically identify *problems*, their *cause*, and their *solution*—they cannot be built without any annotated data. Our goal is to provide an application (TexPrax) to bridge the gap between the lack of annotated task-oriented dialogue data and the increasing need for NLP-based documenting assistance.

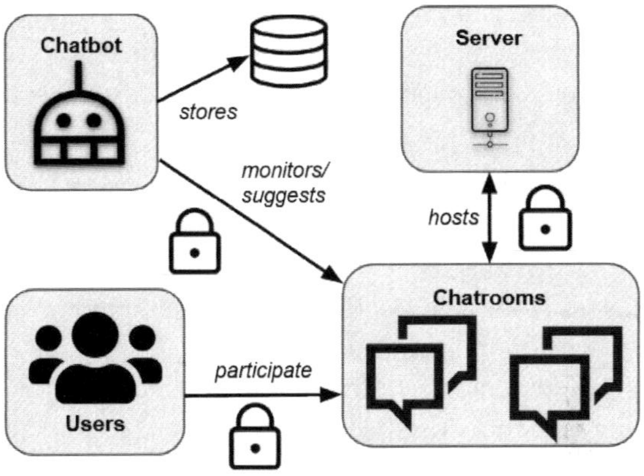

Figure 1: Overview of TexPrax. All users as well as the chatbot communicate via chatrooms that are hosted on a Synapse server instance. All messages are end-to-end encrypted using the Matrix communication protocol.

Figure 1 provides a high-level overview of TexPrax and all involved parties. Our system communicates as a chatbot that acts as the user interface and recording service at the same time. For the server that hosts the messaging application, the bot

[*]Equal contribution
[1]Code and data are published under an open source license: https://github.com/UKPLab/TexPrax

Proceedings of the 2nd Conference of the Asia-Pacific Chapter of the Association for Computational Linguistics and the 12th International Joint Conference on Natural Language Processing: System Demonstrations, pages 9–16
November 20–23, 2022.

appears as an additional user and hence, inherits all privileges and restrictions a user can have; including (1) reading any messages written in a chatroom, (2) being invited and removed by the chatroom moderator, and (3) being able to send messages in chatrooms it was invited to. We use privilege (3) to provide label suggestions from a pre-trained model and collect annotations via a reaction mechanism (Figure 5b); attaining a lightweight annotation process with minimal overhead. We also integrate TexPrax via the REST web API into an internal dashboard to automatically store recognized errors as a first step of the error documentation process.

Directly involving employees in data annotation and curation introduces four key advantages over previous approaches that involve crowdsourcing (Crowston, 2012) or use expert annotation tools such as INCEpTION (Klie et al., 2018). First, they are the very domain experts that hold qualified conversations which concern exactly the target-domain. This allows us to directly collect the dialog data instead of having to generate it semi-automatically or asking crowdworkers who can only provide limited expertise (Raghu et al., 2021). Second, the employees have an immediate benefit from annotating and improving the recommendation model as a dashboard integration saves time they would otherwise have to spend on documenting errors later on (hence, an intrinsic motivation). Third, they have full control over their own data which saves time for NLP practitioners as it alleviates research data management. Finally, the use of an end-to-end encryption protocol ensures that only parties selected by the employees will have access to the data even if the server is breached.[2] Our contributions are:

1. An application for collecting and annotating dialogues in real-time to assist employees during their work. To comply with data privacy and safety regulations such as the GDPR (EU, 2016), TexPrax further has received full clearance by the ethics committee and staff council of TU Darmstadt.

2. A German dataset with 202 dialogues, consisting of 591 turns, and 1,027 annotated sentences collected from a highly specific domain, namely an assembly line in a factory.

[2]Upon creating a chat room, they will explicitly be asked if our chatbot is allowed to join the chatroom (opt-in).

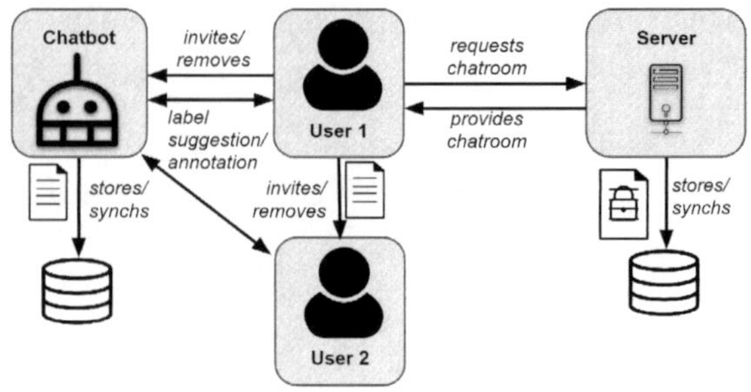

Figure 2: Information flow and privileges between users, server, and chatbot. While staying in a chatroom, the chatbot can decrypt all messages and stores them locally. Messages passed via the server are always encrypted.

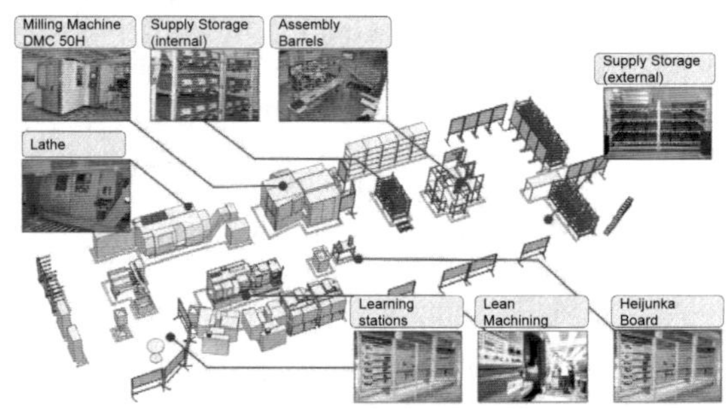

Figure 3: Workstations and machines in the Center for Industrial Productivity (CiP).

2 Use Case

In this work, we focus on assisting employees on the shop floor (the production area in a factory). Our goal is to improve shop floor management (Hertle et al., 2017); a systematic approach for solving processing problems. To efficiently solve such problems, shop floor management defines performance indicators which are used to detect deviations and identify problems which are also used to quantify their successful rectification.

2.1 Production Environment

Our working environment is the learning factory *Center for Industrial Productivity* (CiP) at the Technical University of Darmstadt (TUDa). The factory consists of various assembly stations, machines, and demonstrators (cf. Figure 3) and is run and maintained by ∼15 research assistants and 40 student assistants (Müller et al., 2021b). One substantial challenge is the on-site support in case of problems that occur during their daily work, for instance, if a machine suddenly stops working. Usually, workers then ask their co-workers, technical support support, or the supervising research assistant (who may not be present) for assistance, often via informal communication channels. While this leads to a quick fix of the issue, the knowledge of how to resolve such errors is not explicitly stored and hence, can be forgotten or lost over time.

2.2 Preliminary Survey

To assess the need of an NLP-based assistance system, we rely upon the analysis from a previous survey that was conducted at the CiP (Müller et al., 2021a). In this survey, they identify eight key issues and challenges from an employee's perspective. (1) The most frequently used communication channel are emails. (2) Most questions are answered fast, but in case of a slow return-rate it takes very long to receive an answer which leads to a substantial delay of the assembly line. (3) There are no platforms that pool already encountered problems and solutions. Thus, there is a high demand for such a system. (4) Most employees would use such an application only for work communication. (5) A majority of employees are convinced that such an application could help in substantially reducing the required time to find a solution. (6) Most employees are fine with using such an application on their private phone. (7) All employees agreed to have a chatbot in a group chat monitoring the chatroom, but most stated that this would influence their communication behavior. (8) The most important benefit would be the improvement of knowledge management.

For companies, they identify three important criteria. (1) A high level of data security is essential to avoid any leakage of information outside the company (i.e., the application should be self-hostable). (2) No personal data may be processed to avoid legal complications. (3) The most important benefit would be the improvement of error-reporting and -monitoring processes.

3 System Description

As shown in Figure 1, TexPrax involves three key parties: the users (employees), the chatbot and the server (e.g., hosted by a company). Users communicate via chatrooms; each chatroom including at least two (for a private conversation) or more (for a group conversation) users. Every message a user sends into a room can be read by any other user in the same room. The server is responsible for handling new incoming messages and the distribution of outgoing messages, as well as keeping

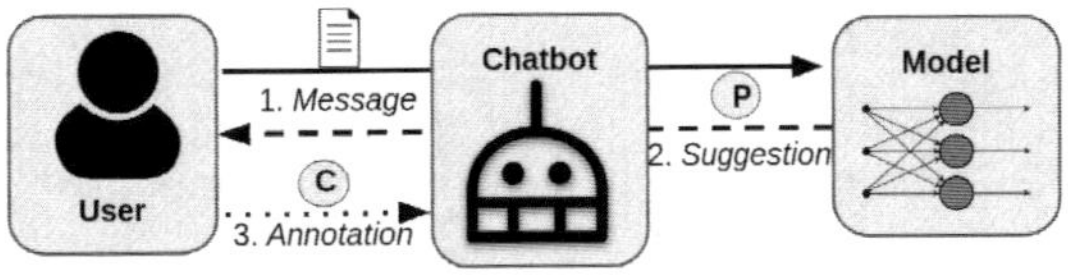

Figure 4: Information flow between the user, chatbot, and the underlying model.

track of currently active conversations and users. Finally, the chatbot is responsible for monitoring conversations, suggesting labels, and storing the relevant data (locally or in an external database).

3.1 Interaction and Privileges

A key focus of TexPrax lies within giving users full control over their data and when their conversation should be monitored. We thus provide them with the option to remove the chatbot from a conversation at any time. Moreover, the matrix communication protocol allows users to modify and remove their messages which are then propagated to other participants in a chatroom including the chatbot. This provides a safer communication space to users as they have full control over what messages are stored. To comply with GDPR regulations (EU, 2016), we further implement a feature to obtain the informed consent of the users for each chatroom.

Upon being invited to a chatroom, the chatbot automatically sends an introductory message and explicitly asks if this room shall be recorded (Figure 5a). The user can then respond to the question with one of the provided reactions. If no reaction is selected but a message is sent, the chatbot will assume that the invitation was not intended and leaves the chatroom automatically without recording any message. Only upon acceptance, the chatbot will notify the user and start monitoring and reacting to new messages (Figure 5b). Note, that the chatbot can be removed by the user at any time and invited back in later. Due to the end-to-end encryption, the chatbot will not be able to read any messages that have been sent while it was not present.

Annotations are then made by the user by accepting the suggested label, or providing a correction.[3] Only when a reaction is provided, the message and its class are stored in the internal database.

[3]We also investigated labeling messages using free-text replies; however, users asked for an easier way of interaction.

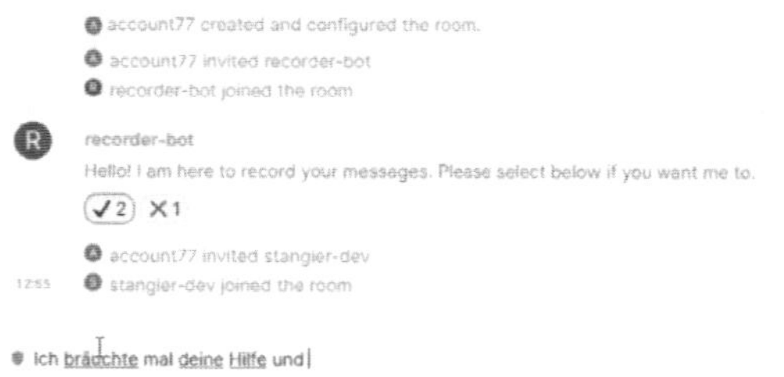

(a) Introductory message after a new room has been created. If at least one user is against recording, the bot will leave the room.

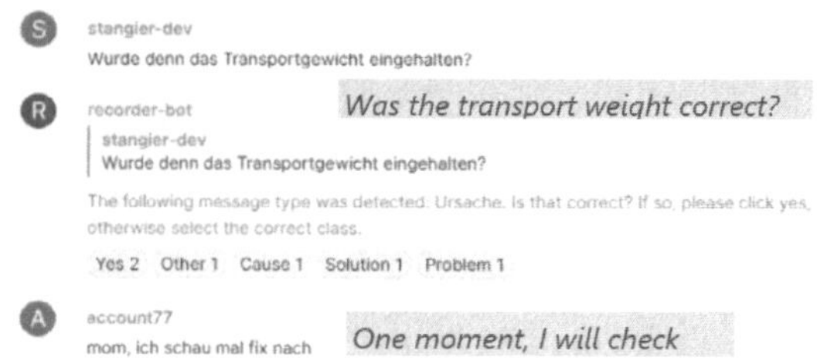

(b) Label suggestion for a recognized cause.

Figure 5: Example messages of TexPrax.

3.2 Server

The server is based on the Synapse implementation of the matrix protocol[4]; an open-source privacy-centric messaging protocol that enables end-to-end encrypted communication while allowing the server to be hosted on custom hardware (Ermoshina et al., 2016). This guarantees that all messages that are passed between users (and the chatbot) remain encrypted on the server and thus, cannot be read even if the server is breached. The usage of Synapse further allows users to use different client applications such as Element[5] across different platforms (i.e., mobile, desktop, and browser) to send and receive messages. For the study and debugging purposes, we further extended the existing implementation to automatically send an invitation to the chatbot every time a new chatroom is created (users will still be asked for their consent before recording any messages). TexPrax is setup on a virtual machine with 4 CPU cores, 8 GB RAM, and 50 GB of storage.

3.3 Chatbot

The chatbot is based on the nio project[6]—a client library for the matrix protocol—written in Python. As soon as the user allows the chatbot to record messages, it will store every new message including the annotation into a local database. Processing messages can freely be extended; for instance, it is also possible to send the messages to an external instance via HTTP instead storing them locally. To provide the system with additional flexibility, the chatbot can be hosted completely separate from the server. It is thus possible to run different chatbots for each chatroom on different hardware, which can be helpful to better comply with data privacy regulations. As shown in Figure 4, we utilize a pre-trained model to provide users with label suggestions. The chatbot will then react to a message with a label suggestion and ask the user to confirm or correct the notification (they can also just ignore the message). All user annotations are stored separately from the model's suggestion.

4 Data Collection

In contrast to our previous work that investigates expert-annotated named entity recognition (Müller et al., 2021b), our goal is to provide a first solution for collecting annotated data and providing assistance with a minimal effort for users. We thus focus on sentence-level annotations that can be easily provided using message reactions and are suitable for existing shop floor management processes.

4.1 Annotation Task

Following existing workflows for shop floor management that are currently done on paper, we identify three crucial classes for our use case:

1. Problem (**P**): The description of a deviation from an expected target state, e.g., machine breakdowns, material delays, incorrect production processes etc. (often formulated as a question).
2. Cause (**C**): The assumed cause of a problem.
3. Solution (**S**): The action to eliminate the root cause of the problem or to help in finding the possible causes and countermeasures.
4. Other (**O**): None of the above classes (e.g., unrelated messages).

To train an initial label suggestion model, we re-annotated the existing dataset with sentence-level

[4] `https://matrix.org/docs/projects/server/synapse`
[5] `https://element.io/`
[6] `https://matrix.org/docs/projects/sdk/matrix-nio`

Part	Dialogues (D)	Turns (T)	T/D	Problem	Solution	Cause	Other	Total	Sents/D
P1	81	246	3.04	127	74	50	302	553	6.83 ± 3.82
P2	97	309	3.19	117	56	114	145	432	4.45 ± 2.11
P3	24	36	1.50	23	12	1	6	42	1.75 ± 0.66
Total	202	591	2.60	267	142	165	453	1,027	5.08 ± 3.28

Table 1: The number of dialogues, turns, and their ratio (left) and the class distribution on a sentence-level (right).

annotations.[7] This was done by three of the authors that are responsible for managing the CiP. Each of them annotated one third of the dataset and cross-examined all other annotations for possible errors or disagreement. Upon disagreeing on a label, all annotators discussed the respective instance to agree upon the best suited one.

4.2 Participants

All participants were student assistants, technical support staff, or researchers that worked in the CiP and are employed at the university; receiving payment according to the official wages (above German minimum wage). They were informed about the purpose of the study in advance, and provided their informed consent before participation. They further received instructions about how to use the application including the features allowing them to modify and remove already sent messages. Participation was strictly voluntary and anonymous; to further obfuscate the identity of our participants, we created a pool of user accounts from which an account was randomly assigned to each user. For data publication we obfuscate the user accounts by hashing the ID of each user. Overall, our study had a total number of 10 participants over the whole duration (October 2021 to July 2022).

4.3 Data Analysis

Table 1 shows the statistics of the collected data. We split the data into three parts; first, the re-annotated dataset that was used to train the label suggestion model (cf. Section 5), second, data collected between October 2021 and June 2022, and third, the data collected in July 2022 to evaluate the our final system which we also use as the test data for our experiments. The second and third batch of data was each collected in a separate chatroom. An overview of the dialogue properties can be found in Table 1. Overall, the dataset consists of 202 dialogues with 591 turns and 1,027 sentences. A close inspection of the data reveals interesting properties (e.g., grammatically incorrect language, abbreviations, etc.). Despite that, we want to emphasize that there was no single case where our participants could not understand a message.

[7]Deploying TexPrax without any suggestion model does not affect the number of reactions provided by users.

Distributional shifts. Table 1 shows varying class distributions across all three splits. One reason for this may be the amount of expertise in chatrooms across different periods of data collection. For instance, between the first and second part of the data collection which were $\sim$10 months apart, there had been a partial change of staff in work force. With new people joining the CiP, we find a higher number of responses looking for potential causes of a problem, but with less success (i.e., less solutions). We further find that the more acquainted workers in the first data collection tend to provide longer explanations and engage themselves more in chitchat which is reflected in the substantially higher number of *Other* class sentences and a higher sentence-per-dialog ratio (Sents/D).

Slang. We find various occurrences of text mimicking spoken language involving grammatically incorrect expressions. For instance, our participants frequently used *ne* instead of *eine* (*Eng.:* a/an) or as the short form of *nein* (*Eng.:* no).

Abbreviations. We find that our participants tend to communicate in short messages that involve abbreviations. While some are easily understandable for native German speakers—e.g., *vllt.* for *vielleicht* (*Eng.:* maybe)—others such as *V8* for *Variante 8* (a product type) or *wimi* for *wissenschaftliche Mitarbeitende* (*Eng.:* researcher) are highly dependent on the domain.

Filler words. Similar to in-person conversations, we also find an abundance of filler words such as *ah*, *hmm*, and *oh*.

Code switching. We find that participants sometimes tend to code switch from German to English (Scotton and Ury, 1977); especially for short, one word responses (e.g., *Nice!*, *Sorry!*).

5 Experiments

We conduct experiments to gain first insights on how well recent models can perform for providing label suggestions for our use case in future studies.

5.1 Experimental Setup

We evaluate two models that are capable of processing German texts as our baselines. First, the XLMR-base model (Conneau et al., 2020) provided by Huggingface (Wolf et al., 2020) that has been shown to have a solid performance across various languages (Malmasi et al., 2022). Second, a German version of BERT (GBERT, Chan et al. 2020). This has been shown to work well for German tweets that have a similar format (i.e., short, German sentences containing informal language) as our messages (Beck et al., 2021). For sentence classification, we use the [CLS] token to predict if a given sentence states a *problem* (P), a *cause* (C), a *solution* (S), or *other* (O). Across all experiments, we train our models for 10 epochs with a learning rate of $2e^{-5}$ and weight decay of 0.01, and a batch size of 16. We use the parts 1 and 2 as presented in Table 1 for training and use part 3 as the most recently collected dataset for testing.

	P1		P2		P1 + P2	
Model	Acc	F1	Acc	F1	Acc	F1
XLMR	0.357	0.216	0.524	0.315	0.476	0.269
GBERT	0.405	0.267	0.310	0.237	0.429	**0.361**

Table 2: Accuracy and macro-averaged F1 scores of both models trained on different temporal datasplits.

5.2 Results

Table 2 shows the results of both models on the P3 data (cf. Table 1). Both models are not able to achieve a marco-averaged F1 score higher than 0.4, showing that even recent language-specific models struggle for sentence classification when applied to a very specific domain and little training data (432–553 sentences). Interestingly, GBERT outperforms XLMR when trained on P1 data as well and when trained on P1 + P2 data in terms of F1 score. Although we initially conjectured that XLMR may be capable of better handling the code switched data, this does not seem to be the case. We further find that the suggested labels from the GBERT model (trained on P1 data) during the collection of P2 achieved an accuracy of 0.683. While this is a moderately high performance, this also implies that 31.7% of the labels needed to be corrected by our participants.

5.3 Usability

To ensure that this did not substantially impact the usability of TexPrax, we asked our voluntary participants to answer the system usability scale (SUS) questionnaire (Brooke, 1996) upon finishing the final round of data collections (P3). SUS quantifies the relative usability with respect to existing benchmarks and ranges from $\mathbf{A}^+$ (84.1–100 SUS) to **F** (0–51.6 SUS) (Lewis and Sauro, 2018). Overall, seven users participated in the usability study. On average, TexPrax receives a system usability scale score of 81.76 with a standard deviation of 5.46, which indicates an **A** level (80.8–84.0 SUS) usability. We thus conclude that TexPrax achieves a high usability despite the label corrections.

6 Conclusion

We presented TexPrax, a system for collecting annotations and assisting employees by directly engaging them as domain-experts during their daily work. TexPrax allows users to exchange, modify, and delete end-to-end encrypted messages at any time, and an opt-in chatbot to ensure a high level of data privacy and security. We evaluate TexPrax in an assembly line at a learning factory (CiP) where we find that daily work communication is noisy, but efficient and very problem-oriented. While existing models still have difficulties to provide the correct label suggestion, TexPrax still maintains a high usability. We conjecture that TexPrax could be especially beneficial to collect data and build assistance systems in domains with a high share of remote work, such as in software development. For future work, we plan to extend TexPrax to identify and suggest solutions for recognized problems and adapt it to new domains, such as our institute's reading group chat where researchers discuss papers relevant for their research.

Acknowledgements

We thank all subjects from the user study and our anonymous reviewers, Max Glockner, and Jan-Christoph Klie for their helpful feedback. This work has been funded by the European Regional Development Fund (ERDF) and the Hessian State Chancellery – Hessian Minister of Digital Strategy and Development under the promotional reference 20005482 (TexPrax).

Ethics Statement

The collection of data from group- and private-chats requires careful consideration about what kind of data is to be expected and how users can control it. To ensure an ethical data collection and usage, we worked closely together with the respective bodies of our university (TUDa) for developing our final workflow. We want to emphasize that such data should never be collected without the explicit and informed consent of the users. Our participants voluntarily participated in this study and furthermore, had an active interest in the system as they could directly benefit from it.

Pre-study clearance from respective bodies. After defining our data collection workflow and annotation task, we hence asked the ethics committee of our university for ethical clearance.[8] To further ensure the (mental) safety of our participants who were employees of TU Darmstadt, we further asked our university's staff council for their clearance.[9] Both bodies provided their full clearance to conduct this study after minor modifications of the initial workflow involving the account distribution to participants (cf. Section 4.2). Both clearance letters for the final study setup can be shared upon request (in German).

Informed consent. All our participants were fully informed about the data collection processes, for what purpose the data was collected, and how it will be used and released (including the surveys). They all provided their informed consent before requesting an anonymous user account for participation in the study (this was a mandatory requirement from the ethics committee and staff council).

Limitations

Interactive assistance. In this work, we focused on data collection and annotation from workers in a factory environment. Although the integration of TexPrax into their existing dashboard[10] alleviates their daily work, additional assistance could be provided by automatically suggesting solutions for identified problems.

Other use cases. While TexPrax received clearance by our university's ethics committee and staff council, it must be noted that this does not automatically transfer to new use cases or even similar ones at different universities/factories. It is crucial to get at least clearance of the respective staff council before deploying TexPrax to avoid any legal issues that may otherwise arise. Moreover, for the collected data to be of use for the NLP community, the company (or a respective organization) must be willing to share their data publicly. This however implies that deploying TexPrax in organizations that handle sensitive data (e.g., security-related or personal user data) can alleviate the work of employees, but will not result in datasets that can be publicly shared.

Different annotation tasks. The current version of TexPrax is designed as a tool for collecting data and annotations on a sentence-level. Explicitly asking for free-text responses could be one solution to tackle different kinds of annotations such as identifying named entities—for instance, a user could reply to a message containing a named entity by repeating it—however, this may hurt usability and lead to a less frequent usage of the application. To extend TexPrax to different annotation tasks one thus first needs to find a good way to interact with the user.

Propagating dataset changes in trained models. Finally, a last limitation is updating the training data that is implicitly stored in the trained model. The lack of efficient methods to update only specific information in trained models can lead to a substantial overhead when implementing changes in the data made by a user as the whole model needs to be retrained.

[8] https://www.intern.tu-darmstadt.de/gremien/ethikkommisson/index.en.jsp

[9] https://www.personalrat.tu-darmstadt.de/personalrat_1/index.de.jsp

[10] https://www.sfmsystems.de/

References

Tilman Beck, Ji-Ung Lee, Christina Viehmann, Marcus Maurer, Oliver Quiring, and Iryna Gurevych. 2021. Investigating label suggestions for opinion mining in German covid-19 social media. In *Proceedings of the 59th Annual Meeting of the Association for Computational Linguistics and the 11th International Joint Conference on Natural Language Processing (Volume 1: Long Papers)*, pages 1–13, Online. Association for Computational Linguistics.

John Brooke. 1996. Sus-a quick and dirty usability scale. *Usability evaluation in industry*, 189(194):4–7.

Branden Chan, Stefan Schweter, and Timo Möller. 2020. German's next language model. In *Proceedings of the 28th International Conference on Computational*

Linguistics, pages 6788–6796, Barcelona, Spain (Online). International Committee on Computational Linguistics.

Alexis Conneau, Kartikay Khandelwal, Naman Goyal, Vishrav Chaudhary, Guillaume Wenzek, Francisco Guzmán, Edouard Grave, Myle Ott, Luke Zettlemoyer, and Veselin Stoyanov. 2020. Unsupervised cross-lingual representation learning at scale. In *Proceedings of the 58th Annual Meeting of the Association for Computational Linguistics*, pages 8440–8451, Online. Association for Computational Linguistics.

Kevin Crowston. 2012. Amazon mechanical turk: A research tool for organizations and information systems scholars. In *Shaping the future of ict research. methods and approaches*, pages 210–221. Springer.

Ksenia Ermoshina, Francesca Musiani, and Harry Halpin. 2016. End-to-end encrypted messaging protocols: An overview. In *International Conference on Internet Science*, pages 244–254. Springer.

EU. 2016. Consolidated text: Regulation (EU) 2016/679 of the European Parliament and of the Council of 27 April 2016 on the protection of natural persons with regard to the processing of personal data and on the free movement of such data, and repealing Directive 95/46/EC (General Data Protection Regulation) (Text with EEA relevance).

Christian Hertle, Michael Tisch, Joachim Metternich, and Eberhard Abele. 2017. Das darmstädter shopfloor management-modell. *Zeitschrift für wirtschaftlichen Fabrikbetrieb*, 112(3):118–121.

Jan-Christoph Klie, Michael Bugert, Beto Boullosa, Richard Eckart de Castilho, and Iryna Gurevych. 2018. The inception platform: Machine-assisted and knowledge-oriented interactive annotation. In *Proceedings of the 27th International Conference on Computational Linguistics: System Demonstrations*, pages 5–9.

James R. Lewis and Jeff Sauro. 2018. Item benchmarks for the system usability scale. *Journal of Usability Studies*, 13(3):158–167.

Shervin Malmasi, Anjie Fang, Besnik Fetahu, Sudipta Kar, and Oleg Rokhlenko. 2022. SemEval-2022 task 11: Multilingual complex named entity recognition (MultiCoNER). In *Proceedings of the 16th International Workshop on Semantic Evaluation (SemEval-2022)*, pages 1412–1437, Seattle, United States. Association for Computational Linguistics.

Marvin Müller, Nicholas Frick, and Joachim Metternich. 2021a. Wissen aus betrieblichen chats nachhaltig nutzen. *wt Werkstattstechnik online*, 111(1-2):93–96.

Marvin Müller, Ji-Ung Lee, Nicholas Frick, Lorenz Stangier, Iryna Gurevych, and Joachim Metternich. 2021b. Extracting problem related entities from production chats to enhance the data base for assistance functions on the shop floor. *Procedia CIRP*, 103:231–236.

Sean A. Newman and Robert C. Ford. 2021. Five steps to leading your team in the virtual covid-19 workplace. *Organizational Dynamics*, 50(1):1–11. Virtual Teams.

Dinesh Raghu, Shantanu Agarwal, Sachindra Joshi, and Mausam. 2021. End-to-end learning of flowchart grounded task-oriented dialogs. In *Proceedings of the 2021 Conference on Empirical Methods in Natural Language Processing*, pages 4348–4366, Online and Punta Cana, Dominican Republic. Association for Computational Linguistics.

Jason Ariel Rajendran, Hanif Baharin, and Fazillah Mohmad Kamal. 2019. Understanding instant messaging in the workplace. In *International Visual Informatics Conference*, pages 640–652. Springer.

Evgeniia Razumovskaia, Goran Glavaš, Olga Majewska, Edoardo Ponti, and Ivan Vulić. 2022. Natural language processing for multilingual task-oriented dialogue. In *Proceedings of the 60th Annual Meeting of the Association for Computational Linguistics: Tutorial Abstracts*, pages 44–50, Dublin, Ireland. Association for Computational Linguistics.

Nithya Sambasivan, Shivani Kapania, Hannah Highfill, Diana Akrong, Praveen Paritosh, and Lora M Aroyo. 2021. "Everyone wants to do the model work, not the data work": Data Cascades in High-Stakes AI. In *proceedings of the 2021 CHI Conference on Human Factors in Computing Systems*, pages 1–15.

Carol Myers Scotton and William Ury. 1977. Bilingual strategies: The social functions of code-switching. *Linguistics. An International Review La Haye*, (193):5–20.

Thomas Wolf, Lysandre Debut, Victor Sanh, Julien Chaumond, Clement Delangue, Anthony Moi, Pierric Cistac, Tim Rault, Remi Louf, Morgan Funtowicz, Joe Davison, Sam Shleifer, Patrick von Platen, Clara Ma, Yacine Jernite, Julien Plu, Canwen Xu, Teven Le Scao, Sylvain Gugger, Mariama Drame, Quentin Lhoest, and Alexander Rush. 2020. Transformers: State-of-the-art natural language processing. In *Proceedings of the 2020 Conference on Empirical Methods in Natural Language Processing: System Demonstrations*, pages 38–45, Online. Association for Computational Linguistics.

PICTALKY: Augmentative and Alternative Communication for Language Developmental Disabilities

Chanjun Park[1,2]†, **Yoonna Jang**[1]†, **Seolhwa Lee**[3]†, **Jaehyung Seo**[1]†, **Kisu Yang**[4], **Heuiseok Lim**[1]*

[1]Korea University, South Korea, [2]Upstage, South Korea,
[3]University of Copenhagen, Denmark, [4]VAIV corp, South Korea

{bcj1210, morelychee, seojae777, limhseok}@korea.ac.kr
chanjun.park@upstage.ai, sele@di.ku.dk, ksyang@vaiv.kr

Abstract

Children with language disabilities face communication difficulties in daily life. They are often deprived of the opportunity to participate in social activities due to their difficulty in understanding or using natural language. In this regard, Augmentative and Alternative Communication (AAC) can be a practical means of communication for children with language disabilities. In this study, we propose PICTALKY, which is an AI-based AAC system that helps children with language developmental disabilities to improve their communication skills and language comprehension abilities. PICTALKY can process both text and pictograms more accurately by connecting a series of neural-based NLP modules. Additionally, we perform quantitative and qualitative analyses on the modules of PICTALKY. By using this service, it is expected that those suffering from language problems will be able to express their intentions or desires more easily and improve their quality of life. We have made the models freely available alongside a demonstration of the web interface [1]. Furthermore, we implemented robotics AAC for the first time by applying PICTALKY to the NAO robot.

1 Introduction

The majority of people with language disabilities suffer in their daily lives as they cannot understand or speak the language. As it is a means of communication, they may be deprived of the opportunity to participate in social activities. Also, they may experience financial difficulties. In general, people with speech disorders have lower employment rates than people with other types of disabilities. What is worse is that the proportion of people with autism disorder has been increasing every year (Zablotsky et al., 2019). Accordingly, a solution is required to ensure their economic freedom.

Meanwhile, augmentative and alternative communication (AAC) has been suggested and applied to solve communication problems for people with language disabilities (Beukelman et al., 1998). This approach enables nonverbal communication by replacing language. Although several AAC software resources are available, existing software packages are expensive, difficult to use, and only provide simple functions. To address these problems, we present a novel AAC system for children with language developmental disabilities. We refer to our AAC software as PICTALKY. Neural-based grammar error correction (GEC) and a symbol-based text-to-pictogram (TP) module are utilized in our model. Thus, PICTALKY offers neural- and symbol-based AAC for the improvement of communication and language learning, which have not been adopted in existing software.

From the perspective of NLP, the speech errors from people with language disabilities can be interpreted as grammatical errors at the morphological and syntactic levels. To handle these errors, neural GEC is applied in PICTALKY. Moreover, we consider both text and image processing for AAC education and communication. After a sentence is entered as an input through the speech-to-text (STT) module, it is passed through the neural GEC and natural language understanding (NLU) modules. Finally, the corresponding pictograms are displayed.

PICTALKY is aimed at children aged 0 to 14 years who have language developmental disabilities caused by intellectual or autism disabilities. The first reason that we focus on children is that early treatment during childhood is critical. According to Lenneberg (1967), language must be acquired during a critical period that ends at approximately the age of puberty with the establishment of the cerebral lateralization of function. Unless language is learned during this period, it is difficult for language to be used freely. This may result in

† All authors contributed equally.
* Corresponding author.
[1] http://nlplab.iptime.org:9062/

Proceedings of the 2nd Conference of the Asia-Pacific Chapter of the Association for Computational Linguistics and the 12th International Joint Conference on Natural Language Processing: System Demonstrations, pages 17–27
November 20–23, 2022.

social deterioration, contraction, aggression, and other problematic behaviors, which eventually affect the overall quality of life and satisfaction of the person (Schwarz et al., 2001).

The second reason is that there is currently insufficient social support for language therapy. Not all children with developmental disabilities can benefit from public systems owing to the limited support. Moreover, in addition to the children, their family and caregivers them experience difficulties.

Therefore, we propose PICTALKY, which complements the limitation of existing products and increases the accessibility of children with language disabilities to appropriate education and treatment. We expect that not only the people with language disabilities but also their caregivers can have more easier education and communication by using this service. Furthermore, in addition to the implementation of the web application, we apply PICTALKY to the NAO robot, thereby providing the first robotics AAC. We expect that robotics AAC can draw interest of children, so that they can use AAC more friendly and easily.

Our contributions are as follows:

- We propose PICTALKY for people with language diabilities, which is the first AAC software with GEC and a synonym-replacement system for accurate language processing.
- We analyze each detailed function of PICTALKY quantitatively and qualitatively. Also, we measure the satisfaction score during the actual services.
- We present a novel metric known as text-to-pictogram accuracy (TPA) to measure the performance of converting texts into pictograms.
- We open PICTALKY in the form of a platform, so that it can help people with language disabilities and contribute to the research in this area.
- We implement robotics AAC for the first time by applying PICTALKY to the NAO robot.

2 Background

2.1 AAC Software for Language Developmental Disabilities

Several AAC software platforms have been developed for language education. TouchChat[2] is a symbol- and text-based AAC tool with a text-to-speech (TTS) service. AVAZ[3] is a language education service that uses pictograms. TalkingBoogie (Shin et al., 2020) is software that supports the caregivers of children.

Systems that use AAC have also been developed for communication in daily life. Proloquo2Go[4] and QuickTalkAAC[5] enable people to communicate by using symbols or text with a TTS service. iCommunicate[6] is a visual and text AAC application that allows for the creation of pictures and storyboards. Although several AAC software platforms have been developed, certain problems remain, such as difficulty of use and high costs. Moreover, existing pictogram-based AAC software is difficult for users to use because they need to select an image from the communication board by themselves.

PICTALKY is the first symbol-based AAC system with neural GEC to provide more accurate and sophisticated language education and communication. PICTALKY automatically outputs the sequence of the pictograms according to the spoken sentences. It can be used for communication between people with disabilities as well as between people with disabilities and non-disabled people. Moreover, it offers the potential to be extended to multilingual versions by using neural machine translation.

2.2 Symbolic AAC

AAC enables nonverbal communication instead of a language, and it can provide practical help for people with cognitive and linguistic disorders.

In the majority of studies on AAC, researchers have employed graphic symbols (i.e., pictograms and picture communication symbols) (Kang et al., 2019) as alternative means of language items to improve the communication skills of children with language developmental disabilities. In this manner, children can be taught how to express their needs and interact with others using symbols (Huang and Lin, 2019).

Most authors have claimed that graphic symbols can enhance the literacy skills and communication of children or support children with disabilities in functional competence (e.g., writing, improving

[2] https://touchchatapp.com/

[3] https://www.avazapp.com/

[4] https://www.assistiveware.com/products/proloquo2go/

[5] https://digitalscribbler.com/quick-talk-aac/

[6] http://www.grembe.com/

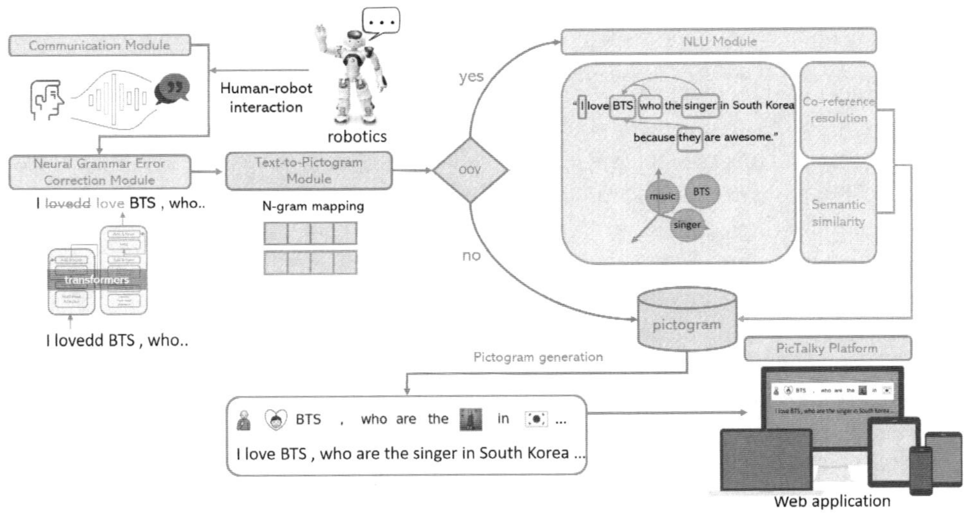

Figure 1: Overall architecture of PICTALKY.

their communication partner knowledge, and learning) (Karal et al., 2016; Nam et al., 2018; Light et al., 2019). Finally, AAC software is a form of symbolic knowledge representation (Beukelman and Mirenda, 2013). That is, symbols are verbal or visual representations of ideas and concepts. Therefore, we adopt both text and image processing mechanisms (i.e., TP) to consider symbolic knowledge with NLP in AAC. Furthermore, we use a deep learning architecture approach for our GEC module. To the best of our knowledge, no such method for a neural and symbol mechanism in AAC has yet been presented.

3 PICTALKY

3.1 Communication Module

Our proposed service uses deep learning-based speech-to-text (STT), which takes the voice of the user as input and converts it into text. We adopt Naver CLOVA Speech (Chung, 2019) for the STT system. The text input can be entered with the keyboard as well as in the form of voice. Users and caregivers can enter the text input easily with the keyboards of their personal computer, tablet, or mobile phone.

3.2 Neural GEC Module

People with language disabilities tend to make grammar and pronunciation errors when speaking. The grammar error correction (GEC) system revises various linguistic errors of users, so it is useful for children to practice correct sentences.

PicTalky is equipped with a neural GEC module that accurately corrects the STT outputs. We denote the sequence-to-sequence model that is applied to the GEC task as neural GEC. From the perspective of machine translation, the neural GEC task is a system whereby a sentence with noise and a correct sentence are entered as the source and target sentences, respectively. Subsequently, translation from the input to the output is trained with the sequence-to-sequence model. In this method, training is conducted without specifying a particular error type; thus, various errors can be detected and processed simultaneously.

PICTALKY enhances the software quality with the latest GEC technique which utilizes noising encoder and denoising decoder proposed by Park et al. (2020b) with copy mechanism (Gu et al., 2016). As a result, the speech errors of people with developmental disorders can be corrected on the text level.

3.3 TP Module

Pictograms are complementary and alternative means of communication that can help people with language difficulties. Unlike languages, which require an understanding of rules and symbolic systems, pictograms deliver the meaning more intuitively and rapidly. Thus, pictograms are utilized in the language rehabilitation field. For example, by using pictograms on communication boards, children can learn how to communicate with others (Calculator and Luchko, 1983). Pictograms provide children who have not learned the language system with practical help in language comprehension and speaking.

This study presents a system that causes the output of the pictogram images to correspond to the input text by using text and image processing. The text-to-pictogram (TP) module is an N-gram base mapping system, and it returns the output images that are morphologically similar to the input text in the pictogram dataset. The pictogram dataset includes texts such as words, phrases or sentences that explain the corresponding images. For more accurate mapping, our TP module makes use of a method that scans the entire sentence by N-gram to 1-gram and provides the most similar image.

3.4 NLU module

The output of the TP module is processed by the natural language understanding (NLU) module to handle the out-of-vocabulary (OOV) text that is not in the pictogram dataset. For this reason, we propose a method that causes the input vocabulary to correspond to a semantically similar image.

In the NLU module, unknown words are replaced with substitute words by measuring the semantic similarities, and a co-reference resolution system is applied to the substitute words. The semantic similarities are measured by Word2Vec (Mikolov et al., 2013) and WordNet (Miller, 1995). Within the input text, substitute words can be resolved through the co-reference resolution function of the spaCy[7] library. The remaining grammatical elements, such as unknown vocabularies, conjunctions, and articles that are not processed by measuring the semantic similarity and replacing unknown words with substitute words are designed not to be printed in the output image.

3.5 Overall Architecture of PICTALKY

When voice input is entered, it is converted into text by the communication module. Subsequently, the text is corrected by the neural GEC system and the corrected texts are changed into pictograms using the TP module. If OOV text exists in the input, the NLU module addresses this problem. Finally, a corresponding pictogram sequence is output.

The overall structure of our proposed service is depicted in Figure 1. If an erroneous sentence `"I lovedd BTS"` is entered as input, the neural GEC corrects the input to `"I love BTS."` Eventually, the text from the pictogram is generated and this module is provided to a form of web service or robotics.

PICTALKY aims to help children with developmental disabilities to communicate and improve their language understanding. The simultaneous encoding and transmission of speech text, both audibly and visually, allows users to understand the speaker's intentions intuitively, in spite of their difficulties in using language. Furthermore, as the text and images are delivered together, implicit learning is possible without directly teaching each element of the language. PICTALKY is intended for children with developmental disabilities, but it can also be applied to rehabilitation for educationally disadvantaged groups.

4 Experiment and Results

4.1 Datasets

To substantiate the performance of PICTALKY qualitatively, we adopted a test set that was provided by a GEC service company[8]. The test set was constructed while performing the actual GEC service, inspired by cases in which people with language developmental disabilities utter grammatically incorrect sentences. Thus, it can be stated that it provides high objectivity and reliability. We refer to this test set as the in-house test set. The test set consists of 100 sentences.

We used parallel corpora as the training data for training our neural GEC model, which were provided by Lang8 (Cho, 2013). We utilized an open-source pictogram dataset that was released by the Aragonese Centre for Augmentative & Alternative Communication[9].

4.2 Verification of Neural GEC Module

Model Although the majority of recent NLP studies have been conducted based on the pretrain-finetuning approach (PFA), it is difficult to service a PFA-based NLP application owing to its slow speed and high computational cost, among other factors (Park et al., 2021). Although state-of-the-art neural models such as mBART (Liu et al., 2020) have been developed, the parameters and model sizes are too large to service in the industry. To overcome this problem, we built a model based on the vanilla transformer, which is easy to service. The hyperparameters were set to the same values

[7] https://spacy.io/

[8] https://www.llsollu.com/

[9] http://arasaac.org

as the settings in Vaswani et al. (2017). The vocabulary size was 32,000 and sentencepiece (Kudo and Richardson, 2018) was adopted for the subword tokenization.

Performance of Neural GEC We used GLEU (Napoles et al., 2015) and BiLingual Evaluation Understudy (BLEU) (Papineni et al., 2002) as evaluation metrics to verify the performance of the neural GEC module. GLEU is similar to BLEU, but it is a more specialized metric for the error correction system, as it considers the source sentences. The overall comparison results are presented in Table 1.

Test set	BLEU	GLEU
In-house (Park et al. (2020c))	63.77	53.99

Table 1: Performance of neural GEC module.

	Case	Deletion setting		Score
		POS	Stopwords	
TPA	(1)	✓	✓	**94.16**
	(2)	-	✓	63.96
	(3)	✓	-	52.77
	(4)	-	-	43.59
TPA W/ PENALTY	(1)	✓	✓	**91.62**
	(2)	-	✓	62.24
	(3)	✓	-	51.35
	(4)	-	-	42.42

Table 2: Experimental results of PICTALKY. POS represents the removal of determiners, prepositions, and conjunctions using POS tagging information.

Algorithm 1 TPA

Initialize S_{pos} = {determiner, preposition, conjunction}
`/* The set of exceptional POS tags */`
Initialize S_{stop} as stopwords predefined by NLTK
procedure TPA($sentence$)
    Initialize $score$ and N as zeros
    $W \leftarrow PosTagger(sentence)$
`/* Split words with POS tags */`
    for each word $w \in W$ **do**
        if $w.pos \notin S_{pos}$ and $w \notin S_{stop}$ **then**
            $score \leftarrow score + \delta_{\hat{y},y}$ where $\hat{y} = M_\theta(w)$
`/* Kronecker delta of TP prediction */`
            $score \leftarrow score - (1 - \delta_{\hat{z},z})$ where $\hat{z} = N_\phi(w)$
`/* Penalty for a misclassified named entity */`
            $N \leftarrow N + 1$
    return $score/(N + \epsilon)$

In the experimental results, BLEU and GLEU scored 63.77 and 53.99, respectively. These results are sufficiently competitive with the results of other neural GEC studies (Im et al., 2017; Choe et al., 2019; Park et al., 2020b,c). This implies that our neural GEC module have an ability to correct the errors from the STT module, as well as the speech errors of users.

4.3 Verification of TP Module

The results of the performance evaluation of the TP module, which is a core function of PICTALKY, are presented in this section.

TPA We propose text-to-pictogram accuracy (TPA), which is a novel metric for measuring the performance of the TP module. TPA is an objective indicator of how effectively the text in PICTALKY input is converted into pictograms. The measurements are performed as follows. First, the input sentences are separated into words and POS tagged. Thereafter, the words that are POS tagged as determiners, prepositions, conjunctions (POS), and stopwords are removed, as we believe that these words are meaningless to be converted into pictograms. Thus, the words that do not contain important contents are removed during this process. The remaining words are used for the measurements and the ratio of the words that are effectively converted into pictograms is used as the TPA value. A named entity recognition (NER) penalty is also implemented when calculating the TPA value. The NER penalty is assigned when the named entities are misclassified by the NER process for the input sentences. As the named entities are important information that should be converted without errors, the NER penalty is assigned in those cases. The pseudo-code for the TPA is described in Algorithm 1.

Case Study We perform comparative experiments on the TPA with various cases of deletion, as indicated in Table 2. There were four cases in total for the deletion cases: (1) both POS (words tagged as determiners, prepositions and conjunctions) and stopwords are deleted, (2) only stopwords are deleted, (3) only POS are deleted, and (4) neither POS nor stopwords are deleted. We also measured how the penalty affected the overall performance. We used NLTK (Bird, 2006) to remove the determiners, prepositions, conjunctions, and stopwords and used the BERT-based (Devlin et al., 2018) NER model provided by Huggingface (Wolf et al., 2019) for the penalty.

The experimental results demonstrated that case (1) of the TPA, which was our proposed method, achieved the highest score of 94.16. In case (2) of the TPA, the score decreased by 30.20 points. When words that were POS tagged as determiners, prepositions, and conjunctions were deleted in case (3), lower performance was exhibited than in case (2). Finally, case (4) achieved the lowest performance. These results demonstrate that excluding both the POS and Stopwords from the subjects of the measurements is the most reasonable evaluation for TP conversion. Moreover, when the NER penalty was applied, the performances decreased in all cases, which means that the NER penalty contributes to more valid measurement. We also conducted a qualitative analysis on the results of PICTALKY (see Appendix B). Finally, we verify the the practicality of PICTALKY with a questionnaire-based satisfaction survey (see Appendix C.

5 PICTALKY with Robotics

We have distributed PICTALKY as a web application (see Appendix D). However, in the case of the web application, there is a possibility that it is difficult or boring for children to handle. Therefore, in addition to the web service, we have applied robotics technology to PICTALKY for arousing interest in children. The NAO robot (Shamsuddin et al., 2011; Jokinen and Wilcock, 2014) is mounted in the communication module of PICTALKY.

NAO is the humanoid robot developed by SoftBank Robotics[10]. Nao has eight full-color RGB LEDs, an inertial sensor, two cameras, and many other sensors. It also has a sonar sensor to check the distance of objects in its vicinity to comprehend its environment with precision and stability. It enables NAO to react its body to move when exposed by interaction. NAO is also available in social robotics (Fong et al., 2003), which focuses on communicating robots capable of interacting and cooperating with humans. All of these characteristics in NAO suit our research pursuit in terms of interacting with a human.

We have created a human-robot interaction system whereby the NAO robot has a conversation with the end users and the pictograms are printed onto the connected screen. As children show substantial interest in robots, this will aid in more familiar education as opposed to web or other applications (Sennott et al., 2019). The video of our demo is also attached with our paper[11].

To the best of our knowledge, this study is the first to apply PICTALKY to the NAO robot and to develop robotics AAC for the first time.

6 Conclusion and Future Work

We have proposed PICTALKY, which is the first AI-based AAC service. With the series of deep learning-based modules, it is able to take a speech or text input from the user, correct error, and converts it into a pictogram automatically for more convenient communication and education of the people with language disabilities. The aim of our proposed system is to provide an opportunity of communication and connection among all people, without anyone being excluded. In the future, we will expand the PICTALKY data to multilingual data for use in various languages and to make it publicly available. In addition, we plan to conduct various AI for accessibility studies to improve the quality of life for the people with disabilities. Starting with our research, we look forward to advances in many other studies so that all members of society can get benefits from AI technology without a financial burden.

Acknowledgments

This work was supported by Institute of Information & communications Technology Planning & Evaluation(IITP) grant funded by the Korea government(MSIT) (No. 2020-0-00368, A Neural-Symbolic Model for Knowledge Acquisition and Inference Techniques) and by the MSIT(Ministry of Science and ICT), Korea, under the ITRC(Information Technology Research Center) support program(IITP-2022-2018-0-01405) supervised by the IITP(Institute for Information & Communications Technology Planning & Evaluation). In addition, This research was supported by Basic Science Research Program through the National Research Foundation of Korea(NRF) funded by the Ministry of Education(NRF-2021R1A6A1A03045425). This work is the extended version of our papers [(Park et al., 2020a)]. Finally, the authors thank Yanghee Kim (rumbinie4@gmail.com) for provide initial ideas and proofreading.

[10]https://www.softbankrobotics.com/emea/en/

[11]https://bit.ly/2SunbaW

References

David Beukelman and Pat Mirenda. 2013. Augmentative and alternative communication: Supporting children and adults with complex communication needs. *4th Edition*.

David R Beukelman, Pat Mirenda, et al. 1998. *Augmentative and alternative communication*. Paul H. Brookes Baltimore.

Steven Bird. 2006. Nltk: the natural language toolkit. In *Proceedings of the COLING/ACL 2006 Interactive Presentation Sessions*, pages 69–72.

Stephen Calculator and Christine D'Altilio Luchko. 1983. Evaluating the effectiveness of a communication board training program. *Journal of speech and Hearing Disorders*, 48(2):185–191.

Young Sang Cho. 2013. Lang-8. *Calico Journal*, 30(2):293–299.

Yo Joong Choe, Jiyeon Ham, Kyubyong Park, and Yeoil Yoon. 2019. A neural grammatical error correction system built on better pre-training and sequential transfer learning. *arXiv preprint arXiv:1907.01256*.

Noam Chomsky. 1964. [the development of grammar in child language]: Discussion. *Monographs of the Society for Research in Child development*, pages 35–42.

Joon Son Chung. 2019. Naver at activitynet challenge 2019–task b active speaker detection (ava). *arXiv preprint arXiv:1906.10555*.

Joost CF de Winter, Samuel D Gosling, and Jeff Potter. 2016. Comparing the pearson and spearman correlation coefficients across distributions and sample sizes: A tutorial using simulations and empirical data. *Psychological methods*, 21(3):273.

Jacob Devlin, Ming-Wei Chang, Kenton Lee, and Kristina Toutanova. 2018. Bert: Pre-training of deep bidirectional transformers for language understanding. *arXiv preprint arXiv:1810.04805*.

Terrence Fong, Illah Nourbakhsh, and Kerstin Dautenhahn. 2003. A survey of socially interactive robots. *Robotics and autonomous systems*, 42(3-4):143–166.

Jiatao Gu, Zhengdong Lu, Hang Li, and Victor OK Li. 2016. Incorporating copying mechanism in sequence-to-sequence learning. *arXiv preprint arXiv:1603.06393*.

Chih-Hsiung Huang and Pei-Jung Lin. 2019. Effects of symbol component on the identifying of graphic symbols from eeg for young children with and without developmental delays. *Applied Sciences*, 9(6):1260.

Daniel Im Jiwoong Im, Sungjin Ahn, Roland Memisevic, and Yoshua Bengio. 2017. Denoising criterion for variational auto-encoding framework. In *Thirty-First AAAI Conference on Artificial Intelligence*.

Kristiina Jokinen and Graham Wilcock. 2014. Multimodal open-domain conversations with the nao robot. In *Natural Interaction with Robots, Knowbots and Smartphones*, pages 213–224. Springer.

Rowon Kang, Young Tae Kim, Seok Jeong Yeon, Rowon Kang, Young Tae Kim, and Seok Jeong Yeon. 2019. Cultural differences on the recognition of social word aac graphic symbols between korean and american undergraduate students. *Communication Sciences & Disorders*, 24(1):71–86.

Yasemin Karal, Hasan Karal, Lokman Şılbır, and Taner Altun. 2016. Standardization of a graphic symbol system as an alternative communication tool for turkish. *Journal of Educational Technology & Society*, 19(1):53–66.

Taku Kudo and John Richardson. 2018. Sentencepiece: A simple and language independent subword tokenizer and detokenizer for neural text processing. *arXiv preprint arXiv:1808.06226*.

Eric H Lenneberg. 1967. The biological foundations of language. *Hospital Practice*, 2(12):59–67.

Janice Light, David McNaughton, David Beukelman, Susan Koch Fager, Melanie Fried-Oken, Thomas Jakobs, and Erik Jakobs. 2019. Challenges and opportunities in augmentative and alternative communication: Research and technology development to enhance communication and participation for individuals with complex communication needs. *Augmentative and Alternative Communication*, 35(1):1–12.

Patsy M Lightbown and Nina Spada. 2021. *How Languages Are Learned 5th Edition*. Oxford university press.

Rensis Likert. 1932. A technique for the measurement of attitudes. *Archives of psychology*.

Yinhan Liu, Jiatao Gu, Naman Goyal, Xian Li, Sergey Edunov, Marjan Ghazvininejad, Mike Lewis, and Luke Zettlemoyer. 2020. Multilingual denoising pre-training for neural machine translation. *Transactions of the Association for Computational Linguistics*, 8:726–742.

Tomas Mikolov, Kai Chen, Greg Corrado, and Jeffrey Dean. 2013. Efficient estimation of word representations in vector space. *arXiv preprint arXiv:1301.3781*.

George A Miller. 1995. Wordnet: a lexical database for english. *Communications of the ACM*, 38(11):39–41.

Sang Nam, Jemma Kim, and Shannon Sparks. 2018. An overview of review studies on effectiveness of major aac systems for individuals with developmental disabilities including autism. *Journal of Special Education Apprenticeship*, 7(2):n2.

Courtney Napoles, Keisuke Sakaguchi, Matt Post, and Joel Tetreault. 2015. Ground truth for grammatical error correction metrics. In *Proceedings of the 53rd*

Annual Meeting of the Association for Computational Linguistics and the 7th International Joint Conference on Natural Language Processing (Volume 2: Short Papers), pages 588–593.

Kishore Papineni, Salim Roukos, Todd Ward, and Wei-Jing Zhu. 2002. Bleu: a method for automatic evaluation of machine translation. In *Proceedings of the 40th annual meeting on association for computational linguistics*, pages 311–318. Association for Computational Linguistics.

Chan-Jun Park, Yang-Hee Kim, Yoonna Jang, Umadevi GR, and Heui-Seok Lim. 2020a. An ai service to support communication and language learning for people with developmental disability. *Journal of the Korea Convergence Society*, 11(6):51–57.

Chanjun Park, Sugyeong Eo, Hyeonseok Moon, and Heui-Seok Lim. 2021. Should we find another model?: Improving neural machine translation performance with one-piece tokenization method without model modification. In *Proceedings of the 2021 Conference of the North American Chapter of the Association for Computational Linguistics: Human Language Technologies: Industry Papers*, pages 97–104.

Chanjun Park, Kuekyeng Kim, YeongWook Yang, Minho Kang, and Heuiseok Lim. 2020b. Neural spelling correction: translating incorrect sentences to correct sentences for multimedia. *Multimedia Tools and Applications*, pages 1–18.

Chanjun Park, Yeongwook Yang, Chanhee Lee, and Heuiseok Lim. 2020c. Comparison of the evaluation metrics for neural grammatical error correction with overcorrection. *IEEE Access*, 8:106264–106272.

Steven M Schwarz, Julissa Corredor, Julie Fisher-Medina, Jennifer Cohen, and Simon Rabinowitz. 2001. Diagnosis and treatment of feeding disorders in children with developmental disabilities. *Pediatrics*, 108(3):671–676.

Samuel C Sennott, Linda Akagi, Mary Lee, and Anthony Rhodes. 2019. Aac and artificial intelligence (ai). *Topics in Language Disorders*, 39(4):389–403.

Syamimi Shamsuddin, Luthffi Idzhar Ismail, Hanafiah Yussof, Nur Ismarrubie Zahari, Saiful Bahari, Hafizan Hashim, and Ahmed Jaffar. 2011. Humanoid robot nao: Review of control and motion exploration. In *2011 IEEE international conference on Control System, Computing and Engineering*, pages 511–516. IEEE.

Donghoon Shin, Jaeyoon Song, Seokwoo Song, Jisoo Park, Joonhwan Lee, and Soojin Jun. 2020. Talkingboogie: Collaborative mobile aac system for nonverbal children with developmental disabilities and their caregivers. In *Proceedings of the 2020 CHI Conference on Human Factors in Computing Systems*, pages 1–13.

J Bruce Tomblin, Xuyang Zhang, Paula Buckwalter, and Marlea O'Brien. 2003. The stability of primary language disorder. *Journal of Speech, Language, and Hearing Research*.

Ashish Vaswani, Noam Shazeer, Niki Parmar, Jakob Uszkoreit, Llion Jones, Aidan N Gomez, Łukasz Kaiser, and Illia Polosukhin. 2017. Attention is all you need. In *Advances in neural information processing systems*, pages 5998–6008.

Thomas Wolf, Lysandre Debut, Victor Sanh, Julien Chaumond, Clement Delangue, Anthony Moi, Pierric Cistac, Tim Rault, Rémi Louf, Morgan Funtowicz, et al. 2019. Huggingface's transformers: State-of-the-art natural language processing. *arXiv preprint arXiv:1910.03771*.

Benjamin Zablotsky, Lindsey I Black, Matthew J Maenner, Laura A Schieve, Melissa L Danielson, Rebecca H Bitsko, Stephen J Blumberg, Michael D Kogan, and Coleen A Boyle. 2019. Prevalence and trends of developmental disabilities among children in the united states: 2009–2017. *Pediatrics*, 144(4).

A Language Developmental Disabilities

Language disorder is a slow-speech phenomenon due to late development of the speech center in the brain (Tomblin et al., 2003). Language disorders can be categorized into four main categories: expressive language disorder, mixed receptive-expressive language disorder, phonological disorder, and stuttering.

People with expressive language disorder have relatively normal receptive language ability to understand other people's words, but difficulty in language expression. They tend to replace simple words or sentences with gestures. People with mixed receptive-expressive language disorder shows a disability in understanding other people's words and in expressing their thoughts in language. In phonological disorder, there is a common occurrence of incorrect pronunciation in consonants, especially mispronouncing consonants or omitting the coda (auslaut) of syllables. Most frequently mispronounced consonants are [s], [z], [ʃ], [ʒ], etc, also, there are mispronunciations in vowels too. The speech of people with stuttering is cut off abnormally often or the speed of which is irregular. The repetition of sounds or syllables, extension of speech sounds, and blockage of speech can be observed. Also, their speech typically begins by repeating the first consonant of a phrase. Children generally do not recognize stuttering, as getting older, they become aware of their speaking problems, and emotional reactions occur to avoid being not fluent.

These disorders can be interpreted as grammatical errors at morphological and syntax levels from the perspective of natural language processing. Thus, deep learning-based grammar error corrector has been developed and loaded into PICTALKY's software .

B Qualitative Analysis

We also perform a qualitative analysis on the results of PICTALKY based on the developmental stages of the First Language Acquisition (FLA) (Lightbown and Spada, 2021).

In Table 3, the input sentences contain grammatical problems, including fronting, infinitive, article, spelling, plural -s, and irregular past form errors. The PICTALKY web application shows users the most appropriate pictograms and the output sentences with the errors corrected.

Examples such as `"I love play the baseball"`, `"I love danceing with a friends"`, and `"He taked my toy!"` occur in telegraphic speech (Chomsky, 1964) in the immature language development stage between the ages of two and three. Grammatical errors for morphemes are not merely an imperfect imitation of adults' speech, and consistency of correction with frequent interactions is required to expand cognitive development.

`"Is the dog is tired?"` and `"Do I can eat a pizza?"` are one of the errors encountered in acquiring basic structures of the first language between the age of 4 and the school years, and this stage requires correction of low frequency and complex systems. Therefore, we reproduce humans' universal language acquisition process, including frequent errors in the early and later development stages.

Note that if the Neural GEC module cannot correct grammatical errors, the NLU module can compensate for it. However, these aspects need to be supplemented through future research.

Input sentence	Output sentence	Pictogram
* Is the dog is tired?	Is the dog tired?	
* Do I can eat a pizza?	Can I eat a pizza?	
* I love play the baseball	I love to play baseball	
* I love danceing with a friends	I love dancing with friends	
* He taked my toy!	He took my toy!	

Table 3: Example sentences and pictograms for qualitative analysis created by PICTALKY web demo.

C PICTALKY Satisfaction Survey

We conducted a satisfaction survey to investigate the user satisfaction. It is difficult to employ the nonverbal child, so we identified the extreme difficulty in performing a large-scale survey. Therefore, we conducted a system satisfaction survey to 53 people with 43 experts in language disabilities and ten nonverbal children. The experts consist of thirty teachers of nonverbal children and the thirteen professionals who majored in language disabilities from Korea University Anam Hospital. PICTALKY Satisfaction Questionnaires are shown in Table 4.

We established a total of five questions and specified the answers using a Likert scale (Likert, 1932) of "Satisfied," "Neither agree nor disagree," and "Dissatisfied.". The survey results are depicted in Figure 2.

Question
Q1. Are you satisfied with the overall performance of PICTALKY?
Q2. Do you think this system will be helpful to people with language developmental disabilities?
Q3. Are you satisfied with the usability and UI of PICTALKY?
Q4. Are you satisfied with the performance of the grammar error correction system?
Q5. Are you satisfied with the results of the text-to-pictogram function?

Table 4: Questions of PICTALKY satisfaction survey.

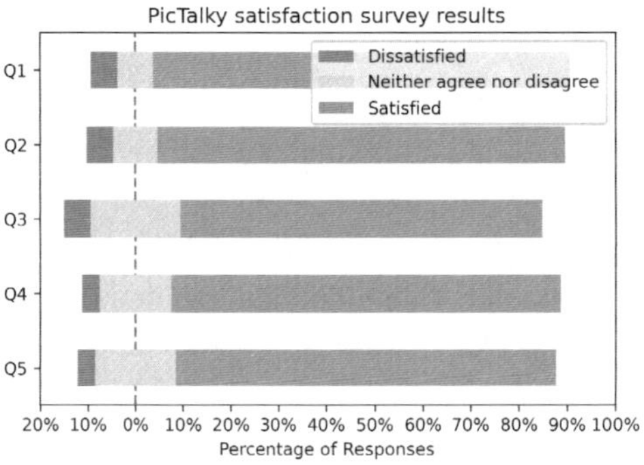

Figure 2: Response results of satisfaction survey regarding PICTALKY.

The survey results revealed that most people were satisfied with the performance of PICTALKY. For each question, 80% to 90% of the responses were satisfied and approximately 90% of the responses stated that it will be helpful to people with developmental disabilities. However, the UI of PICTALKY still requires improvement and the performance of the GEC system should be enhanced. In particular, according to the results of the Spearman correlation (de Winter et al., 2016) of the sentences, as illustrated in Figure 3, the correlation between Q1 and Q2 was high, which indicates that the purpose of this study

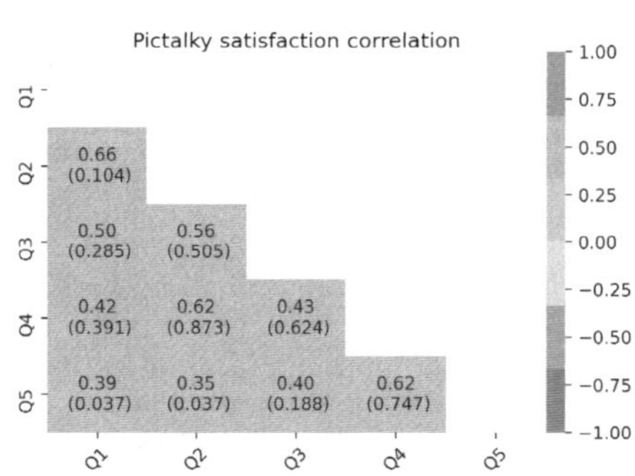

Figure 3: Results of statistical significance test using Spearman correlation between questionnaires. The weight indicates the correlation value and the value in parentheses is the p-value (p-value<0.05 indicates statistical significance).

was well reflected. Although the correlation between Q1 and Q5, and that between Q2 and Q5 were lower than the others, their p-values were lower than 0.05 which means the results were statistically significant.

D PicTalky with Web Application

We released the PicTalky as the form of a web application as shown in Figure 4. Thus, any devices enable our system by responsive user interface. The neural GEC module was connected by Rest API and distributed as both CPU and GPU services. Our system is operated by Flask under a cloud server.

Also, we provide the user input into two modes of both speech and text considering the environment where speech is not possible. For reviewing other situations that people with language disabilities face, these settings are available to people who have deaf-mutism, aphasia. Our system is built on the compact user interface and freely available to advance accessibility.

Overall procedures of the system are illustrated in Section 3.5. The voice recording starts when the user clicks the record button, and our system begins to print out the result.

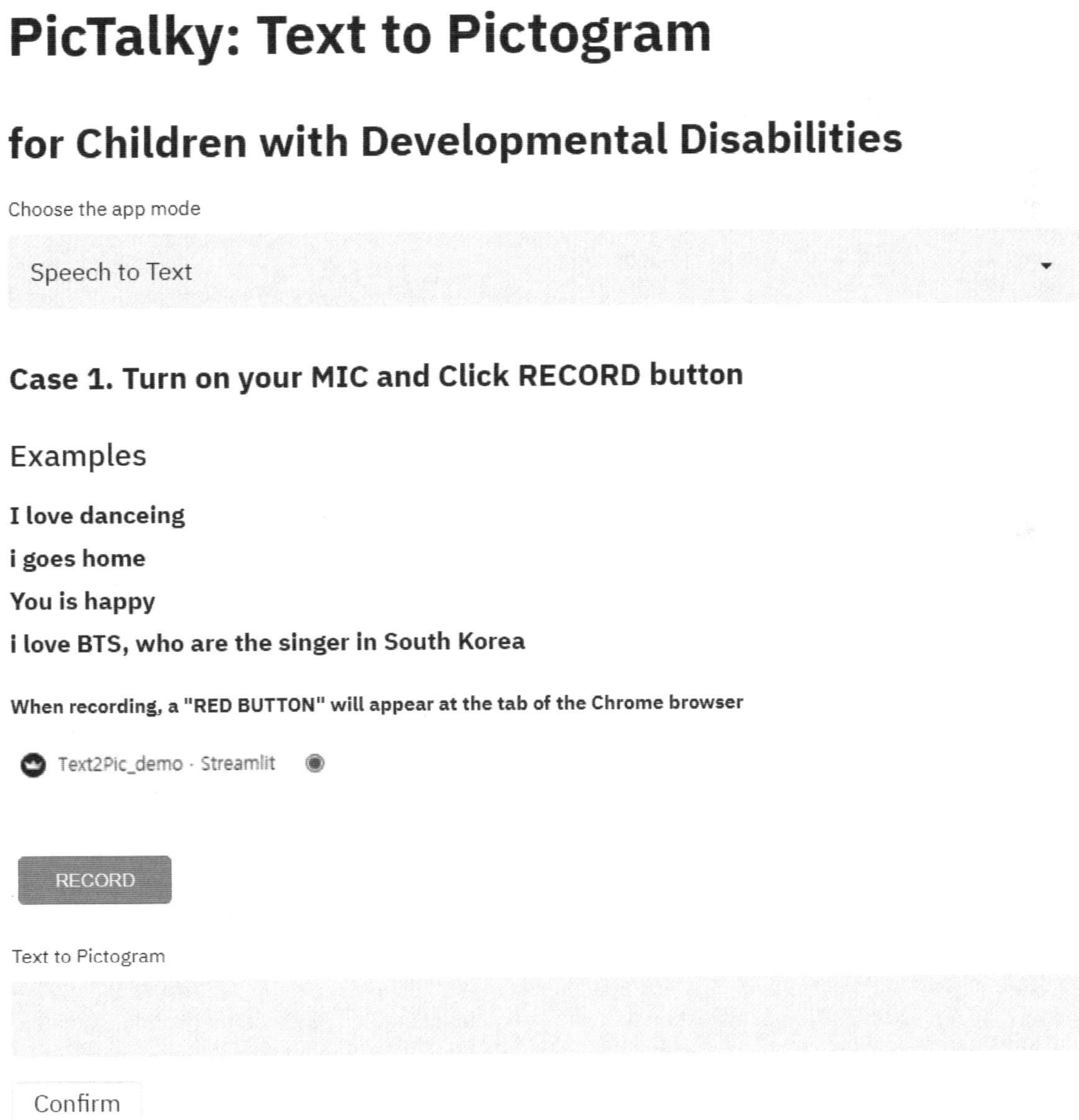

Figure 4: PicTalky web application.

UKP-SQuARE v2
Explainability and Adversarial Attacks for Trustworthy QA

Rachneet Sachdeva*, **Haritz Puerto***, **Tim Baumgärtner, Sewin Tariverdian, Hao Zhang, Kexin Wang, Hossain Shaikh Saadi, Leonardo F. R. Ribeiro, Iryna Gurevych**
Ubiquitous Knowledge Processing Lab (UKP Lab),
Department of Computer Science and Hessian Center for AI (hessian.AI),
Technical University of Darmstadt
www.ukp.tu-darmstadt.de

Abstract

Question Answering (QA) systems are increasingly deployed in applications where they support real-world decisions. However, state-of-the-art models rely on deep neural networks, which are difficult to interpret by humans. Inherently interpretable models or post hoc explainability methods can help users to comprehend how a model arrives at its prediction and, if successful, increase their trust in the system. Furthermore, researchers can leverage these insights to develop new methods that are more accurate and less biased. In this paper, we introduce SQuARE v2, the new version of SQuARE, to provide an explainability infrastructure for comparing models based on methods such as saliency maps and graph-based explanations. While saliency maps are useful to inspect the importance of each input token for the model's prediction, graph-based explanations from external Knowledge Graphs enable the users to verify the reasoning behind the model prediction. In addition, we provide multiple adversarial attacks to compare the robustness of QA models. With these explainability methods and adversarial attacks, we aim to ease the research on trustworthy QA models. SQuARE is available at https://square.ukp-lab.de.[1]

1 Introduction

The recent explosion of Question Answering datasets and models is pushing the boundaries of QA systems and making them widely used by the general public in virtual assistants or chatbots (Rogers et al., 2021). This ubiquitous adoption is making regulators start preparing policies for artificial intelligence with special emphasis on explainability and robustness to adversarial attacks.[2]

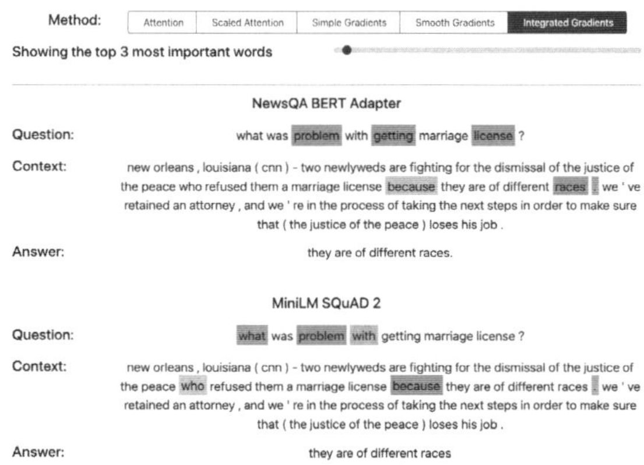

Figure 1: Visualization of two saliency maps computed using integrated gradients. The darker the highlighting color, the higher its importance to get the prediction. Hovering on a word shows its importance value.

There are multiple methods to explain the predictions of AI models (Danilevsky et al., 2020) and analyze their robustness (Zhang et al., 2020). Some explainability methods focus on specific input attributions such as attention- and gradient-based saliency maps (Simonyan et al., 2014). Others design interpretable models instead of using post hoc methods (Yasunaga et al., 2021). Lastly, most approaches that analyze the robustness of AI systems are based on *adversarial attacks*, i.e., the use of inputs such as questions with minor modifications that change the system's output.

However, exploring and comparing these methods is not straightforward for most models. Researchers usually need to manipulate libraries and create interfaces to compare them in a satisfactory manner, which is a slow and complicated process that hinders the research in trustworthy QA.

The SQuARE platform (Baumgärtner et al., 2022) simplifies the process of comparing QA models by empowering NLP researchers with an online platform to deploy, run, and compare the most common QA pipelines while removing technical barriers such as model and infrastructure configu-

*Equal Contribution.

[1]The code is available at https://github.com/UKP-SQuARE/square-core

[2]https://digital-strategy.ec.europa.eu/en/policies/european-approach-artificial-intelligence

Proceedings of the 2nd Conference of the Asia-Pacific Chapter of the Association for Computational Linguistics and the 12th International Joint Conference on Natural Language Processing: System Demonstrations, pages 28–38
November 20–23, 2022.

rations. It includes dozens of models of multiple types, namely open-domain, extractive, multiple choice, and abstractive QA. However, the only explainability method currently implemented is behavioral test (Appendix 3), limiting the comparison between QA models based solely on the models' final predictions.

In this work, we propose SQuARE v2, a new online platform for trustworthy QA research implementing various explainability, interpretability, and robustness methods and interfaces to facilitate research in trustworthy QA models. Specifically, we make the following contributions: 1) SQuARE v2 supports the comparison of models based on different post hoc explainability methods. We create interactive saliency maps that illustrate the importance of each input token for the model's prediction (Simonyan et al., 2014). 2) We extend the Datastores to include support for knowledge graphs (KG), deploy QA-GNN (Yasunaga et al., 2021), an interpretable graph-based model, and create an interactive visualization graph. 3) SQuARE v2 further provides various adversarial attacks, which change the prediction by modifying the input but keeping its semantics in order to evaluate the robustness of QA models (Ebrahimi et al., 2018).

2 Related Work

AllenNLP demo[3] is the closest system to SQuARE v2. They provide a web interface to interact with their library, where users can explore explainability functionalities (Gardner et al., 2018; Wallace et al., 2019). However, only two non-Transformer models include saliency maps and attack methods. In addition, users cannot deploy their models on this web demo, and instead, they would need to install their library and create their own interface.

Among the explainability libraries, Captum (Kokhlikyan et al., 2020) is of special relevance. It is a model interpretability library for PyTorch that includes multiple saliency maps and provides built-in visualizations. However, it does not provide a user interface to run all their methods and compare them at a glance. On the other hand, it provides an adversarial attack method, Fast Gradient Sign Method (Goodfellow et al., 2015), and some variants; however, these are not designed for NLP.

Lastly, there are some efforts to ease the study of adversarial attacks on NLP models. Textattack (Morris et al., 2020) is a library that supports several attacks and is model agnostic. However, they do not provide a web interface, so users must therefore create their own visualizations in order to be able to easily compare attacks on multiple models.

In summary, SQuARE is a single entry-point for NLP practitioners to analyze, compare, and teach QA through models' outputs, explainability, and robustness with a user-friendly interface.

3 UKP-SQuARE

SQuARE (Baumgärtner et al., 2022) is an open-source, online platform for NLP researchers to share, run, compare, and analyze their QA models. The platform implements a flexible and scaleable microservice architecture containing four high-level services:

1. **Datastores:** Provides efficient access to large-scale background knowledge such as Wikipedia.
2. **Models:** Allows the dynamic deployment and inference of a wide variety of models implemented in the Hugging Face transformers library (Wolf et al., 2020) or adapters (Pfeiffer et al., 2020).
3. **Skills:** Implements a configurable QA pipeline (e.g. multiple-choice, open-domain, or extractive QA) leveraging the Datastores and Models service. They can be added dynamically by the users to the system.
4. **Explainability:** provides a set of unit tests (questions and answers in our case) (Ribeiro et al., 2020) to compare the predictions with the expected answers and, in this way, analyze the biases and weaknesses of the Skills.

SQuARE is designed to ease the comparison and analysis of models. Users can deploy their models using a simple interface without the need of any code and then, they can compare outputs of different models side-by-side. This paper describes a new major update of SQuARE.

4 Trustworthy Methods for QA

Modern neural networks have significantly improved in performance in recent years; however, their explainability have not followed the same improvement (Rogers et al., 2020). Additionally, despite their impressive performance, the models

[3] https://demo.allennlp.org

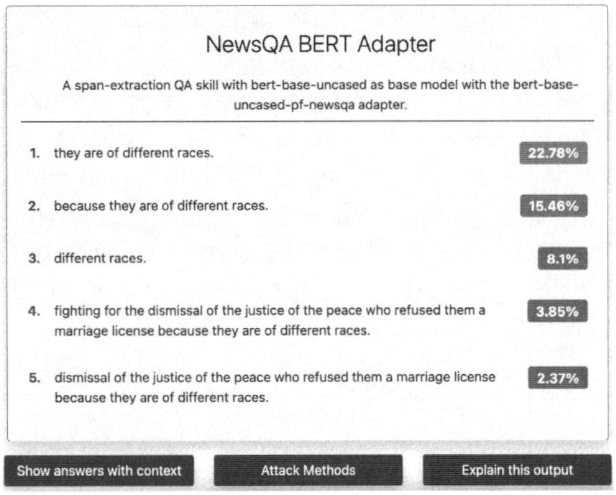

Figure 2: The "Explain this output" and "Attack Methods" are shown under the predictions of the Skill.

are vulnerable to adversarial attacks. The goal of SQuARE v2 is to provide the research community with a set of tools to facilitate the research on trustworthy QA. SQuARE simplifies and provides visualizations for saliency maps, graph-based interpretable models, and adversarial attacks. The following sections briefly describe the methods provided in SQuARE.

4.1 Saliency Maps

Saliency Maps assign an attribution weight to the input tokens to assess their importance in the model prediction, as illustrated in Fig. 1. To obtain this visualization, a user needs to click on the button *"Explain this output"* located after the predictions of any Skill, as shown in Fig. 2.

In SQuARE, we use two families of attribution methods to construct saliency maps: i) Gradient-based methods and ii) Attention-based methods.

4.1.1 Gradient-based Methods

A common approach to obtaining an importance score for the input tokens is to compute the gradients on the embedding layer against the model prediction. The magnitude of the gradient corresponds to the change of the prediction when updating the embedding. Therefore, a large gradient has a large effect on the prediction, indicating the importance of the input.

Vanilla Gradient (Simonyan et al., 2014) utilizes the plain gradients of the embedding layer of the model as importance weights of the inputs.

Integrated Gradient (Sundararajan et al., 2017) integrates the straight line path from the vector of zeros to the input token embedding. The value of this integral is the weight of this token to make the prediction since it represents the amount of information given with respect to the zero vector (i.e., no information).

SmoothGrad (Smilkov et al., 2017) adds gaussian noise to the input to create multiple versions and then average their saliency scores. In this way, this method can smooth the saliency scores and alleviate noise from local variations in the partial derivatives.

4.1.2 Attention Methods

Neural NLP models have broadly incorporated attention mechanisms, which are frequently recognized for enhancing transparency and increasing performance (Vaswani et al., 2017). These methods compute a distribution over the input tokens that can be considered to reflect what the model believes to be important. Following (Jain et al., 2020), we build a saliency map using the average **attention weights** of the heads from the CLS token to the other tokens of the input. However, Serrano and Smith (2019) argue that attention weights are inconsistent and may not always correlate with the human notion of importance. Thus, they propose an alternative, **Scaled Attention**, which we also integrate in SQuARE, that multiplies the attention weights by their corresponding gradients to make it more stable.

4.2 Interpretable Graph-based Models

Knowledge graphs store knowledge in the form of relations (edges) between entities (nodes). In addition to the explicit facts they represent, they enable explainable predictions by providing reasoning paths (Yasunaga et al., 2021). In SQuARE v2, we deploy QA-GNN (Yasunaga et al., 2021), a graph-based QA model, as a Skill (more details on Appendix B) and ConceptNet (Speer et al., 2017) as a graph Datastore. Since QA-GNN uses a KG (i.e., ConceptNet) for QA reasoning, it is possible to analyze its working graph to identify the most important entities and relations for the answer prediction. As shown in Fig. 3 and later discussed in §6.2, we provide an interface that enables the visualization of the graph-based reasoning process executed by the model.

User Interface. In order to plot the graphs, SQuARE provides users with a *"Show graph"* button after the predictions of the QA-GNN Skill at the bottom of the page. Clicking on this button

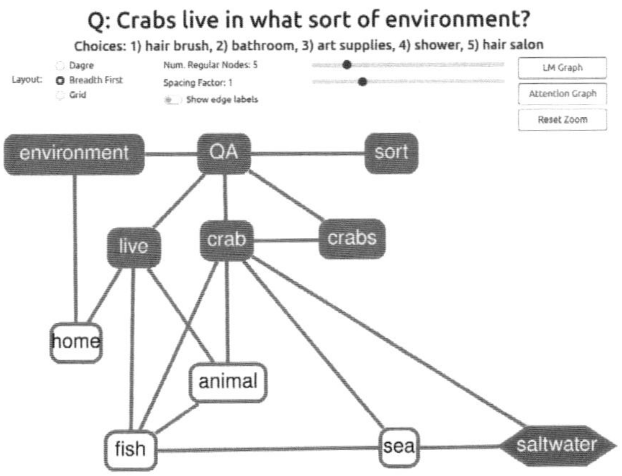

Figure 3: Visualization of the graph used by QA-GNN Skill to answer the question. Question nodes in purple, answer nodes in green.

displays a modal window with multiple options to render the graph, as shown in Fig. 3. Controls include a switch to show or hide edge labels, a slider to show the top k nodes, another slider to select the spacing factor between nodes, and a group of radio buttons to select the layout (Dagre[4], Breath First, and Grid). In addition, we offer two types of visualizations: i) a graph where the nodes are sorted by the relevance scores generated by the model and ii) a graph with the nodes sorted by the sum of the attention scores of their incoming edges.

4.3 Adversarial Attacks

Adversarial attacks make use of inputs that expose vulnerabilities of machine learning models to understand their robustness and identify how to improve them (Ebrahimi et al., 2018). To simplify the exploration of adversarial attacks on a wide range of Skills, we implement the following four methods in SQUARE for span-extraction Skills and leave the other Skills for future updates.

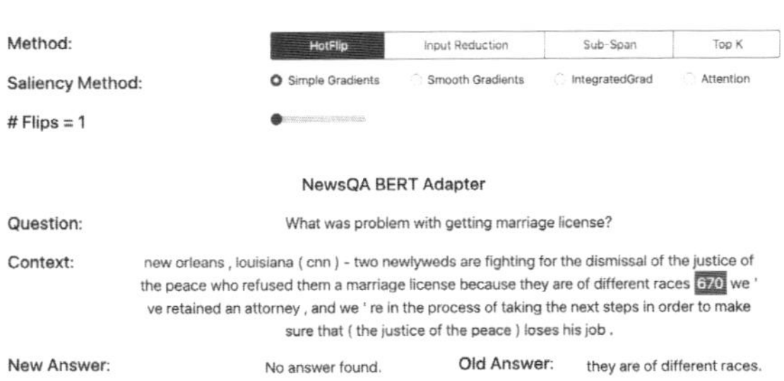

Figure 4: HotFlip Attack. Changing one word changes the prediction.

[4]https://github.com/cytoscape/cytoscape.js-dagre

HotFlip (Ebrahimi et al., 2018) uses a saliency method (§4.1) to score input words and subsequently replaces the top words with semantically similar words to alter the prediction of the model. An example of the interface is shown in Fig. 4. The words highlighted in green are replacements, and when hovering over them, the original word is shown in a tooltip.

Input Reduction (Feng et al., 2018) iteratively removes unimportant words from the question based on their saliency scores (§4.1), without changing the model's prediction. An example is shown in Fig. 5 (Appendix C).

Sub-Span Jain et al. (2020) computes the saliency scores of the input words to select a contiguous span that maximizes the accumulative saliency score and uses this span as an explainability method. Instead, we leverage this method to create an adversarial attack. We identify a sub-span of the context that explains the output and use it as the whole context. In this way, the model has the key information, such as a phrase containing the answer, but not the whole context. Therefore, it is possible to identify a sub-span that lacks the nuance to answer the question properly, but since the answer occurs in the sub-span, the model may retrieve it due to spurious correlations. Fig. 6 (Appendix C) and § 6.3 show an use case of this attack.

Top K. Similarly as in the previous case, Jain et al. (2020) compute the saliency scores of the input words to identify the top k words from the context that explains the output answer. We leverage this method to create an adversarial attack. While the top k words are key to obtaining the answer, they are usually not contiguous. Therefore, creating a new context by concatenating these words yields a grammatically and semantically incorrect text. If the model still identifies the correct answer using this new context, it would be due to spurious correlations. An example of this attack is shown in Fig. 7 (Appendix C).

User Interface After the user queries any Skill, the button *"Attack Method"* is shown under the predictions, as shown in Fig. 2. After clicking on it, a modal page is shown where users can conduct adversarial attacks.

5 Datastores for Knowledge Graphs

To best re-use the existing Datastore while being efficient and robust, we rely on an Elasticsearch instance to store KGs. In particular, we represent nodes and edges as documents and include information to recreate the graph structure, such as their connectivity. We show the schema of these documents in Appendix A.

In addition, we implement two main functionalities: Firstly, users can dynamically add and update new KGs as long as the structure of the KG can be converted to the schema shown in Appendix A. This allows supporting any KG that is requested by the community. For demonstration purposes, we provide ConceptNet (Speer et al., 2017) as a built-in KG. More information is available on the Datastores documentation[5]. Secondly, we implement a subgraph extraction method. Given a list of root nodes (e.g., the entities in a question), it extracts all the nodes and edges in the vicinity of k hops to the roots. Since ConceptNet is densely connected, we limit the maximum number of hops to 3. However, this is a parameter that can be adjusted for any KG. Lastly, after the extraction, we prune the disconnected nodes.

6 Case Study

6.1 Saliency Maps

Our new saliency map interface allows users to compare the explanation of the outputs of up to three Skills. As shown in Fig. 1, thanks to this visualization, we can easily observe that the first Skill, *NewsQA BERT Adapter*, gives the correct answer for the right reasons since it identifies *"races"* as a keyword. Even though the second Skill, *MiniLM SQuAD 2*, also returns the correct answer, the Skill does not seem to understand the context properly. In particular, the most important words for the predictions are not related to the answer. We argue that this interface can provide insights into whether the model understands the task and thus make the Skills more trustworthy.

6.2 Interpretable Models

ConceptNet provides background knowledge that can boost the commonsense abilities of NLP models. As shown in Fig. 3, the QA-GNN Skill makes use of the KG to connect the entities *crab* with *sea* and with *saltwater*, the answer. This explicit path helps to identify why the model returns its answers. However, it still requires some human effort to interpret the graph. For example, ConceptNet does not include the triple (*sea*, *is a*, *environment*), which could be seen as counter-intuitive.

On the other hand, other non-graph-based Skills need post hoc explainability methods such as saliency maps (§4.1) to explain their output. However, post hoc methods have raised concerns about the possibility of not being faithful to the actual computations performed by the model or giving incomplete explanations as in saliency maps (Liu et al., 2021). In particular, saliency maps identify what parts of the input are relevant for the prediction, but they do not explain how or why the model obtains the output.

6.3 Adversarial Attacks

Using the Sub-span attack method shown in Fig. 6 (Appendix C), we can observe that the Skill gives the correct answer even though it does not have information about *Super Bowl 50*, which is needed. A robust Skill should instead return "not enough information." This example suggests that the Skill is conducting a superficial question-context overlap matching without understanding the nuances of the question, a phenomenon previously identified by Lim et al. (2020). Similarly, the input reduction attack shown in Fig. 5 (Appendix C) shows the same phenomenon. After removing most words from the question, the resulting question is not semantically complete, yet the Skill gives the correct answer.

7 Conclusion and Future Work

We present SQuARE v2, a web platform that unifies three families of methods for analyzing QA models: saliency maps, adversarial attacks, and interpretable models. Firstly, we offer an interactive interface that allows users to compare multiple saliency map methods for all the Skills deployed in SQuARE. Secondly, we provide an interface to conduct adversarial attacks. This interface allows the community to study the robustness of QA models. Lastly, we deploy an interpretable graph-based model and provide an interface to visualize the reasoning paths that the model may conduct. To deploy this Skill, we extend the Datastores module to support both text documents and KGs. These contributions give SQuARE a set of tools to compare, analyze, and explain the behavior of QA models. Since SQuARE allows the deployment of almost any Transformer-based model effortlessly, our new explainability interface empowers the community with tools for trustworthy QA research. SQuARE

[5] https://square.ukp-lab.de/docs/api/datastores/

is actively under development. Future updates will include new KGs such as WikiData (Vrandečić and Krötzsch, 2014), automated Skill selection (Geigle et al., 2021), and Skill collaboration (Puerto et al., 2021).

Limitations

Although saliency maps attempt to explain the output of the models, they should be analyzed with skepticism. As discussed in §4.1.2, attention-based saliency maps may not correlate with the human interpretation of importance, and in general, they do not explain how and why the model creates the outputs. Instead, saliency maps only aim to identify regions of the input that upon removal, changes the output.

Currently, we only deploy one graph-based model (QA-GNN) and one knowledge graph (ConceptNet). However, our Datastores §5 and graph visualization interface §4.2 are flexible enough to accommodate any other model, and thus, we invite the community to create pull requests and deploy their graph-based models on SQUARE.

Ethics and Broader Impact Statement

Intended Use. The intended use of SQUARE is to facilitate the comparison of QA models through multiple angles such as performance, explainability, interpretability, and robustness. Our platform allows NLP practitioners to share their models with the community removing technical barriers such as configuration and infrastructure so that any person can reuse these models. This has a straightforward benefit for the research community (i.e., reproducible research and analysis of prior works) but also to the general public because SQUARE allows them to run state-of-the-art models without requiring any special hardware and hiding complex settings such as virtual environments and package management.

Potential Misuse. Our platform makes use of models uploaded by the community. However, this current version does not incorporate any mechanism to ensure that these models are fair and without bias. We hope that the new tools we provide in this work can help the community understand the outputs of QA models and identify potential biases or unfair behaviors. Thus, we currently delegate the fairness checks to the authors of the models. We are not held responsible for errors, false or offensive content generated by the models. Users should use them at their discretion.

Environmental Impact. Since SQUARE empowers the community to run publicly available Skills on the cloud, it has the potential to reduce CO_2 emissions from retraining previous models to make the comparisons needed when developing new models.

Acknowledgements

We thank Irina Bigoulaeva and Haishuo Fang for their insightful comments on a previous draft of this paper. We also thank the anonymous reviewers for their insightful feedback.

This work has been funded by the German Research Foundation (DFG) as part of the UKP-SQuARE project (grant GU 798/29-1), the QASci-Inf project (GU 798/18-3), and by the German Federal Ministry of Education and Research and the Hessian Ministry of Higher Education, Research, Science and the Arts (HMWK) within their joint support of the National Research Center for Applied Cybersecurity ATHENE.

References

Tim Baumgärtner, Kexin Wang, Rachneet Sachdeva, Gregor Geigle, Max Eichler, Clifton Poth, Hannah Sterz, Haritz Puerto, Leonardo F. R. Ribeiro, Jonas Pfeiffer, Nils Reimers, Gözde Şahin, and Iryna Gurevych. 2022. UKP-SQUARE: An online platform for question answering research. In *Proceedings of the 60th Annual Meeting of the Association for Computational Linguistics: System Demonstrations*, pages 9–22, Dublin, Ireland. Association for Computational Linguistics.

Marina Danilevsky, Kun Qian, Ranit Aharonov, Yannis Katsis, Ban Kawas, and Prithviraj Sen. 2020. A survey of the state of explainable AI for natural language processing. In *Proceedings of the 1st Conference of the Asia-Pacific Chapter of the Association for Computational Linguistics and the 10th International Joint Conference on Natural Language Processing*, pages 447–459, Suzhou, China. Association for Computational Linguistics.

Javid Ebrahimi, Anyi Rao, Daniel Lowd, and Dejing Dou. 2018. HotFlip: White-box adversarial examples for text classification. In *Proceedings of the 56th Annual Meeting of the Association for Computational Linguistics (Volume 2: Short Papers)*, pages 31–36, Melbourne, Australia. Association for Computational Linguistics.

Shi Feng, Eric Wallace, Alvin Grissom II, Mohit Iyyer, Pedro Rodriguez, and Jordan Boyd-Graber. 2018.

Pathologies of neural models make interpretations difficult. In *Proceedings of the 2018 Conference on Empirical Methods in Natural Language Processing*, pages 3719–3728, Brussels, Belgium. Association for Computational Linguistics.

Max Franz, Christian Tannus Lopes, Gerardo Huck, Yue Dong, Selçuk Onur Sümer, and Gary D. Bader. 2016. Cytoscape.js: a graph theory library for visualisation and analysis. *Bioinform.*, 32(2):309–311.

Matt Gardner, Joel Grus, Mark Neumann, Oyvind Tafjord, Pradeep Dasigi, Nelson F. Liu, Matthew Peters, Michael Schmitz, and Luke Zettlemoyer. 2018. AllenNLP: A deep semantic natural language processing platform. In *Proceedings of Workshop for NLP Open Source Software (NLP-OSS)*, pages 1–6, Melbourne, Australia. Association for Computational Linguistics.

Gregor Geigle, Nils Reimers, Andreas Rücklé, and Iryna Gurevych. 2021. TWEAC: transformer with extendable QA agent classifiers. *CoRR*, abs/2104.07081.

Ian J. Goodfellow, Jonathon Shlens, and Christian Szegedy. 2015. Explaining and harnessing adversarial examples. In *3rd International Conference on Learning Representations, ICLR 2015, San Diego, CA, USA, May 7-9, 2015, Conference Track Proceedings*.

Sarthak Jain, Sarah Wiegreffe, Yuval Pinter, and Byron C. Wallace. 2020. Learning to faithfully rationalize by construction. In *Proceedings of the 58th Annual Meeting of the Association for Computational Linguistics*, pages 4459–4473, Online. Association for Computational Linguistics.

Narine Kokhlikyan, Vivek Miglani, Miguel Martin, Edward Wang, Bilal Alsallakh, Jonathan Reynolds, Alexander Melnikov, Natalia Kliushkina, Carlos Araya, Siqi Yan, and Orion Reblitz-Richardson. 2020. Captum: A unified and generic model interpretability library for pytorch. *CoRR*, abs/2009.07896.

Doyeon Lim, Haritz Puerto San Roman, and Sung-Hyon Myaeng. 2020. Analysis of the semantic answer types to understand the limitations of mrqa models. *Journal of KIISE : Software and Applications*, 47(3):298–309.

Zixuan Liu, Ehsan Adeli, Kilian M Pohl, and Qingyu Zhao. 2021. Going beyond saliency maps: Training deep models to interpret deep models. In *International Conference on Information Processing in Medical Imaging*, pages 71–82. Springer.

John Morris, Eli Lifland, Jin Yong Yoo, Jake Grigsby, Di Jin, and Yanjun Qi. 2020. TextAttack: A framework for adversarial attacks, data augmentation, and adversarial training in NLP. In *Proceedings of the 2020 Conference on Empirical Methods in Natural Language Processing: System Demonstrations*, pages 119–126, Online. Association for Computational Linguistics.

Jonas Pfeiffer, Andreas Rücklé, Clifton Poth, Aishwarya Kamath, Ivan Vulić, Sebastian Ruder, Kyunghyun Cho, and Iryna Gurevych. 2020. AdapterHub: A framework for adapting transformers. In *Proceedings of the 2020 Conference on Empirical Methods in Natural Language Processing: System Demonstrations*, pages 46–54, Online. Association for Computational Linguistics.

Haritz Puerto, Gözde Gül Sahin, and Iryna Gurevych. 2021. Metaqa: Combining expert agents for multi-skill question answering. *CoRR*, abs/2112.01922.

Marco Tulio Ribeiro, Tongshuang Wu, Carlos Guestrin, and Sameer Singh. 2020. Beyond accuracy: Behavioral testing of NLP models with CheckList. In *Proceedings of the 58th Annual Meeting of the Association for Computational Linguistics*, pages 4902–4912, Online. Association for Computational Linguistics.

Anna Rogers, Matt Gardner, and Isabelle Augenstein. 2021. QA dataset explosion: A taxonomy of NLP resources for question answering and reading comprehension. *arXiv*, abs/2107.12708.

Anna Rogers, Olga Kovaleva, and Anna Rumshisky. 2020. A primer in BERTology: What we know about how BERT works. *Transactions of the Association for Computational Linguistics*, 8:842–866.

Sofia Serrano and Noah A. Smith. 2019. Is attention interpretable? In *Proceedings of the 57th Annual Meeting of the Association for Computational Linguistics*, pages 2931–2951, Florence, Italy. Association for Computational Linguistics.

Karen Simonyan, Andrea Vedaldi, and Andrew Zisserman. 2014. Deep inside convolutional networks: Visualising image classification models and saliency maps. In *2nd International Conference on Learning Representations, ICLR 2014, Banff, AB, Canada, April 14-16, 2014, Workshop Track Proceedings*.

Daniel Smilkov, Nikhil Thorat, Been Kim, Fernanda B. Viégas, and Martin Wattenberg. 2017. Smoothgrad: removing noise by adding noise. *CoRR*, abs/1706.03825.

Robyn Speer, Joshua Chin, and Catherine Havasi. 2017. Conceptnet 5.5: An open multilingual graph of general knowledge. In *Proceedings of the Thirty-First AAAI Conference on Artificial Intelligence, February 4-9, 2017, San Francisco, California, USA*, pages 4444–4451. AAAI Press.

Mukund Sundararajan, Ankur Taly, and Qiqi Yan. 2017. Axiomatic attribution for deep networks. In *Proceedings of the 34th International Conference on Machine Learning, ICML 2017, Sydney, NSW, Australia, 6-11 August 2017*, volume 70 of *Proceedings of Machine Learning Research*, pages 3319–3328. PMLR.

Ashish Vaswani, Noam Shazeer, Niki Parmar, Jakob Uszkoreit, Llion Jones, Aidan N. Gomez, Lukasz Kaiser, and Illia Polosukhin. 2017. Attention is all you need. In *Advances in Neural Information Processing Systems 30: Annual Conference on Neural Information Processing Systems 2017, December 4-9, 2017, Long Beach, CA, USA*, pages 5998–6008.

Denny Vrandečić and Markus Krötzsch. 2014. Wikidata: A free collaborative knowledgebase. *Commun. ACM*, 57(10):78–85.

Eric Wallace, Jens Tuyls, Junlin Wang, Sanjay Subramanian, Matt Gardner, and Sameer Singh. 2019. AllenNLP interpret: A framework for explaining predictions of NLP models. In *Proceedings of the 2019 Conference on Empirical Methods in Natural Language Processing and the 9th International Joint Conference on Natural Language Processing (EMNLP-IJCNLP): System Demonstrations*, pages 7–12, Hong Kong, China. Association for Computational Linguistics.

Thomas Wolf, Lysandre Debut, Victor Sanh, Julien Chaumond, Clement Delangue, Anthony Moi, Pierric Cistac, Tim Rault, Remi Louf, Morgan Funtowicz, Joe Davison, Sam Shleifer, Patrick von Platen, Clara Ma, Yacine Jernite, Julien Plu, Canwen Xu, Teven Le Scao, Sylvain Gugger, Mariama Drame, Quentin Lhoest, and Alexander Rush. 2020. Transformers: State-of-the-art natural language processing. In *Proceedings of the 2020 Conference on Empirical Methods in Natural Language Processing: System Demonstrations*, pages 38–45, Online. Association for Computational Linguistics.

Michihiro Yasunaga, Hongyu Ren, Antoine Bosselut, Percy Liang, and Jure Leskovec. 2021. QA-GNN: Reasoning with language models and knowledge graphs for question answering. In *Proceedings of the 2021 Conference of the North American Chapter of the Association for Computational Linguistics: Human Language Technologies*, pages 535–546, Online. Association for Computational Linguistics.

Wei Emma Zhang, Quan Z Sheng, Ahoud Alhazmi, and Chenliang Li. 2020. Adversarial attacks on deep-learning models in natural language processing: A survey. *ACM Transactions on Intelligent Systems and Technology (TIST)*, 11(3):1–41.

A Knowledge Graph Document Schema

The nodes of a knowledge graph are stored in the Datastore as a json document using the following schema:

```
{
    "node_id": {
        "_id": "keyword",
        "name": "keyword",
        "description": "text",
        "type": "keyword"
    }
}
```

The edges of a knowledge graph are stored in the Datastore as a json document using the following schema:

```
{
    "edge_id": {
        "_id": "keyword",
        "name": "keyword",
        "description": "text",
        "type": "keyword",
        "in_id": "keyword",
        "out_id": "keyword",
        "weight": "double"
    }
}
```

B QA-GNN Implementation

We implement the QA-GNN inference pipeline on SQUARE based on the official implementation of QA-GNN model.[6] We disregard the training code since training QA models is not in the scope of SQUARE and connect the model with the Datastores service holding the KG. This makes it more flexible for future updates of ConceptNet. Lastly, the retrieved nodes with corresponding attention weights and relevance scores are accessible along with the answer prediction. With this information, we plot the graph using the JavaScript library Cytoscape.js (Franz et al., 2016).

[6] https://github.com/michiyasunaga/qagnn

C Adversarial Attack Figures

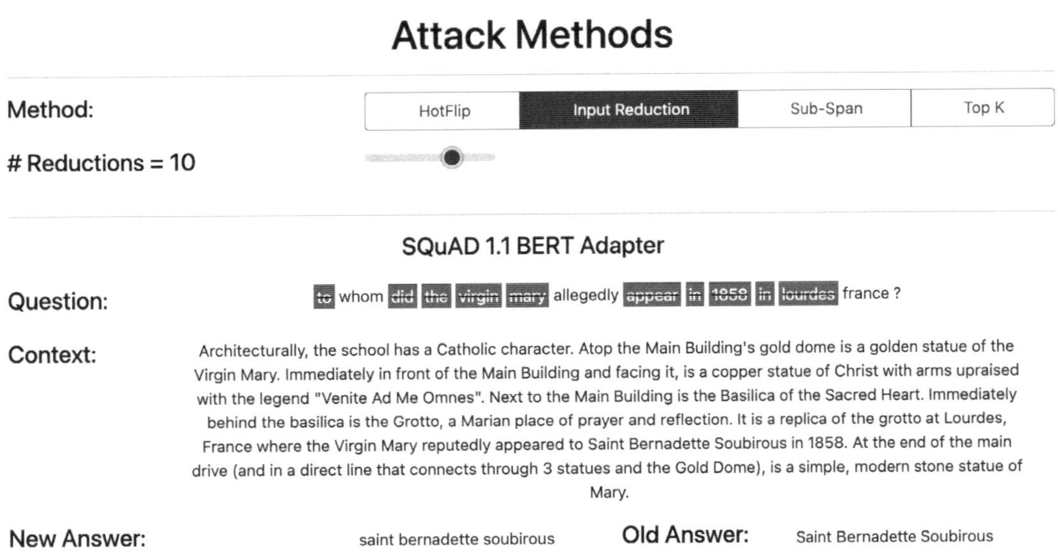

Figure 5: Input Reduction. After removing tokens from the question, the new question is not specific enough to be answerable. Yet, the model still gives the same answer evidencing a spurious correlation.

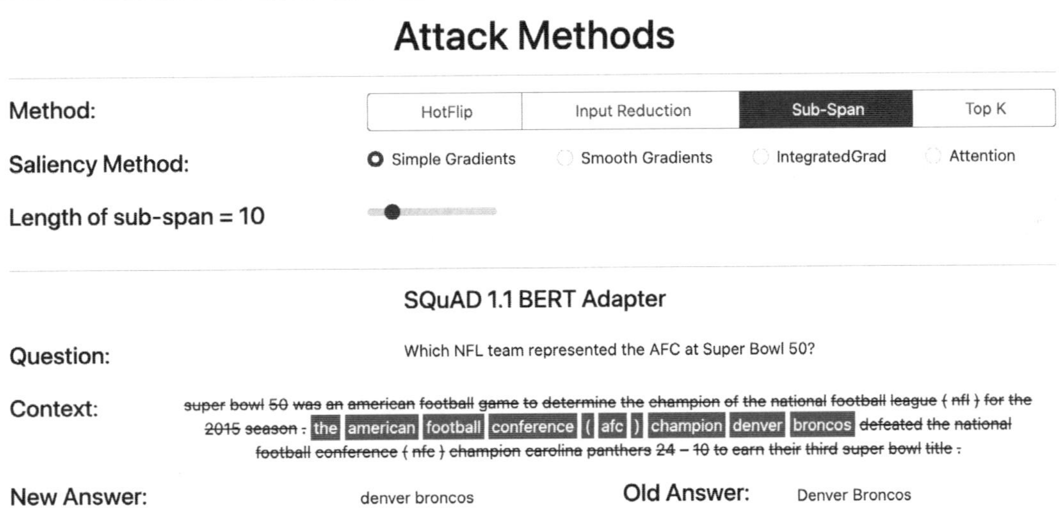

Figure 6: Sub-Span Attack. Removing part of the context leaves a new context without the nuances needed to properly respond to the question (i.e., *at Super Bowl 50*).

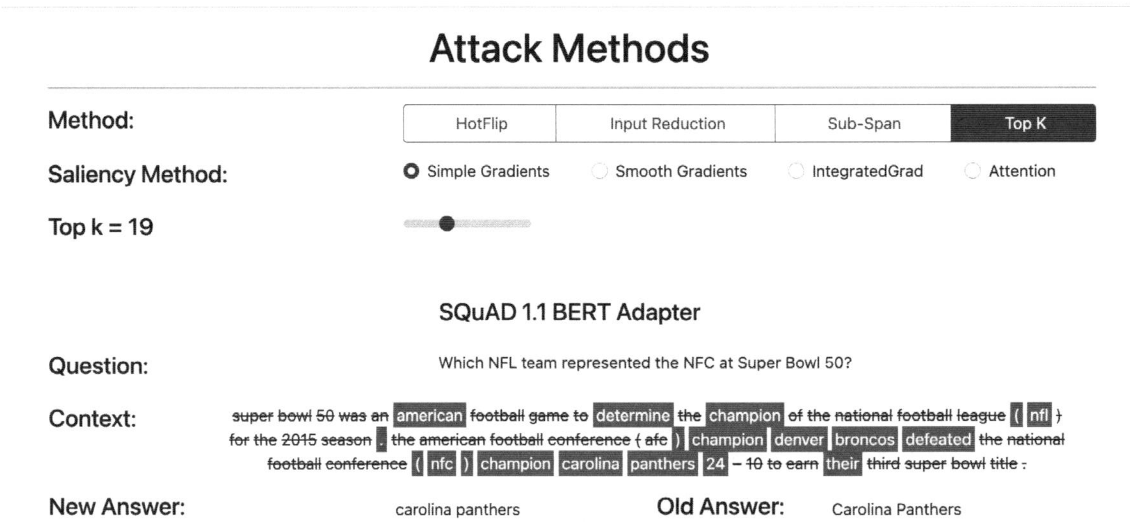

Figure 7: Top K Attack. Using as context the highlighted words, the Skill still gives the same answer even though the context is semantically and grammatically incomplete and does not include *Super Bowl 50*.

TaxFree: a Visualization Tool for Candidate-free Taxonomy Enrichment

Irina Nikishina[1] , Ivan Andrianov, Alsu Vakhitova[2], and Alexander Panchenko[2]
[1]Universität Hamburg
[2]Skolkovo Institute of Science and Technology
irina.nikishina@uni-hamburg.de, i.a.andrianov@gmail.com, alsu.vakhitova@gmail.com,
a.panchenko@skoltech.ru

Abstract

Taxonomies are widely used in a various number of downstream NLP tasks and, therefore, should be kept up-to-date. In this paper, we present **TaxFree**, an open source system for taxonomy visualisation and automatic Taxonomy Enrichment without pre-defined candidates on the example of WordNet-3.0. As opposed to the traditional task formulation (where the list of new words is provided beforehand), we provide an approach for automatic extension of a taxonomy using a large pre-trained language model. As an advantage to the existing visualisation tools of WordNet, **TaxFree** also integrates graphic representations of synsets from ImageNet. Such visualisation tool can be used for both updating taxonomies and inspecting them for the required modifications.

1 Introduction

In this paper, we focus on visualisation of taxonomic structures which are quite relevant for many Natural Language Processing (NLP) tasks, e.g. lexical entailment (Herrera et al., 2005) and entity linking (Moro and Navigli, 2015; Sevgili et al., 2022). Taxonomies are tree-like structures where words are considered as nodes (synsets) and the edges are the relations between them. Such kind of relationship is called a hypo-hypernym relationship. For instance, let us consider two words: “apple” and “fruit”. The former word is hyponym (“child”) to the latter and the latter is hypernym (“parent”) to the former.

However, taxonomies are hard to maintain, while the manual taxonomy annotation process is very expensive and time-consuming. Moreover, it requires expertise in the field. The process of selection new words is even more challenging for the large existing taxonomies like WordNet (Miller, 1995), as most existing words already present there. We expect that the large pre-trained language models such as BERT (Devlin et al., 2019) and GPT (Brown et al., 2020) could be useful in the task, as they are pre-trained on large-scale corpora. It has been proven that language models possess syntactic, semantic and word knowledge which could be applied for further language inference (Radford et al., 2019).

In this demo we demonstrate how the existing taxonomy can be enriched automatically without predefined candidates on WordNet-3.0. Figure 1 demonstrates the candidate-free task setting where the node “milk.n.01” (“n” stands for “noun”, “01” denotes the ordinal number of word sense, the standard notation for the synset in WordNet) is extended with multiple synsets of different types of milk: “’low-fat milk”, “chocolate milk”, “dry milk”, etc.

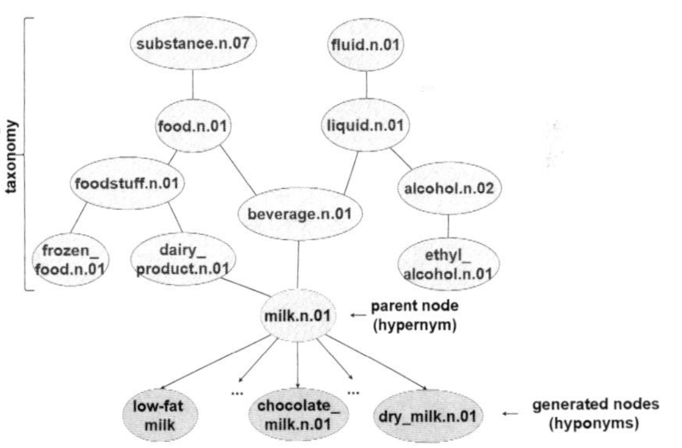

Figure 1: Candidate-free Taxonomy Enrichment task solved by **TaxFree**. The node “milk.n.01” is enriched with hyponyms (different types of milk).

TaxFree (see example of the visualisation page in Figure 2) is an open source, web-based visualisation and enrichment tool for taxonomies. We demonstrate the capacities of **TaxFree** on WordNet-3.0 with support for visual representation of WordNet synsets using ImageNet (Deng et al., 2009). The tool demonstrates an approach of automatic taxonomy graph extension by predicting new nodes (synsets) using BERT (Devlin et al., 2019) as a pre-trained language model. It allows the user to search

Proceedings of the 2nd Conference of the Asia-Pacific Chapter of the Association for Computational Linguistics and the 12th International Joint Conference on Natural Language Processing: System Demonstrations, pages 39–47
November 20–23, 2022.

in WordNet by words (lemma) or nodes (synset), to visualise the context of the query word (with $hop = 2$), to generate new leaf nodes or nodes between the two existing ones. To generate new nodes we apply the Cross-modal Contextualized Hidden State Projection Method (Nikishina et al., 2022b). The approach includes several stages: (i) learning embeddings of the WordNet taxonomy and new synsets at the required places that we want to predict (ii) projecting all graph embeddings into the hidden states space of BERT, and (iii) decoding them back to text candidates.

Thus, the contribution of this demonstration system is three-fold:

- Firstly, it allows users to search and visualize the query node within its context (on the example of the English WordNet-3.0);
- Secondly, it allows users to automatically extend the existing taxonomy without predefined (or manually defined) nodes using Cross-modal Contextualized Hidden State Projection Method (Nikishina et al., 2022b);
- Thirdly, it integrates ImageNet representations to the WordNet synset description card.

The link to the demo is as follows: **`https://taxgen.ltdemos.informatik.uni-hamburg.de`**.

The code link: **`https://github.com/skoltech-nlp/taxgen-demo`**. Link to the screencast video demonstrating the system: **`https://youtu.be/GF2AVlnWGag`**.

2 Related Work

In this section we review the existing approaches for Taxonomy Enrichment as well as the existing tools for taxonomy visualization.

2.1 Taxonomy Enrichment

To the best of our knowledge, there are no existing approaches for Candidate-free Taxonomy Enrichment. All methods require the list of pre-defined words to be added to the taxonomy. There exist several recent papers on Taxonomy Enrichment that make use of word vector representations and/or large pre-trained language models. For instance, (Nikishina et al., 2022a) present an approach applying numerous of text and graph embeddings as well as their combinations; (Takeoka et al., 2021) solves the same problem, but for the low-resource scenario using BERT-based classifier and Hearst Patterns (Roller et al., 2018); (Cho et al., 2020) regard the taxonomy enrichment task as a sequence-to-sequence problem and train an LSTM model on the WordNet data. A detailed overview of other taxonomy-related tasks is presented in (Jurgens and Pilehvar, 2016; Nikishina et al., 2022a).

2.2 Taxonomy Visualisation

Plenty of tools are available for generic visualisation of networks like Gephi (Bastian et al., 2009), GraphX (Gonzalez et al., 2014), D3[1], GraphViz (Ellson et al., 2001). At the same time, there might be found some tools specific for the visualisation of wordnets, which are not available from the original interface of WordNet. For example, (Collins, 2006) is one of the earliest papers that present a design paradigm. Visualisation from (Kamps and Marx, 2002) demonstrates not only the relations between synsets, but also denotes lemmas as graph nodes. WordNet Atlas (Abrate and Bacciu, 2012) is designed for "users like computer scientists that are not familiar with computational linguistics and/or WordNet.

Another paper (Giabelli et al., 2020) presents NEO: a tool for Taxonomy Enrichment that allows to enhance the standard occupation and skill taxonomy. The authors collect the terms from the Online Job Vacancies corpus and add them to the taxonomy automatically. Another visualisation of lexical graphs based on WordNet[2] is very similar to the one we present in our paper, however, it is lemma-based and does not allow dynamic extension of the graph using taxonomy enrichment technology.

3 Candidate-free Taxonomy Enrichment

This section presents Candidate-free Taxonomy Enrichment — the problem of new word prediction in order to enhance the existing taxonomy. We briefly describe the Cross-modal Contextualized Hidden State Projection Method (CHSP) used in the demo and the results obtained on the dataset based on WordNet-3.0.

3.1 Task Formulation

Formally, the task of candidate-free taxonomy enrichment may be formulated as follows: given taxonomy T and the position of the synset $s_i \in S$

[1]`https://github.com/d3/d3`

[2]`https://github.com/aliiae/lexical-graph`

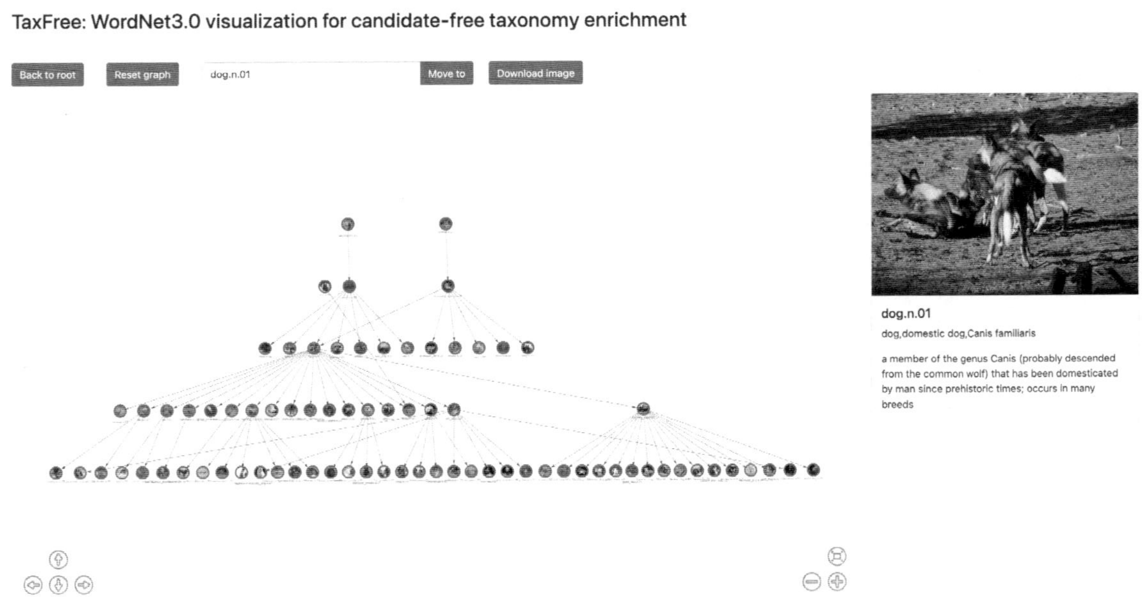

Figure 2: Visualisation example for the node "dog.n.01"

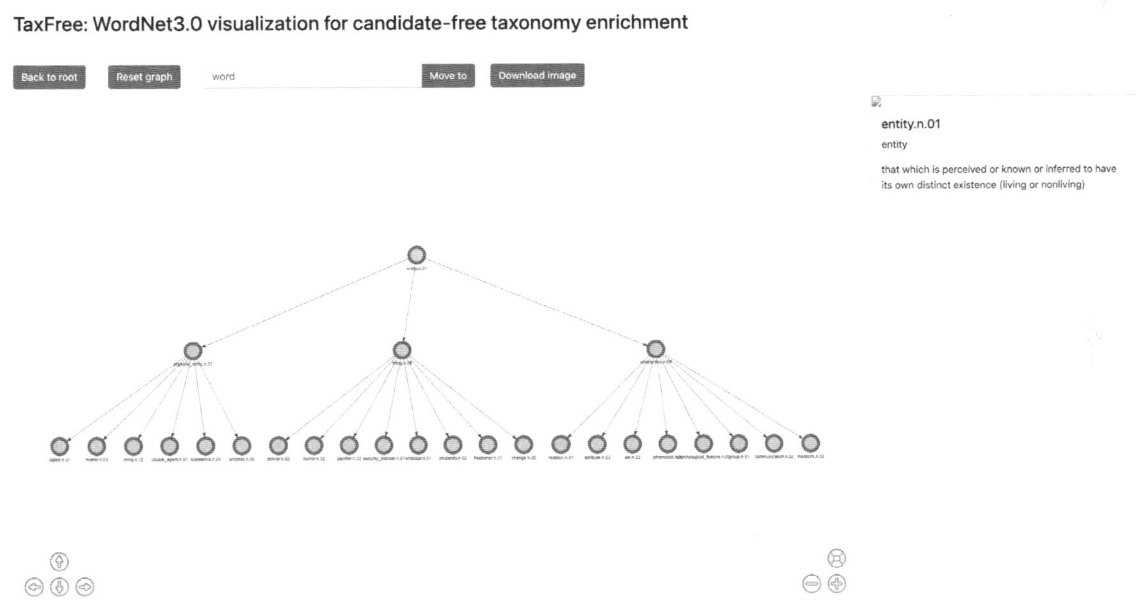

Figure 3: Default search page with the root "entity.n.01"

in this taxonomy, the task aims at predicting hyponyms $H_s \subseteq \{h_{s1}, ..., h_{sn}\}$ such that $H_s \notin E$, where E are edges in the taxonomy. Such formulation allows us to avoid the need of pre-supplied candidates making the task more challenging yet realistic. It might be expected that the information about new words could be already present in the large pre-trained networks.

3.2 Method Description

The Contextualized Hidden State Projection Method (CHSP) is a graph-based BERT architecture introduced by Nikishina et al. (2022b) that makes use of both node and text embeddings. Figure 4 demonstrates the overall architecture of the approach that we use in our demonstration system.

First, we train a graph representation model to compute GraphBERT (Zhang et al., 2020) embed-

Table 1: CHSP prediction scores for single-token hyponyms generation for different source graph embeddings, replacement strategies and substitution layer (x100).

Method	Context	Replaced	Layer	MRR@5	MRR@10	MRR@20	P@1	P@5	P@10
Pattern comparison (Hanna and Mareček, 2021)									
"[MASK] is a {parent}"	Yes	No	-	2.461	2.704	3.091	1.546	1.289	1.057
"My favourite {parent} is a [MASK]"	Yes	No	-	0.554	0.863	1.001	0.000	0.464	0.490
"A {parent} such as a [MASK]"	Yes	No	-	0.168	0.193	0.235	0.000	0.155	0.103
BERT (parent embedding on inference)	No	No	-	1.003	1.083	1.203	0.940	0.251	0.188
fastText (nearest neighbours)	No	No	-	2.400	3.500	4.000	0.130	1.839	2.100
CHSP (Graph-BERT)	Yes	Yes	1st	4.502	4.995	5.371	3.093	1.598	1.340
		Mix	1st	1.448	1.813	2.033	0.773	0.876	0.979
		Yes	6th	5.503	6.216	6.453	3.093	2.371	2.010
		Mix	6th	2.981	3.500	3.836	1.546	1.649	1.495
		Yes	12th	5.215	5.674	6.027	3.093	2.113	1.598
		Mix	12th	**7.229**	**8.037**	**8.624**	**3.608**	**3.247**	**2.474**

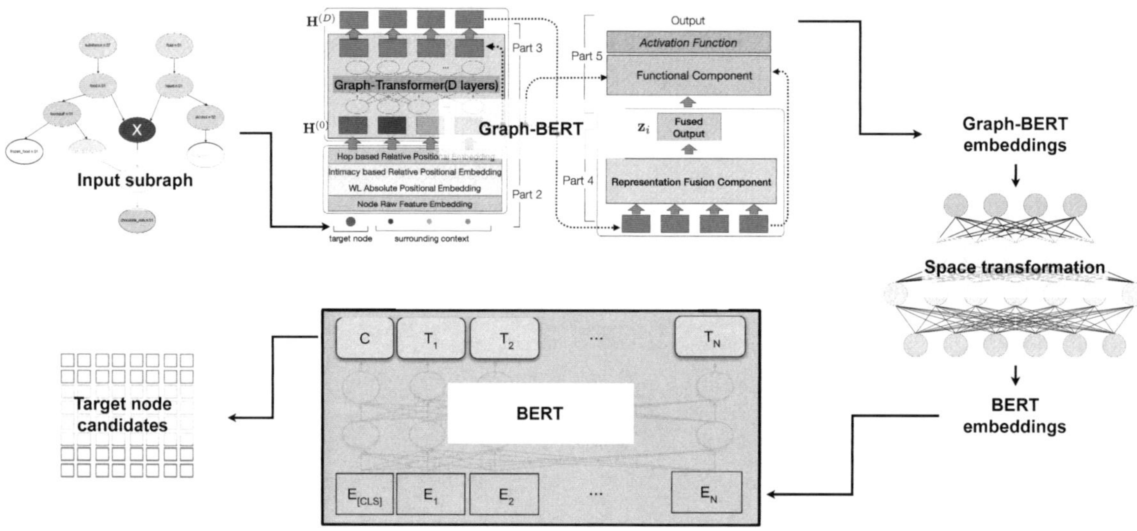

Figure 4: Cross-modal Contextualized Hidden State Projection Method (CHSP): graph-based BERT architecture that makes use of both node and text embeddings. Graph-BERT illustration source: (Zhang et al., 2020), BERT illustration source (Devlin et al., 2019). The computed GraphBERT embeddings from a taxonomy are projected from graph space to BERT space. Then BERT was used to predict candidates from the projected embeddings.

dings. Then we learn a feed-forward neural network as a projection layer to transform target graph embeddings to the BERT vector space. We use the SemCor dataset (Langone et al., 2004) that maps WordNet entities with the corresponding words in the context and learn the projection from Graph-BERT space to BERT. The next step is to apply the projected embeddings as input to the masked language modelling part of BERT model. We have evaluated three different context constructions suggested in (Hanna and Mareček, 2021): 1. "[MASK] is a/an {parent}"; 2. "My favourite {parent} is a [MASK]"; 3. "{parent} such as a [MASK]" . The scores for the amount of true hyponyms in a list of predicted candidates are presented in the first three lines of Table 1.

Then we incorporate the result graph embedding into the language model prediction using mixed (or contextualised) prediction: embedding of "[MASK]" token is averaged with projected graph embedding. The replacement can happen at three different stages: after first layer of BERT encoder, after sixth (middle) or after twelfth (last). Thus, the prediction head generates new lemmas that are treated as candidate hyponyms for the target nodes.

3.3 Experiments and Results

In this research, we perform experiments on WordNet 3.0 (Miller, 134 1995) nouns (82,115 synsets, 117,798 lemmas). For each "parental" hypernym all its hyponyms (leaves) were replaced by a single "masked" node. This place in the taxonomy was then considered for extension and the candidates predicted for the masked node could be compared against true hyponyms. All in all, we masked 4,376 leaves out of 65,422 noun leaves to 1000 "[MASK]" tokens. We limit our experiments to leaves only, replacing all children with one mask in order to be able to compare with a wide range of possible answers, as one synset might have several hyponyms.

We utilize Precision@k (P@k), Recall (R@k), and Mean Reciprocal Rank (MRR) for evaluation. The results are presented in Table 1. We observe that the patterns from (Hanna and Mareček, 2021) show results are mostly far from the top ones. This happened because the context encapsulated in the patterns in general contains little information. We also see that our method outperforms the BERT (parent embedding on inference) baseline (which is a simple prediction of encoded parent synset) and a simple approach on fastText nearest neighbours candidates.

4 System Design

TaxFree is designed to help lexicographers in their work on updating taxonomies and inspecting them for the required modifications. In the current section we discuss each part of the tool and its usage in detail.

4.1 Software Architecture

The system consists of a web-based user interface through which users can explore the WordNet-3.0 taxonomy. The front-end is implemented with JavaScript library **vis.js**[3] used to display networks consisting of nodes and edges. It supports the hierarchical layout and allows us to integrate with the network. Back-end is written in Python using **Flask**[4] framework. It has an API with several "GET" and "POST" queries that maintain functioning of the system: (i) searching for synsets, (ii) getting image by node id, (iii) getting the current node graph context, (iv) generating new nodes.

4.2 Main Page

As a start page 3 , you see the highest level of the taxonomy, a tree with the root node "entity.n.01" which is highlighted with green color. Normally, the target node is displayed within its two-hop neighbourhood. To the right of the graph visualization there is a card with the description of the current node: its image from ImagNet (if any), definition and the list of lemmas. Above the graph visualization box there are two buttons: **"Reset graph"**, **"Back to root"** and a search box with a **"Move to"** button. **"Reset graph"** means that all generated nodes will be deleted from memory and only the initial WordNet-3.0 graph will be displayed. **"Back to root"** will return the user to the display of the root of the taxonomy, leaving all generated nodes untouched. Search bar allows to easily navigate through the taxonomy and display subgraphs for the queried node. More details for each box are provided in the corresponding subsections.

4.3 Synset Search

The search bar accepts both synset names and lemmas and helps to disambiguate unclear queries to WordNet-3.0. The user can enter a word or a phrase separated with spaces or underscores. Moreover, noun synsets are also accepted, e.g. "cat.n.01" or "standard_poodle.n.01". If the synset name is not recognized there will be no error displayed, but the search bar will be empty again. For the entered lemma(s) there is a special pipeline that the query word goes through:

1. If there is only one synset corresponding to the query lemma, then this synsets will be displayed.

2. If there are more than one synset, therefore, the user is forwarded to the subgraph of the most common synset, displaying other disambiguation options under the synset description card (see Figure 6 as an example). Each disambiguated synset is presented with its synset name and definition.

After the query synset has been identified (either manually or automatically), the tool opens the required page with the query synset as the target node in context. Subgraph display and synset description card are described in the following subsections.

4.4 Subgraph Display

Central (query) synset is displayed with the closest "relatives" two hops away from the query (it might be less if there are no neighbours at the certain step away of the target node) in the central box of the page. It has green borders that highlight that the current image is the target one. However, if the image from the ImageNet is not presented, then the

[3] https://visjs.github.io/vis-network/docs/network/

[4] https://flask.palletsprojects.com/en/2.2.x/

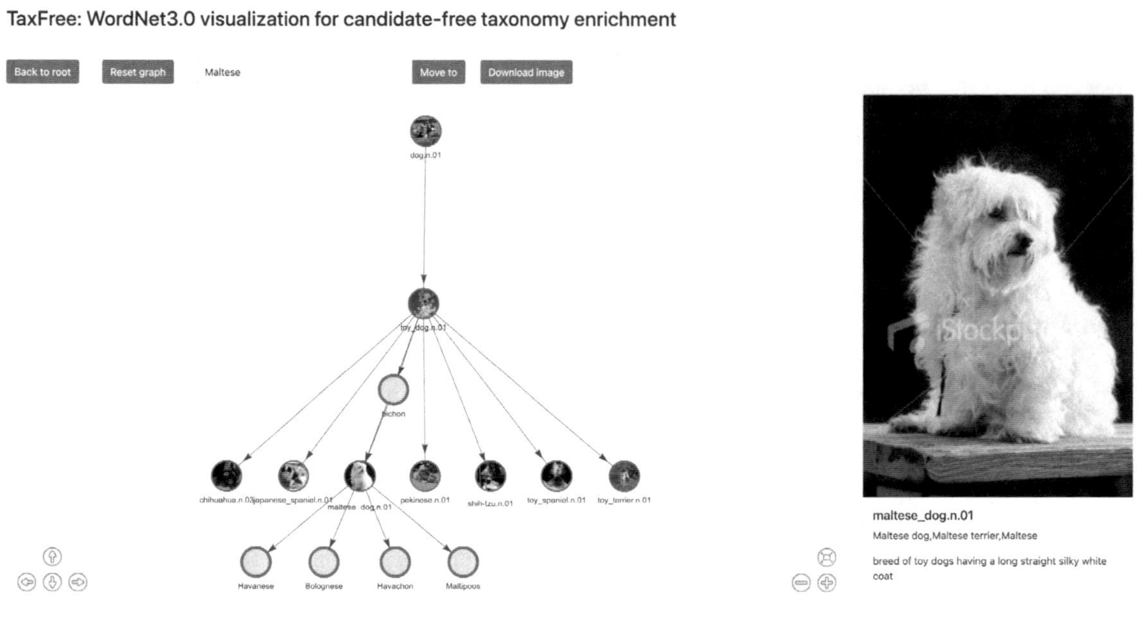

Figure 5: Generation of a new node for the leaf node "maltese_dog.n.01"

whole node is colored in green. Other nodes are not highlighted and colored in blue (in case there is no image to display).

Figure 5 shows the result page for the synset "maltese_dog.n.01" as an example to demonstrate synsets with images. Here we can see that all nodes have their representations from WordNet-3.0. The node "maltese_dog.n.01" is a leaf node, therefore, it is placed in the bottom of the graph and has only co-hyponyms at the same level and one hypernym "toy_dog.n.01" and one hypo-hypernym "dog.n.01". The arrows always have the same direction: from abstract words to more concrete. By clicking on a node twice it will open you a subgraph for this node, as it would consider it as a next query word. Therefore, you might be able to navigate through the graph even without queries. The graph might be downloaded when pressing the **"Download graph" button**.

In the bottom of the visualization box there are buttons to zoom in/out and centering. You can also move the graph using "left", "right", "up" and "down" buttons on the screen or simply use mouse.

4.5 Synset Description Card

To the right of the subgraph display, there is a card with the summary of the query node. It consists of a definition, image from the ImageNet (if any), synset name, list of lemmas. If any information about the node is missing, then the row is skipped. Image for the node is selected randomly, normally the first one from the ImageNet dataset. According to the statistics, only 19,167 synsets have their images.

4.6 New Synsets Prediction

Figure 5 demonstrates the process of adding new nodes to the taxonomy using the algorithm described in Section 3.2. First, you can generate a new node starting from a leaf. By clicking twice on it, we can generate children for the "maltese_dog" synset, which does not possess hyponyms. Otherwise, they would be displayed, as "maltese_dog" is the central node. Therefore, by clicking twice on the target (query) node we can predict a candidate child for it. Figure 5 shows that there were generated new nods - the names of dog breeds. Another option for new synset generation is to predict a new node which is placed between two nodes (in this case it means that on of them is hypernym to the other). To generate this node, the user should click twice on the edge that connects them. This option has been added in case there are unaccounted words that should be placed in the middle of the graph. Figure 5 also depicts the "dog.n.01" and "toy_dog" nodes. By clicking twice on the edge between them, a new node is generated which is supposed to be more general then its hyponym "maltese_dog" and narrower than the word "toy_dog". However, we have not evaluated the performance of this specific

dog.n.01

dog,domestic dog,Canis familiaris

a member of the genus Canis (probably descended from the common wolf) that has been domesticated by man since prehistoric times; occurs in many breeds

Maybe you meant:

frump.n.01	a dull unattractive unpleasant girl or woman
dog.n.03	informal term for a man
cad.n.01	someone who is morally reprehensible
frank.n.02	a smooth-textured sausage of minced beef or pork usually smoked; often served on a bread roll
pawl.n.01	a hinged catch that fits into a notch of a ratchet to move a wheel forward or prevent it from moving backward
andiron.n.01	metal supports for logs in a fireplace

Figure 6: Disambiguation blog for the "dog" lemma

type of node insertion, so we leave the application of our method for this subtask for further research.

5 Conlusion

The growing popularity of implementing taxonomies in different research and industry tasks has created the need for a platform for visualization of tree-like taxonomic subgraphs (query node in context). **TaxFree** provides such a platform for the visualisation and analysis of hypo-hypernymy subgraphs. The tool allows users to explore wordnet synsets in context and predict new synsets for the leaf nodes. Our work aims to bring taxonomies to a broader audience, by making WordNet interface user-friendly in comparison to the standard WordNet[5] visualization.

Limitations

Despite multiple advantages of the presented system it still has several limitations we list below:

1. Firstly, currently our system cannot predict new hyponyms for synsets that are not leaves. Yet, methodologically it's possible.

2. Secondly, we demonstrate only the first image of the synset, while there might be several images for one concept.

Ethics Statement

In general, we do not see any ethical issues or negative consequences within the current work. At the same time, as we apply the pre-trained language model we may inherit social bias learned from the Web corpora.

References

Matteo Abrate and Clara Bacciu. 2012. Visualizing word senses in WordNet atlas. In *Proceedings of the Eighth International Conference on Language Resources and Evaluation (LREC'12)*, pages 2648–2652, Istanbul, Turkey. European Language Resources Association (ELRA).

Mathieu Bastian, Sebastien Heymann, and Mathieu Jacomy. 2009. Gephi: an open source software for exploring and manipulating networks. In *Proceedings of the international AAAI conference on web and social media*, volume 3, pages 361–362.

Tom Brown, Benjamin Mann, Nick Ryder, Melanie Subbiah, Jared D Kaplan, Prafulla Dhariwal, Arvind Neelakantan, Pranav Shyam, Girish Sastry, Amanda Askell, Sandhini Agarwal, Ariel Herbert-Voss, Gretchen Krueger, Tom Henighan, Rewon Child, Aditya Ramesh, Daniel Ziegler, Jeffrey Wu, Clemens Winter, Chris Hesse, Mark Chen, Eric Sigler, Mateusz Litwin, Scott Gray, Benjamin Chess, Jack Clark, Christopher Berner, Sam McCandlish, Alec Radford, Ilya Sutskever, and Dario Amodei. 2020. Language models are few-shot learners. In *Advances in Neural Information Processing Systems*, volume 33, pages 1877–1901. Curran Associates, Inc.

Yejin Cho, Juan Diego Rodriguez, Yifan Gao, and Katrin Erk. 2020. Leveraging WordNet paths for neural hypernym prediction. In *Proceedings of the 28th*

[5]http://wordnet.princeton.edu

International Conference on Computational Linguistics, pages 3007–3018, Barcelona, Spain (Online). International Committee on Computational Linguistics.

Christopher Collins. 2006. Wordnet explorer: applying visualization principles to lexical semantics. *Computational Linguistics Group, Department of Computer Science, University of Toronto, Toronto, Ontario, Canada.*

Jia Deng, Wei Dong, Richard Socher, Li-Jia Li, Kai Li, and Li Fei-Fei. 2009. Imagenet: A large-scale hierarchical image database. In *2009 IEEE Conference on Computer Vision and Pattern Recognition*, pages 248–255.

Jacob Devlin, Ming-Wei Chang, Kenton Lee, and Kristina Toutanova. 2019. BERT: Pre-training of deep bidirectional transformers for language understanding. In *Proceedings of the 2019 Conference of the North American Chapter of the Association for Computational Linguistics: Human Language Technologies, Volume 1 (Long and Short Papers)*, pages 4171–4186, Minneapolis, Minnesota. Association for Computational Linguistics.

John Ellson, Emden Gansner, Lefteris Koutsofios, Stephen C North, and Gordon Woodhull. 2001. Graphviz—open source graph drawing tools. In *International Symposium on Graph Drawing*, pages 483–484. Springer.

Anna Giabelli, Lorenzo Malandri, Fabio Mercorio, Mario Mezzanzanica, and Andrea Seveso. 2020. Neo: a tool for taxonomy enrichment with new emerging occupations. In *International Semantic Web Conference*, pages 568–584. Springer.

Joseph E Gonzalez, Reynold S Xin, Ankur Dave, Daniel Crankshaw, Michael J Franklin, and Ion Stoica. 2014. {GraphX}: Graph processing in a distributed dataflow framework. In *11th USENIX symposium on operating systems design and implementation (OSDI 14)*, pages 599–613.

Michael Hanna and David Mareček. 2021. Analyzing BERT's knowledge of hypernymy via prompting. In *Proceedings of the Fourth BlackboxNLP Workshop on Analyzing and Interpreting Neural Networks for NLP*, pages 275–282, Punta Cana, Dominican Republic. Association for Computational Linguistics.

Jesús Herrera, Anselmo Peñas, and Felisa Verdejo. 2005. Textual entailment recognition based on dependency analysis and *WordNet*. In *Machine Learning Challenges, Evaluating Predictive Uncertainty, Visual Object Classification and Recognizing Textual Entailment, First PASCAL Machine Learning Challenges Workshop, MLCW 2005, Southampton, UK, April 11-13, 2005, Revised Selected Papers*, volume 3944 of *Lecture Notes in Computer Science*, pages 231–239. Springer.

David Jurgens and Mohammad Taher Pilehvar. 2016. SemEval-2016 task 14: Semantic taxonomy enrichment. In *Proceedings of the 10th International Workshop on Semantic Evaluation (SemEval-2016)*, pages 1092–1102, San Diego, California. Association for Computational Linguistics.

Jaap Kamps and Maarten Marx. 2002. Visualizing wordnet structure. In *Proc. of the 1st International Conference on Global WordNet*, pages 182–186.

Helen Langone, Benjamin R. Haskell, and George A. Miller. 2004. Annotating WordNet. In *Proceedings of the Workshop Frontiers in Corpus Annotation at HLT-NAACL 2004*, pages 63–69, Boston, Massachusetts, USA. Association for Computational Linguistics.

George A. Miller. 1995. Wordnet: A lexical database for english. *Commun. ACM*, 38(11):39–41.

Andrea Moro and Roberto Navigli. 2015. SemEval-2015 task 13: Multilingual all-words sense disambiguation and entity linking. In *Proceedings of the 9th International Workshop on Semantic Evaluation (SemEval 2015)*, pages 288–297, Denver, Colorado. Association for Computational Linguistics.

Irina Nikishina, Mikhail Tikhomirov, Varvara Logacheva, Yuriy Nazarov, Alexander Panchenko, and Natalia V. Loukachevitch. 2022a. Taxonomy enrichment with text and graph vector representations. *Semantic Web*, 13(3):441–475.

Irina Nikishina, Alsu Vakhitova, Elena Tutubalina, and Alexander Panchenko. 2022b. Cross-modal contextualized hidden state projection method for expanding of taxonomic graphs. In *Proceedings of TextGraphs-16: Graph-based Methods for Natural Language Processing*, pages 11–24, Gyeongju, Republic of Korea. Association for Computational Linguistics.

Alec Radford, Jeffrey Wu, Rewon Child, David Luan, Dario Amodei, Ilya Sutskever, et al. 2019. Language models are unsupervised multitask learners. *OpenAI blog*, 1(8):9.

Stephen Roller, Douwe Kiela, and Maximilian Nickel. 2018. Hearst patterns revisited: Automatic hypernym detection from large text corpora. In *Proceedings of the 56th Annual Meeting of the Association for Computational Linguistics (Volume 2: Short Papers)*, pages 358–363, Melbourne, Australia. Association for Computational Linguistics.

Özge Sevgili, Artem Shelmanov, Mikhail Y. Arkhipov, Alexander Panchenko, and Chris Biemann. 2022. Neural entity linking: A survey of models based on deep learning. *Semantic Web*, 13(3):527–570.

Kunihiro Takeoka, Kosuke Akimoto, and Masafumi Oyamada. 2021. Low-resource taxonomy enrichment with pretrained language models. In *Proceedings of the 2021 Conference on Empirical Methods in Natural Language Processing*, pages 2747–2758, Online and Punta Cana, Dominican Republic. Association for Computational Linguistics.

Jiawei Zhang, Haopeng Zhang, Congying Xia, and Li Sun. 2020. Graph-bert: Only attention is needed for learning graph representations. *CoRR*, abs/2001.05140.

F-COREF: Fast, Accurate and Easy to Use Coreference Resolution

Shon Otmazgin[1] **Arie Cattan**[1] **Yoav Goldberg**[1,2]
[1]Computer Science Department, Bar Ilan University
[2]Allen Institute for Artificial Intelligence
{shon711,arie.cattan,yoav.goldberg}@gmail.com

Abstract

We introduce *fastcoref*, a python package for fast, accurate, and easy-to-use English coreference resolution. The package is pip-installable, and allows two modes: an accurate mode based on the LINGMESS architecture, providing state-of-the-art coreference accuracy, and a substantially faster model, F-COREF, which is the focus of this work. F-COREF allows to process 2.8K OntoNotes documents in 25 seconds on a V100 GPU (compared to 6 minutes for the LINGMESS model, and to 12 minutes of the popular AllenNLP coreference model) with only a modest drop in accuracy. The fast speed is achieved through a combination of distillation of a compact model from the LingMess model, and an efficient batching implementation using a technique we call leftover batching.[1]

1 Introduction

Coreference Resolution consists of identifying textual mentions that refer to the same entity in a given text (Karttunen, 1969). This fundamental NLP task can benefit various applications such as Information Extraction (Luan et al., 2018; Li et al., 2020; Jain et al., 2020), Question Answering (Dasigi et al., 2019; Chen and Durrett, 2021), Machine Translation (Stojanovski and Fraser, 2018; Voita et al., 2018), and Summarization (Christensen et al., 2013; Falke et al., 2017; Pasunuru et al., 2021). However, compared to other core tasks such as POS Tagging, named-entity recognition or syntactic parsing, existing packages and state-of-the-art models for coreference resolution are challenging to apply: there are few easy-to-use packages implementing state-of-the-art models, and the available packages consume a lot of GPU memory, and take very long to process each document. For example, the coreference model in the popular AllenNLP package (Gardner et al., 2017), implementing the model of Joshi et al. (2020), requires 27GB of GPU memory and takes 12 minutes to process the 2.8K documents of the OntoNotes corpus, on a V100 GPU.

In this work, we introduce F-COREF, a new open source Python package for simply running an efficient coreference model using a few lines of code. F-COREF predicts coreference clusters 29 times faster than the AllenNLP model (processing the OntoNotes corpus in 25 seconds) and requires only 15% of its GPU memory use, with only a small drop in performance (78.5 vs 79.6 average F1). The package also includes LINGMESS (Otmazgin et al., 2022), a state-of-the-art coreference model, which is almost twice as fast as the AllenNLP model, while being more accurate (81.4 average F1), under the same API.

To achieve F-COREF's speed, we use two additive techniques: model distillation of the strong-but-slow LINGMESS model using large unlabeled data, and an effective batching technique that reduces the number of padded tokens in a batch.

2 The F-COREF API

The *fastcoref* Python package is pip installable (`pip install fastcoref`) and provides an easy and fast API for coreference information with only few lines of code without any prepossessing steps.

The F-COREF constructor initializes our pretrained model on a single device:

```
from fastcoref import FCoref

model = FCoref(device='cuda:0')
```

The main functionally of the package is the *predict* function, which accepts a list of texts.

```
preds = model.predict(
    texts=['We are so happy to see you
    using our coref package.
    This package is very fast!']
)
```

[1]https://github.com/shon-otmazgin/fastcoref

Proceedings of the 2nd Conference of the Asia-Pacific Chapter of the Association for Computational Linguistics and the 12th International Joint Conference on Natural Language Processing: System Demonstrations, pages 48–56
November 20–23, 2022. ©2022 Association for Computational Linguistics

The return value of the *predict* function is a list of *CorefResult* objects, from which one can extract the coreference clusters (either as strings or as character indices over the original texts), as well as the logits for each corefering entity pair:

```
preds[0].get_clusters()
> [[(0, 2), (33, 36)],
   [(33, 50), (52, 64)]
  ]

preds[0].get_clusters(string=True)
> [['We', 'our'],
   ['our coref package', 'This package']
  ]

preds[0].get_logit(
    span_i=(33, 50), span_j=(52, 64)
)

> 18.852894
```

Processing can be applied to a collection of texts of any length in a batched and parallel fashion:

```
texts = ['text 1', 'text 2',.., 'text n']

# control the batch size
# with max_tokens_in_batch parameter

preds = model.predict(
    texts=texts, max_tokens_in_batch=100
)
```

The `max_tokens_in_batch` parameter can be used to control the speed vs. memory consumption tradeoff, and can be tuned to maximize the utilization of the associated hardware.

To control speed vs. accuracy tradeoff, use the larger but more accurate LINGMESS model, simply import LingMessCoref instead of FCoref:

```
from fastcoref import LingMessCoref

model = LingMessCoref(device='cuda:0')
```

On top of the provided models, the package also provides the ability to train and distill coreference models on your own data, opening the possibility for fast and accurate coreference models for additional languages and domains.

To summarize, the package provides a simple API that makes predicting coreference entities straightforward and easy-to-use. The package supports any text length as input, and performs efficient batching. The package's F-COREF model is 29 times faster and 4 times smaller than the popular coreference model in the AllenNLP package, while the provided LINGMESS mode is twice as fast the AllenNLP implementation, and more accurate.

3 Background: Neural Coreference

Lee et al. (2017) present the first end-to-end model that jointly learns mention detection and coreference decision. Successive follow-up works kept improving performance through the incorporation of widely popular pretrained architectures (Lee et al., 2018; Joshi et al., 2019; Kantor and Globerson, 2019; Joshi et al., 2020). However, as the dimensionality of contextualized encoders increases, keeping in memory all possible span representations becomes highly costly and computationally untractable for long documents.

3.1 Faster Neural Coreference

Several methods have been proposed to address this memory constraint at the cost of the computation time and a slight performance deterioration (Xia et al., 2020; Toshniwal et al., 2020; Thirukovalluru et al., 2021). The *s2e* model of Kirstain et al. (2021) managed to improve computation time with a slight *increase* in accuracy.

s2e Our F-COREF is based on the architecture of the *s2e* model by Kirstain et al. (2021). Like other neural coreference models, *s2e* scores each pair of spans in the text to be co-referring to each other. However, in order to achieve lower memory footprint s2e moves to representing each span as a function of its start and end tokens. Consequently, the model avoids holding vector representation for each of the $O(n^2)$ spans in memory, and instead stores only $O(n)$ vectors. This reduced memory footprint allows it to handle longer sequences.

The *s2e* architecture includes three components: (1) Longformer (Beltagy et al., 2020), a contextualized encoder; (2) a parameterized *mention scoring function* f_m; and (3) a parameterized *pairwise antecedent scoring function* f_a. To score any pair of spans to be co-referring, the model starts by encoding the text using Longformer into vectors $x_1, ..., x_n$. Using these vectors, for each possible span $q = (x_k, x_\ell)$ the mention scoring function $f_m(q)$, scores how likely q ("query") being a mention. Then for a pair of spans $c = (x_i, x_j)$, $q = (x_k, x_\ell)$ where c ("candidate") appears before q, the pairwise antecedent scoring function, $f_a(c, q)$, scores how likely is c being an antecedent of q. In practice, to avoid complexity of $\mathcal{O}(n^4)$, the antecedent function scores only the λT spans with highest mention scores (where T is the number of tokens). Finally, the final pairwise score for a coreference link between c and q is composed by the score of q being a mention, c being a mention, and how likely is c being an antecedent of q:

$$F(c,q) = \begin{cases} f_m(c) + f_m(q) + f_a(c,q) & c \neq \varepsilon \\ 0 & c = \varepsilon \end{cases}$$

where ε is the null antecedent.

The computation of f_m and f_q for the entire sequence can be efficiently batched.

Word-level coreference Dobrovolskii (2021) proposed moving from scoring pairs of spans to scoring pairs of words, establishing coreference relations between the words, and then expanding each of the relevant words into their mention boundaries. This reduces the model complexity from $\mathcal{O}(n^4)$ to $\mathcal{O}(n^2)$.

3.2 What remains slow?

While the *s2e* and the word-level models are considered lightweight and efficient, and substantally improve in speed over Joshi et al. (2019), their computation time is still dominated by their expensive contextualized encoding stage. They also use relatively large hidden layers in their scoring functions (the s2e model has 26 layers and 494M parameters). Thus, one avenue for improving coreference speed is by reducing the model size. Additionally, while batching computations can improve parallelism and thus also throughput, the implementation of batching long documents of varying lengths is often sub-optimal, and results in many padded tokens which translate to wasted computation.

3.3 Accurate Neural Coreference

Our recent LINGMESS model (Otmazgin et al., 2022) improves coreference accuracy by observing that different types of entities require different strategies to score, and replacing the single mention-pair scorer with a set of specialized scorers. During inference, each mention pair is deterministically routed to one of the scorers, based on the the type of mentions being scored. This results in state-of-the-art coreference accuracy, while being somewhat less efficient to run and to batch than the *s2e* model.

4 Method

We employ two complementary directions in order to obtain a fast and efficient coreference model. First, we substantially reduce the size of the *s2e* model using knowledge distillation (§4.1) from the LINGMESS model. Second, our implementation aims to maximize parallelism via batching while limiting the number of unnecessary computations such as padded tokens (§4.2).

4.1 Knowledge Distillation

Knowledge Distillation is the process of learning a small student model from a large teacher model.

Teacher model We use the state-of-the-art LINGMESS model of Otmazgin et al. (2022) as the teacher model.

Student model we build our student model as a variant of the *s2e* model with fewer layers and parameters. The "expensive" Longformer (Beltagy et al., 2020) encoder was replaced with DistilRoBERTa (Sanh et al., 2019), which is on average $\times 8$ faster than Longformer. The number of parameters of the mention and the antecedent pairwise scorers was reduced by a factor of 6. This reduces the total number of parameters from 494M to 91M. In addition, the number of sequential layers in the network reduced from 26 layers to only 8 layers (6 encoder layers, 1 mention scorer and 1 antecedent scorer). As a result, our student combines the strengths of the *s2e* model by not constructing span representation with a lightweight encoder and substantially less model parameters.

Hard distillation Traditional approaches for knowledge distillation trains the student on the logits of the teacher model's predictions on unlabeled data (Gou et al., 2021). However, as we will further elaborate in Section §5.1, applying such an approach to a coreference model with all its components (i.e. encoder, mention scorer, pruning, antecedent scorer) achieves poor performance. To remedy this issue, we employ *hard* target knowledge distillation, where the teacher model acts as an annotator for the unlabeled data and the student model learns from these "silver" annotations.

4.2 Maximizing Parallelism and Reducing Unnecessary Computations

Mention pruning As mentioned in Section 3, the coreference model computes antecedent scores only for the λT spans with highest mention scores, where T is the number of tokens. As the number of coreferring spans cannot be known in advance, the common approach is to use a soft pruning coefficient ($\lambda = 0.4$) to guarantee high mention recall,

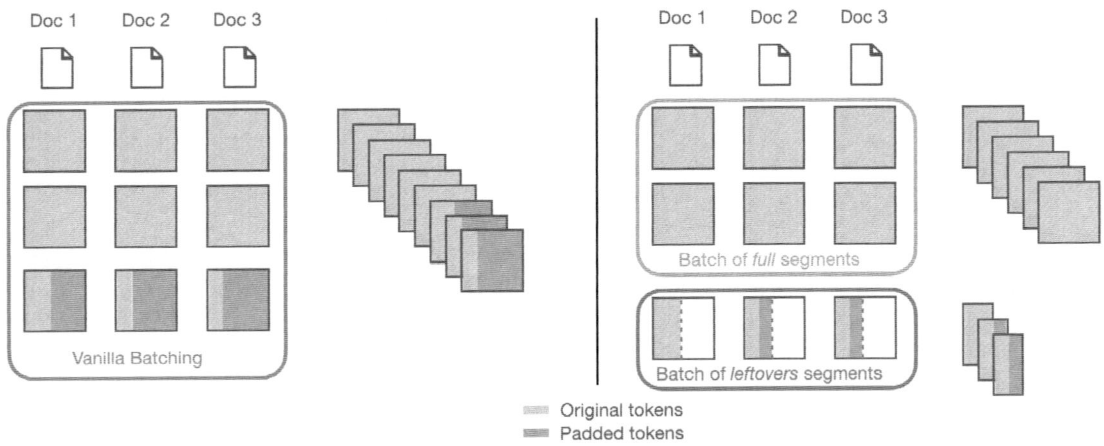

Figure 1: Illustration of document batching using vanilla batching (left) and our leftovers approach (right). In our leftover batching, we create two separate batches, one for the full segments without padding (orange) and one for the leftover segments (green), thus substantially reducing the number of padded tokens (red) compared to the vanilla approach.

while expecting the antecedent scorer to assign a negative score to pairs involving a wrong mention span (Lee et al., 2017; Kirstain et al., 2021). In F-COREF, we adopt a more aggressive pruning ($\lambda = 0.25$), which decreases the number of pairwise comparisons by a factor of 2.56 without harming performance.

Dynamic batching We adopt a dynamic batching approach which, given a large number of documents, batches documents until we reach a certain maximum number of tokens. Compared with the naive approach of batching a fixed number of documents together, dynamic batching enables to fully exploit the available memory in our hardware (this approach was also used by Kirstain et al. (2021) when *training* the *s2e* model, but not for inference).

Leftovers batching Figure 1 illustrates our document batching strategy, in comparison with the common approach.

As mentioned in Section 3, the first step in our coreference model consists of encoding the document using a transformer-based encoder. The common approach for encoding long documents with transformer encoders is to split the document into non-overlapping segments of *max_length*, where each segment is encoded separately (Joshi et al., 2019; Xu and Choi, 2020). With that approach, for each long document, we obtain two[2] types of segment lengths: (1) one or more segments of *max_length* i.e. FULL tokens segment, (2) exact one segment $\leq$ *max_length*, i.e the LEFTOVERS tokens segment.

Then to batch multiple documents, a naive but popular approach consists of padding each document's LEFTOVERS segment to *max_length*. This results in a high number of padded tokens, e.g., 34.7% of all tokens are padded when batching 2802 OntoNotes (Pradhan et al., 2012) training set documents with *max_length* $= 512$. Padded tokens result in unnecessary computations in each layer of the network, as well as unnecessary memory allocation.

To avoid such unnecessary computations, we split each batch into two batches such that the first batch is for the FULL segments and the second batch is for the LEFTOVERS tokens segment of each document. Then we pad the second batch to the max leftovers length rather than padding the leftovers segments to *max_length*. Finally we run the two batches separately and combine them afterwards. With this technique, the padded tokens in the OntoNotes training set reduced dramatically to 0.6%. It should be noted that the aforementioned batching technique is not specific for coreference resolution and can be applied for other tasks that require processing long documents.

5 Experiments and Results

Experiments setup In our experiments, we use the Multi-news (Fabbri et al., 2019) dataset to train our teacher-student architecture. The Multi-news

[2]A document with fewer tokens than *max_length* has only one segment.

	MUC			B^3			$CEAF_{\phi_4}$			
	P	R	F1	P	R	F1	P	R	F1	Avg. F1
Joshi et al. (2020)	85.8	84.8	85.3	78.3	77.9	78.1	76.4	74.2	75.3	79.6
Kirstain et al. (2021)	86.5	85.1	85.8	80.3	77.9	79.1	76.8	75.4	76.1	80.3
Dobrovolskii (2021)	84.9	87.9	86.3	77.4	82.6	79.9	76.1	77.1	76.6	81.0
Otmazgin et al. (2022) (Teacher)	88.1	85.1	86.6	82.7	78.3	80.5	78.5	76.0	77.3	81.4
F-COREF OntoNotes only	78.5	84.3	81.3	68.2	74.8	71.4	64.1	72.9	68.2	73.7
F-COREF Multi-News	84.8	82.8	83.4	76.8	73.7	75.2	73.8	72.7	73.2	77.4
+ FT OntoNotes	85.0	83.9	84.4	77.6	75.5	76.6	74.7	74.3	74.5	78.5

Table 1: Performance on the test set of the English OntoNotes 5.0 dataset. The averaged F1 of MUC, B^3, $CEAF_\phi$ is the main evaluation metric.

	Masc	Fem	Bias	Overall
Otmazgin et al. (2022) (Teacher)	91.3	87.8	0.96	89.6
F-COREF	87.8	83.5	0.95	85.7

Table 2: Performance on the test set of the GAP coreference dataset. The reported metrics are F1 scores.

	Runtime	Memory
Joshi et al. (2020)[1]	12:06	27.4
Otmazgin et al. (2022) (Teacher)	06:43	4.6
+ Batching[2]	06:00	6.6
Kirstain et al. (2021)	04:37	4.4
Dobrovolskii (2021)	03:49	3.5
F-COREF	00:45	**3.3**
+ Batching[2]	00:35	4.5
+ Leftovers batching[2]	**00:25**	4.0

[1] AllenNLP package implementation.
[2] 10K tokens in a single batch.

Table 3: The inference time(Min:Sec) and memory(GiB) for each model on 2.8K documents. Average of 3 runs. Hardware, NVIDIA Tesla V100 SXM2.

	#Docs	#Chains	#Mentions
OntoNotes	2.8K	35K	155K
Multi-News	123K	2M	9M

Table 4: Coreference statistics of the training set of OntoNotes and Multi-News.

dataset is an open source dataset aimed at NLP summarization. Each entry in the dataset contains multiple documents and a summary of these documents. For our purposes, we ignored the summaries, and train our student model on the documents, a total of 123,227 documents in the news domain. We chose Multi-News because it contains a large number of documents in the news genre, which would result in a large number of coreference clusters (see Table 4 for statistics). Furthermore, we use the English portion of the OntoNotes (Pradhan et al., 2012) dataset to evaluate the student model performance (on the test set) and to further fine-tune the student model (on the train set).

The student training procedure includes three phases. In the first phase, we predict coreference clusters on MultiNews using the teacher model (Otmazgin et al., 2022). Secondly, following (Wu et al., 2020; Dobrovolskii, 2021), we pre-train the mention scorer of the student on the output mentions of the teacher, then train the full student model on the predicted teacher coreference clusters. Finally, we finetune the student model on the OntoNotes training set.

Accuracy Table 1 shows F-COREF's performance on the OntoNotes test set according to the standard evaluation metrics for coreference resolution. F-COREF achieved 78.5 F1 with knowledge distillation and finetuning on OntoNotes. When trained only on OntoNotes, F-COREF achieved only 73.7 F1 (−4.8 F1), showing a substantial benefit from knowledge distillation on the Multi-news dataset (Fabbri et al., 2019). In comparison with other coreference models, F-COREF degrades by 1.1 point compared to the Joshi et al. (2019) model in the AllenNLP package, by 2.9 F1 points compared to LINGMESS (Otmazgin et al., 2022), the teacher, and by 1.8 F1 points versus Kirstain et al. (2021), the *s2e* model, which F-COREF is a variant of. Table 2 shows similar trends for the GAP dataset (Webster et al., 2018). This degradation comes in favor to the model efficiency, which we will discuss in the next paragraph.

Speed and Memory Usage Table 3 summarizes the efficiency of the different coreference models. Using the techniques described in Section §4 which reduces the model size, maximize batching and avoids unnecessary computation, the inference time on 2.8K documents is significantly reduced by factor of 9 from the 03:49 minutes of Dobrovol-

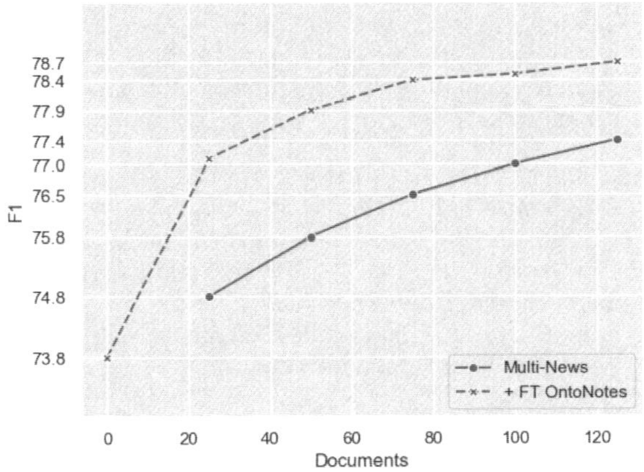

Figure 2: The knowledge distillation learning curve. The x-axis is the number of documents we took from the Multi-News dataset to train the student model. The y-axis is the student F1 score for each size.

skii (2021)—the fastest model to date—to only 25 seconds for F-COREF.[3]

Most of the speed increase (80%) is due to the smaller model size achieved through distillation, which alone reduces the runtime to 45 seconds. However, introducing batching further reduces the runtime by additional 22% to 35 seconds, and our novel leftover batching reduces further 29%, and gets us to 25 seconds. The more aggressive mention pruning (not shown in the table) had only a negligible additive effect in our experiments, reducing the runtime from 25 to 24 seconds.

Without batching, F-COREF also consumes less memory then Dobrovolskii (2021), a model that recently reduces the coreference complexity from $\mathcal{O}(n^4)$ to $\mathcal{O}(n^2)$.

Finally, compared to one of the most widely used coreference models, the Joshi et al. (2020) model available through the AllenNLP package (Gardner et al., 2017), F-COREF is 29 times faster and consumes 85% less memory.

5.1 Further Analysis

Effect of Unlabeled Data Size We first analyze the effect of the amount of unlabeled data used in distillation, by training the student model on different amounts of training data. As Figure 2 shows the performance gain between 25K documents and 50K documents is 1 F1 point while the gain between 100K and 125K documents decreases to 0.4 points. This indicates that the gain margin is decreasing, but overall, increasing the dataset size continuously improves the model performance and there is a room for improvement with more data. Fine-tuning the distilled model on the in-domain OntoNotes data consistently improves the results, but is also additive with the distillation: the fine-tuned performance also increases with more unlabaled data in distillation.

Effect of the Teacher Model To estimate the effect of the teacher model, we compare the LINGMESS teacher to a *s2e* model (Kirstain et al., 2021) teacher on the same unlabeled data. We obtain 76.6 F1 with *s2e* (vs. 77.4 F1 with LINGMESS) on the OntoNotes (test set) when training only on Multi-News and 78.3 F1 with *s2e* (vs. 78.5 F1 with LINGMESS) after further fine-tuning on OntoNotes (training set). This indicates that the student accuracy increases when more accurate models are used in knowledge distillation, even with hard labels.

Soft VS. Hard Distillation Our first attempt to transfer the coreference knowledge from the teacher model to the student model was the traditional knowledge distillation, i.e. soft targets knowledge distillation. For each example in the training set, we forward it first in the teacher model and obtained the top-scoring spans indices, and the pairwise coreference logits. Then we forward the example in the student network (at pruning stage we use the teacher's top-scoring spans indices) to obtain the student coreference pairwise logits. Following common training objective (Hinton et al., 2015; Sanh et al., 2019; Jiao et al., 2020), we optimize the student model using the soft cross entropy loss between the student and the teacher logits.

Our student model reached only 64 F1, while achieving 73.7 F1 without knowledge distillation. Soft distillation presents challenges in coreference models. The main challenge we encounter is at the pruning stage, where both teacher and student should prune the exact same mentions from their individual mention scorer. This forces the student model to learn from a conditional antecedent distribution of the teacher spans indices instead of the full antecedent distribution.

Additionally, we observe that learning to mimic the teacher logits may trouble the training because logits can violate transitivity (e.g positive score for the mention pairs (a, b) and (b, c) but a negative score for (a, c)) and propagate contradictory

[3]These experiments used batch sizes of 10k tokens. Increasing the batch sizes increase memory consumption, but does not improve overall speed on our NVIDIA Tesla V100 hardware.

information. Specifically, we build the coreference clusters based on the positive pairwise scores, and verify whether all pairwise scores within the same coreference clusters are positive, as we would naturally expect. In fact, 53.8% of the pairwise scores within the same coreference cluster are negative. In contrast, this undesired behavior does not happen in hard distillation because we assign positive labels for all coreferring antecedents for each mention.

6 Conclusions

We introduce the *fastcoref* python package for coreference resolution, and hope its speed an ease of use will facilitate work that utilizes coreference resolution at scale.

Acknowledgements

This project has received funding from the European Research Council (ERC) under the European Union's Horizon 2020 research and innovation programme, grant agreement No. 802774 (iEXTRACT). Arie Cattan is partially supported by the Data Science Institute at Bar-Ilan University.

References

Iz Beltagy, Matthew E. Peters, and Arman Cohan. 2020. Longformer: The long-document transformer. *ArXiv*, abs/2004.05150.

Jifan Chen and Greg Durrett. 2021. Robust question answering through sub-part alignment. In *Proceedings of the 2021 Conference of the North American Chapter of the Association for Computational Linguistics: Human Language Technologies*, pages 1251–1263, Online. Association for Computational Linguistics.

Janara Christensen, Mausam, Stephen Soderland, and Oren Etzioni. 2013. Towards coherent multi-document summarization. In *Proceedings of the 2013 Conference of the North American Chapter of the Association for Computational Linguistics: Human Language Technologies*, pages 1163–1173, Atlanta, Georgia. Association for Computational Linguistics.

Pradeep Dasigi, Nelson F. Liu, Ana Marasović, Noah A. Smith, and Matt Gardner. 2019. Quoref: A reading comprehension dataset with questions requiring coreferential reasoning. In *Proceedings of the 2019 Conference on Empirical Methods in Natural Language Processing and the 9th International Joint Conference on Natural Language Processing (EMNLP-IJCNLP)*, pages 5925–5932, Hong Kong, China. Association for Computational Linguistics.

Vladimir Dobrovolskii. 2021. Word-level coreference resolution. In *Proceedings of the 2021 Conference on Empirical Methods in Natural Language Processing*, pages 7670–7675, Online and Punta Cana, Dominican Republic. Association for Computational Linguistics.

Alexander Fabbri, Irene Li, Tianwei She, Suyi Li, and Dragomir Radev. 2019. Multi-news: A large-scale multi-document summarization dataset and abstractive hierarchical model. In *Proceedings of the 57th Annual Meeting of the Association for Computational Linguistics*, pages 1074–1084, Florence, Italy. Association for Computational Linguistics.

Tobias Falke, Christian M. Meyer, and Iryna Gurevych. 2017. Concept-map-based multi-document summarization using concept coreference resolution and global importance optimization. In *Proceedings of the Eighth International Joint Conference on Natural Language Processing (Volume 1: Long Papers)*, pages 801–811, Taipei, Taiwan. Asian Federation of Natural Language Processing.

Matt Gardner, Joel Grus, Mark Neumann, Oyvind Tafjord, Pradeep Dasigi, Nelson F. Liu, Matthew Peters, Michael Schmitz, and Luke S. Zettlemoyer. 2017. Allennlp: A deep semantic natural language processing platform.

Jianping Gou, B. Yu, Stephen J. Maybank, and Dacheng Tao. 2021. Knowledge distillation: A survey. *ArXiv*, abs/2006.05525.

Geoffrey E. Hinton, Oriol Vinyals, and Jeffrey Dean. 2015. Distilling the knowledge in a neural network. *ArXiv*, abs/1503.02531.

Sarthak Jain, Madeleine van Zuylen, Hannaneh Hajishirzi, and Iz Beltagy. 2020. SciREX: A challenge dataset for document-level information extraction. In *Proceedings of the 58th Annual Meeting of the Association for Computational Linguistics*, pages 7506–7516, Online. Association for Computational Linguistics.

Xiaoqi Jiao, Yichun Yin, Lifeng Shang, Xin Jiang, Xiao Chen, Linlin Li, Fang Wang, and Qun Liu. 2020. TinyBERT: Distilling BERT for natural language understanding. In *Findings of the Association for Computational Linguistics: EMNLP 2020*, pages 4163–4174, Online. Association for Computational Linguistics.

Mandar Joshi, Danqi Chen, Yinhan Liu, Daniel S. Weld, Luke Zettlemoyer, and Omer Levy. 2020. SpanBERT: Improving pre-training by representing and predicting spans. *Transactions of the Association for Computational Linguistics*, 8:64–77.

Mandar Joshi, Omer Levy, Luke Zettlemoyer, and Daniel Weld. 2019. BERT for coreference resolution: Baselines and analysis. In *Proceedings of the 2019 Conference on Empirical Methods in Natural Language Processing and the 9th International Joint Conference on Natural Language Processing (EMNLP-IJCNLP)*, pages 5803–5808, Hong Kong, China. Association for Computational Linguistics.

Ben Kantor and Amir Globerson. 2019. Coreference resolution with entity equalization. In *Proceedings of the 57th Annual Meeting of the Association for Computational Linguistics*, pages 673–677, Florence, Italy. Association for Computational Linguistics.

Lauri Karttunen. 1969. Discourse referents. In *International Conference on Computational Linguistics COLING 1969: Preprint No. 70*, Sånga Säby, Sweden.

Yuval Kirstain, Ori Ram, and Omer Levy. 2021. Coreference resolution without span representations. In *Proceedings of the 59th Annual Meeting of the Association for Computational Linguistics and the 11th International Joint Conference on Natural Language Processing (Volume 2: Short Papers)*, pages 14–19, Online. Association for Computational Linguistics.

Kenton Lee, Luheng He, Mike Lewis, and Luke Zettlemoyer. 2017. End-to-end neural coreference resolution. In *Proceedings of the 2017 Conference on Empirical Methods in Natural Language Processing*, pages 188–197, Copenhagen, Denmark. Association for Computational Linguistics.

Kenton Lee, Luheng He, and Luke Zettlemoyer. 2018. Higher-order coreference resolution with coarse-to-fine inference. In *Proceedings of the 2018 Conference of the North American Chapter of the Association for Computational Linguistics: Human Language Technologies, Volume 2 (Short Papers)*, pages 687–692, New Orleans, Louisiana. Association for Computational Linguistics.

Manling Li, Alireza Zareian, Ying Lin, Xiaoman Pan, Spencer Whitehead, Brian Chen, Bo Wu, Heng Ji, Shih-Fu Chang, Clare Voss, Daniel Napierski, and Marjorie Freedman. 2020. GAIA: A fine-grained multimedia knowledge extraction system. In *Proceedings of the 58th Annual Meeting of the Association for Computational Linguistics: System Demonstrations*, pages 77–86, Online. Association for Computational Linguistics.

Yi Luan, Luheng He, Mari Ostendorf, and Hannaneh Hajishirzi. 2018. Multi-task identification of entities, relations, and coreference for scientific knowledge graph construction. In *Proceedings of the 2018 Conference on Empirical Methods in Natural Language Processing*, pages 3219–3232, Brussels, Belgium. Association for Computational Linguistics.

Shon Otmazgin, Arie Cattan, and Yoav Goldberg. 2022. Lingmess: Linguistically informed multi expert scorers for coreference resolution. *ArXiv*, abs/2205.12644.

Ramakanth Pasunuru, Mengwen Liu, Mohit Bansal, Sujith Ravi, and Markus Dreyer. 2021. Efficiently summarizing text and graph encodings of multi-document clusters. In *Proceedings of the 2021 Conference of the North American Chapter of the Association for Computational Linguistics: Human Language Technologies*, pages 4768–4779, Online. Association for Computational Linguistics.

Sameer Pradhan, Alessandro Moschitti, Nianwen Xue, Olga Uryupina, and Yuchen Zhang. 2012. CoNLL-2012 shared task: Modeling multilingual unrestricted coreference in OntoNotes. In *Joint Conference on EMNLP and CoNLL - Shared Task*, pages 1–40, Jeju Island, Korea. Association for Computational Linguistics.

Victor Sanh, Lysandre Debut, Julien Chaumond, and Thomas Wolf. 2019. Distilbert, a distilled version of bert: smaller, faster, cheaper and lighter. *ArXiv*, abs/1910.01108.

Dario Stojanovski and Alexander Fraser. 2018. Coreference and coherence in neural machine translation: A study using oracle experiments. In *Proceedings of the Third Conference on Machine Translation: Research Papers*, pages 49–60, Brussels, Belgium. Association for Computational Linguistics.

Raghuveer Thirukovalluru, Nicholas Monath, Kumar Shridhar, Manzil Zaheer, Mrinmaya Sachan, and Andrew McCallum. 2021. Scaling within document coreference to long texts. In *Findings of the Association for Computational Linguistics: ACL-IJCNLP 2021*, pages 3921–3931, Online. Association for Computational Linguistics.

Shubham Toshniwal, Sam Wiseman, Allyson Ettinger, Karen Livescu, and Kevin Gimpel. 2020. Learning to Ignore: Long Document Coreference with Bounded Memory Neural Networks. In *Proceedings of the 2020 Conference on Empirical Methods in Natural Language Processing (EMNLP)*, pages 8519–8526, Online. Association for Computational Linguistics.

Elena Voita, Pavel Serdyukov, Rico Sennrich, and Ivan Titov. 2018. Context-aware neural machine translation learns anaphora resolution. In *Proceedings of the 56th Annual Meeting of the Association for Computational Linguistics (Volume 1: Long Papers)*, pages 1264–1274, Melbourne, Australia. Association for Computational Linguistics.

Kellie Webster, Marta Recasens, Vera Axelrod, and Jason Baldridge. 2018. Mind the GAP: A balanced corpus of gendered ambiguous pronouns. *Transactions of the Association for Computational Linguistics*, 6:605–617.

Wei Wu, Fei Wang, Arianna Yuan, Fei Wu, and Jiwei Li. 2020. CorefQA: Coreference resolution as query-based span prediction. In *Proceedings of the 58th Annual Meeting of the Association for Computational Linguistics*, pages 6953–6963, Online. Association for Computational Linguistics.

Patrick Xia, João Sedoc, and Benjamin Van Durme. 2020. Incremental neural coreference resolution in constant memory. In *Proceedings of the 2020 Conference on Empirical Methods in Natural Language Processing (EMNLP)*, pages 8617–8624, Online. Association for Computational Linguistics.

Liyan Xu and Jinho D. Choi. 2020. Revealing the myth of higher-order inference in coreference resolution. In *Proceedings of the 2020 Conference on Empirical Methods in Natural Language Processing (EMNLP)*, pages 8527–8533, Online. Association for Computational Linguistics.

PIEKM: ML-based Procedural Information Extraction and Knowledge Management System for Materials Science Literature

Huichen Yang
Kansas State University
Manhattan, Kansas, USA

Carlos Aguirre
Johns Hopkins University
Baltimore, Maryland, USA

William Hsu
Kansas State University
Manhattan, Kansas, USA

Abstract

The published materials science literature contains abundant description information about synthesis procedures that can help discover new material areas, deepen the study of materials synthesis, and accelerate its automated planning. Nevertheless, this information is expressed in unstructured text, and manually processing and assimilating useful information is expensive and time-consuming for researchers. To address this challenge, we develop a Machine Learning-based procedural information extraction and knowledge management system (PIEKM) that extracts procedural information (*recipe steps*), figures, and tables from materials science articles, and provides information retrieval capability and the statistics visualization functionality. Our system aims to help researchers to gain insights and quickly understand the connections among massive data. Moreover, we demonstrate that the machine learning-based system performs well in low-resource scenarios (i.e., limited annotated data) for domain adaption.

1 Introduction

The procedural information in materials science literature aims to help researchers reproduce experiments and gain insights to speed up the process of new materials synthesis development (Vaucher et al., 2020; Kononova et al., 2019). It takes the form of *recipes* (e.g., Figure 4) and is normally defined as a series of actions and their corresponding conditions and results. Such information contains imperatives, action verbs, steps of operations, and constructions (Yang et al., 2019). This information can be commonly found in method sections of materials science research literature. However, a great amount of scientific literature is published every year by the growing materials science research community. These well-established works provide a foundation to enlighten researchers and explore new materials development simultaneously. Acquiring valuable information from the year-over-year increasing scientific literature efficiently and effectively remains one of the great challenges (Kononova et al., 2021). The existing scholarly literature search engines, such as Google Scholar and Semantic Scholar, provide a good service to discover the relevant publications, but they cannot directly deliver the recipe steps of the experiments that are included in the literature. Therefore, an intelligent system that provides the functions of procedural information searching and viewing, visualization, and analysis is highly demanded.

Information Extraction (IE) which is a sub-area of Natural Language Processing (NLP) provides an efficient way to automatically extract structured information from large unstructured text data. Likewise, in the materials science domain, IE has been applied to similar tasks, such as experimental steps classification with unsupervised approaches of probabilistic methods for inorganic materials (Huo et al., 2019) and named entity recognition in materials science domain (Kim et al., 2017; Yang and Hsu, 2021). One of the biggest challenges of extracting information in materials science articles is that the annotated datasets are insufficient (Olivetti et al., 2020), which can be overcome by machine learning, particularly transfer learning, with pre-trained models obtained from other large training datasets (Zhang et al., 2021). Transfer learning can help with domain adaptation in materials science. We use transfer learning through fine-tuning a pre-trained language model with datasets in the materials science domain for chemical entity extraction. The trained model is integrated into the PIEKM system and performs well. This solves real cases where the number of training data in the materials science domain is very small for information extraction.

This paper presents PIEKM, a prototype of a machine learning-based procedural information extraction and knowledge management system based

Proceedings of the 2nd Conference of the Asia-Pacific Chapter of the Association for Computational Linguistics and the 12th International Joint Conference on Natural Language Processing: System Demonstrations, pages 57–62
November 20–23, 2022. ©2022 Association for Computational Linguistics

on materials scientific literature. The goal of PIEKM is to demonstrate procedural information extraction and information retrieval capabilities. Three crucial contributions of PIEKM are summarized as follows:

- This system helps researchers to obtain materials science-related procedural information efficiently and effectively from massive publications.
- The system utilizes transfer learning approaches, such as chemical entity extraction, which can solve the issues with the small size of training dataset.
- The system is flexible and can be easily deployed in other domains.

2 System Architecture

In this section, we describe the detailed architecture of PIEKM system. The proposed system consists of three modules: (A) Information Processing, (B) User Interface, and (C) Query Processing and Information Storage. Figure 1 shows the architecture of PIEKM system. Figure 2 shows the home page of PIEKM system. The details of each module are introduced as follows.

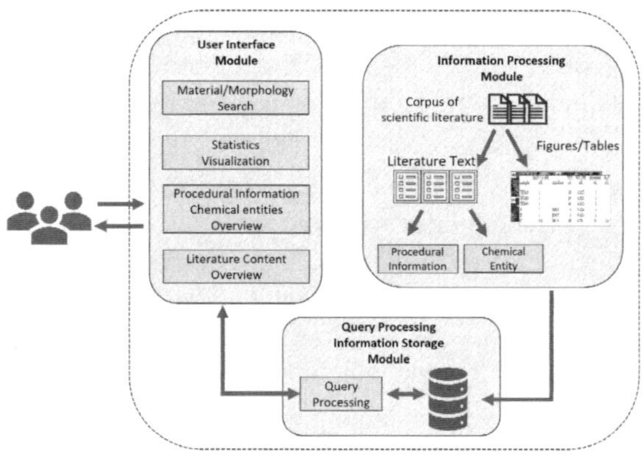

Figure 1: Architecture of PIEKM system

(A) Information Processing Module: This module processes the information from the digital scientific literature. We focus on Portable Document Format (PDF) digital scientific literature in the PIEKM system. The input corpus of digital scientific literature has been segmented into text and non-text (figures, tables) parts (section 3.1). Then the procedural information (section 3.2) and name entities (section 3.3) are extracted from these texts.

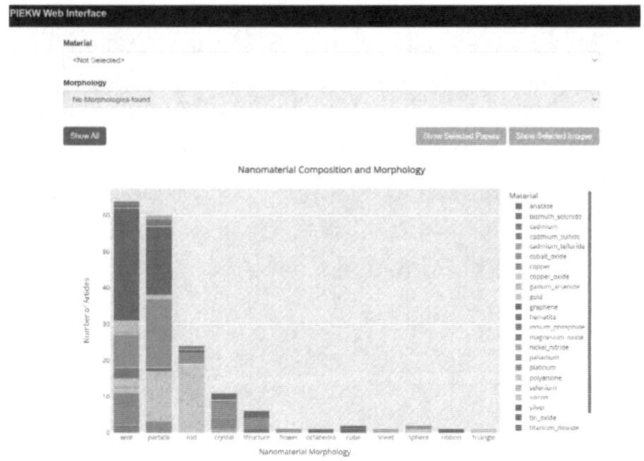

Figure 2: Home page of PIEKM system

The extracted figures and tables are stored in the corresponding folders. The rest of extracted text information is stored in as a semi-structured format in the database for quick query response.

(B) User Interface Module: This module is in charge of responding to user queries and showing the result corresponding to each query, providing the preview of figures and tables of articles available in the system, and presenting the details of every single article which includes procedural information and chemical entities.

(C) Query Processing and Information Storage Module: This module is responsible for query processing and information storage. The queries are sent by users, then the answers would be acquired from the information storage database and returned back to the user interface module for display. The module supports different material compositions and morphology searches.

The PIEKM system is deployed by Flask[1] framework and written in Python. We use MongoDB[2] to store the information data and respond to queries. The Plotly[3] and Dash[4] are used for interactive visualizations.

3 Information processing

In this section, we present the implementation details of the information processing module in PIEKM system. This module serves as a pipeline including free-text extraction, procedural information extraction, and chemical entity recognition. The details of each stage are described as follows.

[1]https://flask.palletsprojects.com/
[2]https://www.mongodb.com/
[3]https://plotly.com/javascript/
[4]https://plotly.com/dash/

3.1 Free-Text Extraction

The first step is to extract the text from the digital scientific literature, such as Portable Document Format (PDF) files, which is not in readable format and cannot be processed by computer directly, before processing it further. However, the very diverse formats and structures of scientific literature corpora could make text extraction and section classification difficult. The existing tools, such as PDFMiner (Shinyama, 2007) and PDFReader (Polshcha, 2020), may not fully extract the sections (e.g., methodology, experiment, results), and leave them in the wrong order. This could significantly affect recipe extraction if the recipe steps are not in sequential order. We, therefore, make use of heuristic rule-based Metadata-Analytic Text and Section Extractor (MATESC) (Maria et al., 2018) system to solve the issues of different formats. MATESC is a heuristic rule-based pattern analysis tool that is used for extracting text and classifying sections from the scientific literature. The key purpose of this tool is to accelerate the extraction of information and semantic knowledge among variant formats of scientific literature across different domains. We can extract text spans and utilize metadata features (i.e., spatial layout location, font type, and size) via MATESC. By doing so, we are able to create grouped blocks of text which can be then classified into groups and subgroups depending on characterized paper sections.

MATESC extracts text including the metadata features of all characters (i.e., font type and size, spatial layout location) from PDF scientific articles which are considered as input. It is worth noting that the irrelevant text left in the margins of every page of these documents can be automatically removed from the extracted text based on the corresponding spatial layout location. Following that, words will be placed into the appropriate line, and then the different fonts and locations of characters will be considered to differentiate between section titles and section content. Lastly, the lines created will be merged into paragraphs which will then be ordered sequentially by the computation of the bounding box of paragraphs.

MATASC has been evaluated with 300 scientific articles, including 150 articles that are related to the materials science domain, and the others are randomly selected from online resources. All sections of these 300 articles are extracted as ground truth for MATASC performance evaluation. We choose

Table 1: Evaluation results comparison between MATESC and GROBID

Article	Name	Accuracy	F1
Random	MATESC	**0.85**	**0.57**
Random	GROBID	0.82	0.44
Relevant	MATESC	**0.88**	**0.72**
Relevant	GROBID	0.76	0.40

GROBID (Lopez, 2009) which is a prevailing tool for metadata extraction from scholarly articles. The Longest Common Subsequence (LCS) that compares the longest common subsequence between ground truth and automatic extracts serves as the evaluation metric. Table 1 reports the performance evaluation results.

3.2 Procedural Information Extraction

The procedural information takes the form of the recipe in our PIEKM system. It describes the main synthesis steps of experiments in materials science literature. We use two approaches to ensure the quality of extracted procedural information: relevant synthesis sentence classification and checking if a relevant sentence contains recipe entities.

Relevant sentences classification: We applied the binary Naïve Bayes (NB) classifier to relevant sentence classification in the experiment section which was output by the free-text extraction. The sentences can be considered relevant if they contain the *recipe* elements (e.g., named compounds, chemical entities, unit operations or sub-procedures). We annotated 2600+ sentences from 98 relevant literature for training the classification model. Particularly, two domain experts annotated 120 sentences from 5 relevant literature and the rest of the annotation work was done by three trained annotators. To better predict the class attribute of the input sentence, we train the NB classifier with word term frequency as count features to achieve a leaned function with 80% accuracy of prediction.

Relevant sentences entities checking: We use ChemicalTagger (Hawizy et al., 2011), an open-source tool for semantic text-mining in the chemistry domain, for recipe sentence checking. The ChemicalTagger uses regex expression to tag different entities, such as conditions, molecules, actions, and phrases, from sentences. In our PIEKM system, the procedural information or recipe should include at least one action which can be represented by a verb word (e.g., dry, distill, dissolve). The system will ignore the sentence even if it has been classified as a relevant sentence.

3.3 Chemical Entity Extraction

Chemical entity extraction is considered as named entity recognition (NER) which is used to recognize and classify the concepts in texts to identify the objects of semantic value. We are able to broadly pre-define the name entities, such as material names, material properties, and sample deceptions, in materials science contexts, based on the task requirements (Mysore et al., 2019). Large, annotated corpora are required to be able to train a machine learning model for NER tasks, which brings a challenge in the materials science domain due to the insufficient annotated dataset. Additionally, manually labeling based on an enormous number of articles would be very time-consuming and expensive for domain exports. We address this issue with transfer learning that is based on the combination of attention-based pre-trained language model SciBERT (Beltagy et al., 2019), Bidirectional Long Short-term Memory (BiLSTM) (Huang et al., 2015), and Conditional Random Fields (CRF), or SciBERT-BiLSTM-CRF for short. Specifically, the pre-trained SciBERT model serves as the embedding layer which takes raw sentences as input and outputs the contextual embedding vectors for each word to the BiLSTM layer. BiLSTM layer takes these inputs for syntactic and semantic feature representation learning and outputs the predicted scores of each label which then will be fed into the CRF layer. Finally, the CRF layer will select the label sequence with the highest predicts score as output.

Considering the insufficient annotated datasets that are available for chemical entity extraction, we merged two annotated corpora in the materials science domain to train the model. One of them is materials synthesis procedural text corpus (**MSP**) (Mysore et al., 2019), which has 230 experiment paragraphs regarding synthesis procedure in the materials science domain and 21 different pre-defined named entities. The other corpus is in the field of solid oxide fuel cell (**SOFC**) (Friedrich et al., 2020), including 45 open-access scholarly articles and 5 different pre-defined named entities. In addition, the BIO format is used to annotate both of the corpora mentioned above, where B indicates the word beginning entity, I represents the words inside the entity, and O is the outside of the entity.

Table 2: Evaluation results comparison

Model	Precision	Recall	F1
SciBERT-BiLSTM-CRF	**0.93**	**0.91**	**0.92**
ChemDataExtractor	0.88	0.83	0.85

We keep only the material name as the predefined named entity in the corpus to train the SciBERT-BiLSTM-CRF model since PIEKM system only focuses on the chemical entity extraction rather than the extraction of other named entities. We compared our model with ChemDataExtractor (Swain and Cole, 2016), a tool for the automated extraction of chemical information from the scientific literature. Table 2 shows the comparison of evaluation results between SciBERT-BiLSTM-BRF and ChemDataExtractor. Note that the ChemDataExtractor is not trained on this merged corpora but only for evaluation comparison.

4 Query processing and information storage

We use the model that is fine-tuned from section **3.3** to extract the key information from the title of the paper. The key information in our system could be considered into two types: **material** and **morphology**. For example, *copper* and *gold* are the type of material; *nanocube* and *nanowire* are the type of morphology. We integrate all this information and store it into the database as a query feature for users.

5 Demonstration

The demonstration covers all of the features of PIEKM system. Figure 2 shows the home page of PIEKM system. It visualizes the overview of the association between the number of articles within the database of nanomaterial composition and the corresponding morphology. The user can click the material name to see the number of relevant articles across different morphology. The relevant literature can be searched by material or morphology name, and the search result page will show a preview figure browser that offers all different options of material or morphology names to select and provides all figures included in the relevant articles (Figure 3). In addition, the chemical entities, recipe, and the full content of extracted literature can be displayed after clicking the title on the top of each figure on the browser (Figure 4).

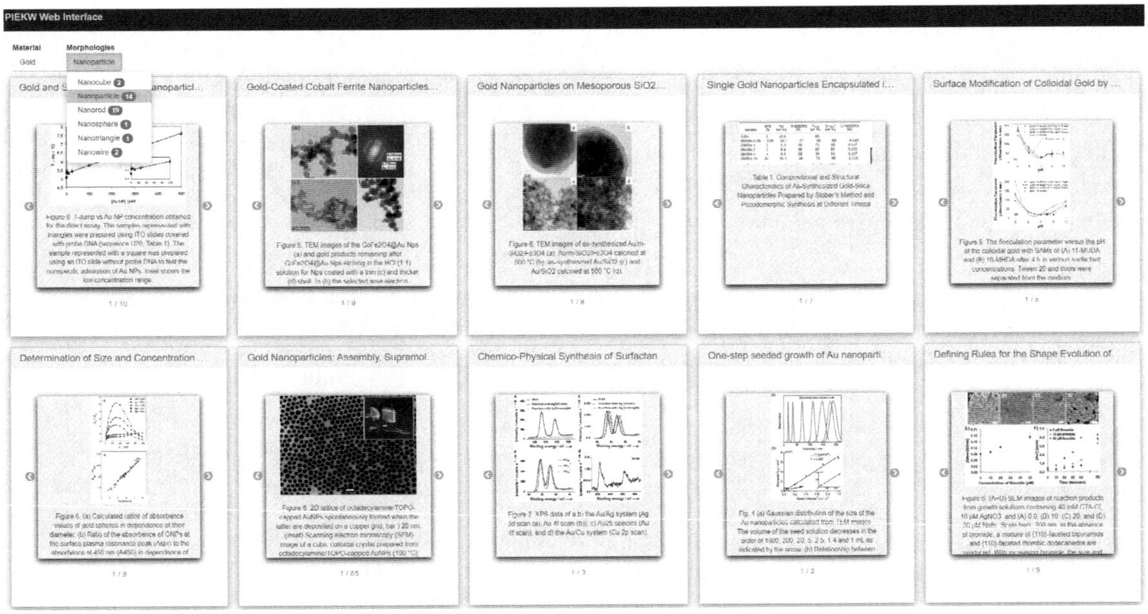

Figure 3: Search result page showing extracted papers and a preview figure browser

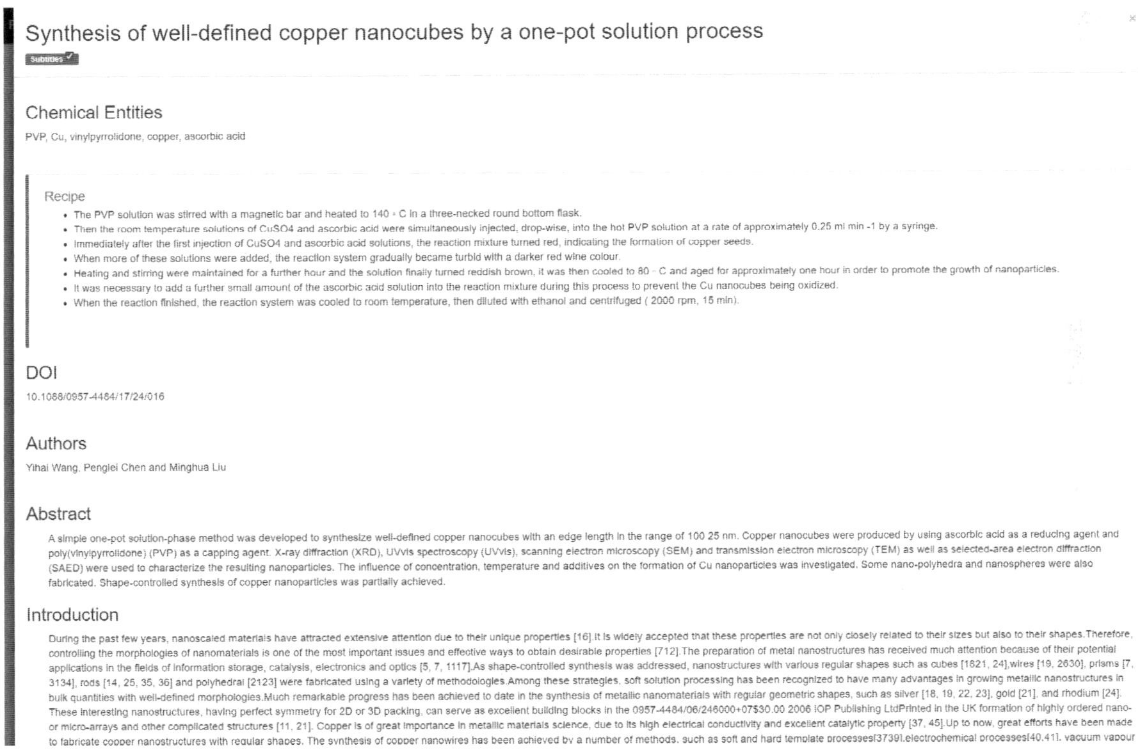

Figure 4: Chemical entities, recipe, and full content of extracted literature

6 Conclusion

This work presents a machine learning-based procedural information extraction and knowledge management system, namely PIEKM, for the materials science domain. PIEKM system integrates multiple functionalities, such as procedural information extraction, chemical entities extraction, information retrieval capabilities, and statistics interactive visualization, into a single web interface. This system provides an efficient way for researchers to gain insights from an enormous number of well-established literature and offers a feasible way to manage knowledge and publications in not only materials science but also other domains.

References

Iz Beltagy, Kyle Lo, and Arman Cohan. 2019. SciBERT: A pretrained language model for scientific text. In *Proceedings of the 2019 Conference on Empirical Methods in Natural Language Processing and the 9th International Joint Conference on Natural Language Processing (EMNLP-IJCNLP)*, pages 3615–3620, Hong Kong, China. Association for Computational Linguistics.

Annemarie Friedrich, Heike Adel, Federico Tomazic, Johannes Hingerl, Renou Benteau, Anika Marusczyk, and Lukas Lange. 2020. The SOFC-exp corpus and neural approaches to information extraction in the materials science domain. In *Proceedings of the 58th Annual Meeting of the Association for Computational Linguistics*, pages 1255–1268, Online. Association for Computational Linguistics.

Lezan Hawizy, David M Jessop, Nico Adams, and Peter Murray-Rust. 2011. Chemicaltagger: A tool for semantic text-mining in chemistry. *Journal of cheminformatics*, 3(1):1–13.

Zhiheng Huang, Wei Xu, and Kai Yu. 2015. Bidirectional lstm-crf models for sequence tagging. *arXiv preprint arXiv:1508.01991*.

Haoyan Huo, Ziqin Rong, Olga Kononova, Wenhao Sun, Tiago Botari, Tanjin He, Vahe Tshitoyan, and Gerbrand Ceder. 2019. Semi-supervised machine-learning classification of materials synthesis procedures. *npj Computational Materials*, 5(1):1–7.

Edward Kim, Kevin Huang, Adam Saunders, Andrew McCallum, Gerbrand Ceder, and Elsa Olivetti. 2017. Materials synthesis insights from scientific literature via text extraction and machine learning. *Chemistry of Materials*, 29(21):9436–9444.

Olga Kononova, Tanjin He, Haoyan Huo, Amalie Trewartha, Elsa A Olivetti, and Gerbrand Ceder. 2021. Opportunities and challenges of text mining in materials research. *Iscience*, 24(3):102155.

Olga Kononova, Haoyan Huo, Tanjin He, Ziqin Rong, Tiago Botari, Wenhao Sun, Vahe Tshitoyan, and Gerbrand Ceder. 2019. Text-mined dataset of inorganic materials synthesis recipes. *Scientific data*, 6(1):1–11.

Patrice Lopez. 2009. Grobid: Combining automatic bibliographic data recognition and term extraction for scholarship publications. In *International conference on theory and practice of digital libraries*, pages 473–474. Springer.

F Maria, De La Torre, Carlos A Aguirre, BreAnn M Anshutz, and William H Hsu. 2018. Matesc: Metadata-analytic text extractor and section classifier for scientific publications. In *KDIR*, pages 259–265.

Sheshera Mysore, Zachary Jensen, Edward Kim, Kevin Huang, Haw-Shiuan Chang, Emma Strubell, Jeffrey Flanigan, Andrew McCallum, and Elsa Olivetti. 2019. The materials science procedural text corpus: Annotating materials synthesis procedures with shallow semantic structures. In *Proceedings of the 13th Linguistic Annotation Workshop*, pages 56–64, Florence, Italy. Association for Computational Linguistics.

Elsa A Olivetti, Jacqueline M Cole, Edward Kim, Olga Kononova, Gerbrand Ceder, Thomas Yong-Jin Han, and Anna M Hiszpanski. 2020. Data-driven materials research enabled by natural language processing and information extraction. *Applied Physics Reviews*, 7(4):041317.

Maksym Polshcha. 2020. Pdfreader. `https://github.com/maxpmaxp/pdfreader`.

Yusuke Shinyama. 2007. Pdfminer. `https://github.com/pdfminer/pdfminer.six`.

Matthew C Swain and Jacqueline M Cole. 2016. Chemdataextractor: a toolkit for automated extraction of chemical information from the scientific literature. *Journal of chemical information and modeling*, 56(10):1894–1904.

Alain C Vaucher, Federico Zipoli, Joppe Geluykens, Vishnu H Nair, Philippe Schwaller, and Teodoro Laino. 2020. Automated extraction of chemical synthesis actions from experimental procedures. *Nature communications*, 11(1):1–11.

Huichen Yang, Carlos A Aguirre, F Maria, Derek Christensen, Luis Bobadilla, Emily Davich, Jordan Roth, Lei Luo, Yihong Theis, Alice Lam, et al. 2019. Pipelines for procedural information extraction from scientific literature: Towards recipes using machine learning and data science. In *2019 International Conference on Document Analysis and Recognition Workshops (ICDARW)*, volume 2, pages 41–46. IEEE.

Huichen Yang and William H Hsu. 2021. Named entity recognition from synthesis procedural text in materials science domain with attention-based approach. In *SDU@ AAAI*.

Zixuan Zhang, Nikolaus Parulian, Heng Ji, Ahmed Elsayed, Skatje Myers, and Martha Palmer. 2021. Fine-grained information extraction from biomedical literature based on knowledge-enriched Abstract Meaning Representation. In *Proceedings of the 59th Annual Meeting of the Association for Computational Linguistics and the 11th International Joint Conference on Natural Language Processing (Volume 1: Long Papers)*, pages 6261–6270, Online. Association for Computational Linguistics.

BiomedCurator: Data Curation for Biomedical Literature

Mohammad Golam Sohrab*, Khoa N. A. Duong*, Masami Ikeda, Goran Topić, Yayoi Natsume-Kitatani, Masakata Kuroda, Mari Nogami Itoh, Hiroya Takamura
Artificial Intelligence Research Center (AIRC)
National Institute of Advanced Industrial Science and Technology (AIST), Japan
National Institutes of Biomedical Innovation, Health and Nutrition (NIBIOHN), Japan
{sohrab.mohammad, goran.topic}@aist.go.jp
{ikeda-masami, takamura.hiroya}@aist.go.jp
{natsume, m-kuroda, mari}@nibiohn.go.jp

Abstract

We present BiomedCurator[1], a web application that extracts the structured data from scientific articles in PubMed and ClinicalTrials.gov. BiomedCurator uses state-of-the-art natural language processing techniques to fill the fields pre-selected by domain experts in the relevant biomedical area. The BiomedCurator web application includes: text generation based model for relation extraction, entity detection and recognition, text classification model for extracting several fields, information retrieval from external knowledge base to retrieve IDs, and a pattern-based extraction approach that can extract several fields using regular expressions over the PubMed and ClinicalTrials.gov articles. Evaluation results show that different approaches of BiomedCurator web application system are effective for automatic data curation in the biomedical domain.

1 Introduction

Scientific article contains a lot of valuable information. For example, reports on clinical studies provide the pieces of information including the applied drug, the target disease, the dose, the dosing period, the ages of the human subjects, and the results. Such pieces of information are useful in data mining and statistical analysis for drug discovery and drug development, if they are properly structured. We call this structurization process *data curation* in this paper, aiming at two-dimensional spreadsheet style structured data as illustrated in Figure 1. Data curation is usually conducted by human experts, who are supposed to read and understand scientific papers, and fill in the spreadsheet. The purpose of this paper is to develop a web application system for automatic data curation in the biomedical domain, which we name *BiomedCurator*. Specifically, for a PubMed/ClinicalTrials.gov ID given by a user, BiomedCurator returns values for 61 information pieces (henceforth, *fields*).

The task of data curation requires a number of different NLP techniques including named entity recognition (NER), entity linking, relation extraction, and text classification. One notable characteristic of this task is that datasets curated by human experts provide spreadsheet-style supervision signal, but do not tell where in the paper each information piece is described; we cannot annotate BIO tags to the paper unlike the training data for NER.

One approach to perform automatic data curation is to use both structured data obtained from the literature and the original literature as training data. The advantage of this approach is that it can output important fields in a data format that is needed by intended users. On the other hand, disadvantages emerge, as typified by the following. (1) Since only information that is important to intended users is included in the structured data, information that is important in NLP (e.g., where each data field is described in the original literature) tends to be omitted. (2) In the process of creating such structured data, the words are often bundled into a notation different from that used in the original literature for the correction of word distortions. In this study, we have developed a web application that can easily realize automated data curation by solving these technical issues with the methods described in Section 2.2.

2 BiomedCurator: Data Curation System for Biomedical Domain

We first describe the dataset for this task, and then the natural language processing techniques used in the system, followed by the description of our system as a web application.

*Equal Contribution

[1]BiomedCurator is publicly available at `https://biomed-text.airc.aist.go.jp/biomedcurator/` as well as its GitHub repository at `https://github.com/aistairc/BiomedCurator`.

Proceedings of the 2nd Conference of the Asia-Pacific Chapter of the Association for Computational Linguistics and the 12th International Joint Conference on Natural Language Processing: System Demonstrations, pages 63–71
November 20–23, 2022.

Reference Information				Intervention Characteristics						Disease Characreristics			...	Reference details		
reference_type	reference_id	associated_clinical trials	...	drug/therapy	refererence_drug therapy	dose	duration	CAS id	...	disease name	stage	...		source	...	Year
PubMed	23868010	UMIN000001779		Prednisolone	[NA]	80 mg	[NA]	50-24-8		Lung Cancer/Non-Small Cell	IIA, IIB			Full Text		2013
...																
PubMed	27924059	CEEOG0106, ML20033		Erlotinib	[NA]	150 mg	[NA]	183321-74-6		Lung Cancer	IIIB, IV			Full Text		2017
ClinicalTrial	NCT02759835	[NA]		Osimertinib	[NA]	80 mg	[NA]	1421373-65-0		Lung Cancer, Non-Small Cell	[NA]			Clinicaltrial-No result		2016
...																
ClinicalTrial	NCT02773238	[NA]		Radiotherapy	[NA]	[NA]	[NA]	[NA]		Lung Cancer, Non-Small Cell	IIB, IIIB			Clinicaltrial-No result		2016

Figure 1: A quick overview of spreadsheet style structured data. The first and second rows refer to categories and their associated fields. The first column indicates PubMed and ClinicalTrials.gov articles and the other columns are the lists of information pieces of PubMed and ClinicalTrials.gov respectively. "..." indicates more other categories and fields.

2.1 Dataset for BiomedCurator

The information required by the intended user is extracted from the articles in a comprehensive manner and structured. As information required by the intended user, 11 categories of articles in PubMed and ClinicalTrials.gov were selected, and each category was further divided into subcategories for a total of 61 fields (lists of information pieces). In the selection process, freely available PubMed articles from the last five years were screened according to whether they were about Idiopathic Pulmonary Fibrosis (IPF), Idiopathic Pulmonary (IP), or fibrosis. From these, priority was given to those with a text as well as an abstract, and the words were extracted manually to a pre-determined DESCRIPTION. A similar screening was then carried out for papers on lung cancer, with similar prioritization and extraction. To assess the quality of data curation for selecting the 11 categories and its 61 fields is based on two criterion. (1) Determination of items: Necessary information in various processes of drug discovery was extracted by dividing it into categories. This was determined by a pharmacologist with experience in drug discovery in discussion with a curator biologist. (2) For curation, a primary curator and an editor in the field of biology were provided, and further quality assurance and quality control checks were conducted.

We developed NLP models trained on a dataset from which information was manually extracted by biologists with domain knowledge as a supervisory dataset. Figure 1 shows a quick overview of spreadsheet style structured data [2]. We refer to the readers to visit our project page `https://github.com/aistairc/BiomedCurator` to learn more details about 11 categories and its 61 fields, as well as the models used for each field. See Appendix A for a quick overview of 11 categories and its 61 fields.

[2]Releasing of the structured data set is under consideration through the project page `https://github.com/aistairc/BiomedCurator`.

2.2 NLP Approaches in BiomedCurator

We address the task of data curation by five main components: (1) Generative relation extraction, (2) Named entity recognition, (3) Text classification, (4) Pattern-based extraction and (5) Information retrieval from external knowledge-base (KB).

2.2.1 Generative Relation Extraction

To extract relations in BiomedCurator, we address two main challenges: (1) the system needs to return the entities and relations where their positions are not given in the training data as mentioned in Introduction, and (2) many entities and relations in our gold data were rephrased/normalized in different ways; pure extraction might not work. These make the preparation of training data and training the discriminative relation extraction model more difficult.

In order to address these challenges, we formalize n-ary relation extraction task as a template generation problem. For a given paragraph, we expect to train a model that can generate a sequence in our predefined structure. For the sequence-to-sequence model, we utilize the BigBirdPegasus model[3] which is designed for summarization tasks to deal with long sequences. For instance, here is a simple training example for extracting relations of drug and dose entities from a given input text: *eligible patients received up to six cycles of pemetrexed, 500 mg/m(2) plus cisplatin, 75 mg/m(2) (day 1) or gemcitabine, 1000 mg/m(2) (days 1 and 8) plus cisplatin, 75 mg/m(2) (day 1). os and toxicity were assessed.*

```
TARGET OUTPUT:
[start]
  [drug] gemcitabine [/drug]
  [dose] 1000 mg/m2 [/dose]
  [and]
  [drug] cisplatin [/drug]
```

[3]`https://huggingface.co/google/bigbird-pegasus-large-pubmed`

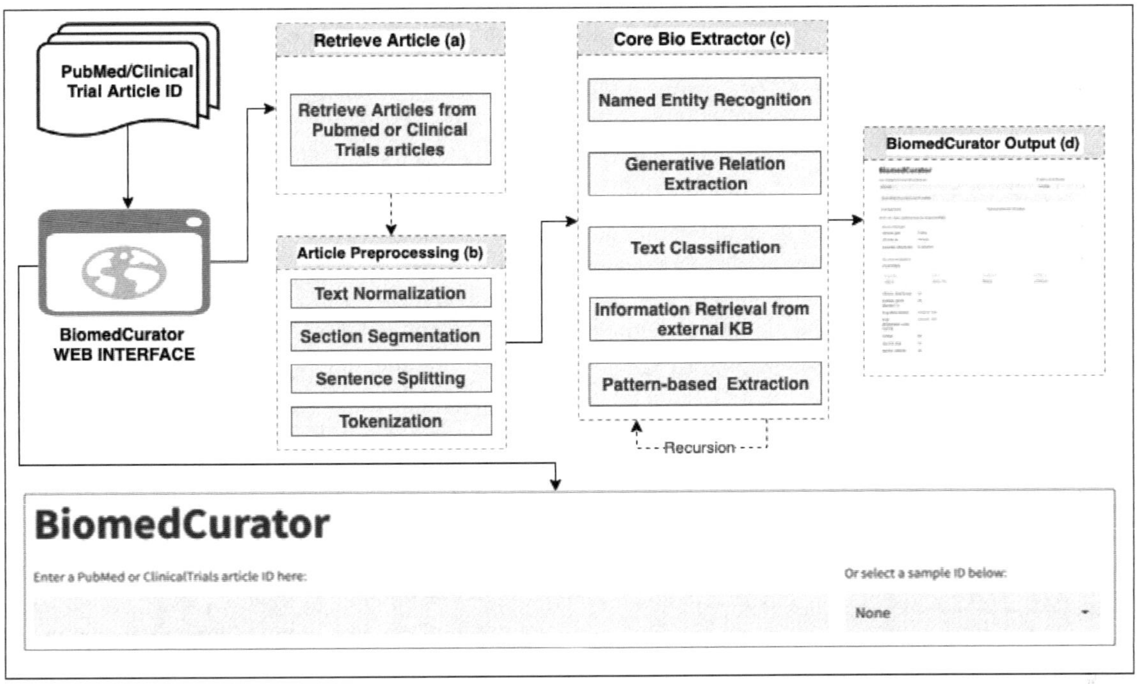

Figure 2: An overview of the workflow of BiomedCurator. The articles from PubMed and ClinicalTrials.gov are parsed through the processes (a) to (d) to extract the value of each field.

```
    [dose] 75 mg/m2 [/dose]
  [or]
    [drug] pemetrexed [/drug]
    [dose] 500 mg/m2 [/dose]
    [and]
    [drug] cisplatin [/drug]
    [dose] 75 mg/m2 [/dose]
  [end]
```

The target output can be expressed as

```
Combination 1:
Rel_1(gemcitabine, 1000 mg/m2)
+ Rel_2(cisplatin, 75 mg/m2)

Combination 2:
Rel_3(pemetrexed, 500 mg/m2)
+ Rel_4(cisplatin, 75 mg/m2)
```

where `[start]` and `[end]` are special tokens to indicate the beginning and the end of the template. Similarly, `[drug]`, `[/drug]`, `[dose]`, and `[/dose]` are special tokens to denote the beginning and the end of entity drug and dose. `[and]` and `[or]` are special tokens that act as operators for combining different relations together. We propose `[and]` and `[or]` to help the model be able to predict multiple relations at the same time. `[and]` is used to combine two relations together and `[or]` is used to separate two relations. When parsing a generated output to extract relations, `[and]` is greater precedence than `[or]`. `Rel` indicates relation of `[drug]` and `[dose]` entities.

BigBird Encoder-Decoder Model The BigBird architecture can process up to 8x longer sequences than BERT (Devlin et al., 2019). Therefore, for the sequence-to-sequence model, we utilize the BigBirdPegasus (Zaheer et al., 2020) model to extract the relations from a given paragraph which is an input to the BigBirdPegasus model. Unlike discriminative model, we address the relation extraction task based on generative model to fill the fields of `dose`, `drug`, and `route of administration`.

2.2.2 Named Entity Recognition

In the named entity recognition (NER) task, we employ pre-trained BERT-based NER models as they have been proven to be effective in many downstream tasks (Devlin et al., 2019). We also make use of the spaCy[4] library which is very well integrated with BERT-based models to simplify our prediction process. To extract the required information to fill the `ethnicity` field, we use BERT-

[4] `https://spacy.io/`

based NER model finetuned on OntoNotes 5 (Pradhan et al., 2007) dataset using SciBERT (Beltagy et al., 2019) as initial weights. In contrast to fill the `Biomarker name` field, SciBERT NER model finetuned on BioNLP13CG (Pyysalo et al., 2015) is used. For other fields, we first generate training data using distant supervision as our curated dataset do not provide position information of gold entities. Then, we finetune separate SciBERT NER models on each noisy generated data and use the trained models to extract the required information.

2.2.3 Text Classification

To extract the information of some fields, we implement two multi-class classification models: (1) SciBERT-based and (2) RandomForest-based[5] classification models. The SciBERT-based classification model is used to predict the labels of a given text input. In contrast, the RandomForest-based classification model is used to predict the labels for a combination of feature vectors as an input data. For instance, to predict the labels of the field `association` where we encode the output of three fields `marker_type`, `marker_nature`, `phenotype` as a feature vector.

2.2.4 Pattern-based Extraction

We observe that pattern-based extraction can be applied to extract the information of many fields (e.g. `reference_id`, `grade`, `stage`, `total_sample_number`, etc.). In this approach, it needs to find a substring that matches a pre-specified regular expression pattern in the text and extract the information. We refer to the readers through our project page to know more about the data fields and its corresponding approaches.

2.2.5 Information Retrieval from External Knowledge Base

Given a field information which is extracted from an article, the task is to retrieve its corresponding ID from a knowledge base (KB). This task is an entity linking problem without context. Instead of building our own model from scratch, we use existing KB API services. We look up the fields `CAS ID`, `ChEMBL ID`, `DrugBank ID`, `Entrez ID`, `Uniprot ID`, `HGVS Name`, `Rs ID`, and `KEGG Pathway Name` by using the keywords of `CAS ID`[6], `ChEMBL`[7], `DrugBank Accession`[8], `Entrez ID`[9], `Uniprot ID`[10], `HGVS`[11], `RSID`[12], `Pathway ID`[13], respectively.

2.3 Web Application of BiomedCurator

The overall workflow of BiomedCurator is illustrated in Figure 2.

Given an article ID, the system first retrieves its corresponding article from the online databases; PubMed or ClinicalTrials.gov. The article is then preprocessed before feeding into the five core components, which are designed to extract different types of information from the input article. Finally, the extracted information is returned and displayed to the user. The recursion connection below the core components in the diagram denotes that some predictions are reused and combined as input features to predict other fields. For instance, the system requires the results of `marker_type`, `marker_nature`, and `phenotype` to be able to predict the label for the field `association`.

3 Experimental Settings

In this section, we evaluate our system on our datasets.

3.1 Datasets

We conduct experiments on our curated datasets based on PubMed and ClinicalTrials.gov to address the biomedical data curation tasks. The PubMed and ClinicalTrials.gov datasets consist of 2,570 and 2,371 PubMed and ClinicalTrials.gov related scientific articles respectively. For ClinicalTrials.gov and PubMed datasets, the predefined template is labeled into 11 main categories that labeled further into several subcategories to make 61 fields. The details of 61 fields are stated on the project page[14]. Statistics of both datasets is shown in Table 1.

[5] https://scikit-learn.org/stable/modules/generated/sklearn.ensemble.RandomForestClassifier.html

[6] https://commonchemistry.cas.org, https://go.drugbank.com

[7] https://go.drugbank.com

[8] https://go.drugbank.com

[9] https://www.ncbi.nlm.nih.gov/gene/, https://www.genecards.org

[10] https://www.uniprot.org/uniprot/, https://www.genecards.org

[11] https://www.ncbi.nlm.nih.gov/CBBresearch/Lu/Demo/LitVar/api.html

[12] https://www.ncbi.nlm.nih.gov/CBBresearch/Lu/Demo/LitVar/api.html

[13] https://www.genome.jp/kegg/pathway.html

[14] https://github.com/aistairc/BiomedCurator

3.2 Data Preprocessing

The data preprocessing component includes 4 main steps: (1) Text normalization, (2) Sentence splitting, (3) Section or paragraph segmentation, and (4) Tokenization.

Text normalization This step is to eliminate XML tags and multiple white spaces in the article, and special characters are converted to spaces. We then apply NFC normalization using ftfy (Speer, 2019) to convert letters followed by combining characters into single combined characters.

Sentence Splitting After the normalization step, we apply the GENIA sentence splitter model[15] to the articles to split into sentences.

Section or Paragraph Segmentation In our curated data, there are several fields that require the system to work on paragraph level instead of sentence level. For example, the relation of fields `drug` and `dose` could span across multiple sentences in the article. Therefore, we propose a simple two-step method to split the entire article into smaller chunks, namely sections and paragraphs. The first step is to leverage the article's metadata provided by PubMed and ClinicalTrials.gov in XML format. Unfortunately, there are cases where we do not have the needed metadata to be able to perform the segmentation, such as not all PubMed articles exist in the PubMed Central[16] database to be downloadable in XML format, or there are sections in ClinicalTrials.gov articles provided in a plain text format. For instance, the section `criteria` in ClinicalTrials.gov articles usually contains sub-sections `Inclusion Criteria` and `Exclusion Criteria` in a plain text format. For that reason, our second step is to utilize a rule-based classifier to predict whether a sentence is a heading/sub-heading or not. Then, we use those headings as splitting points to separate the article into different sections. Our rule-based approach is based on an observation that headings often contain some phrases like Abstract, Introduction, Method, Approach, Results etc. at the beginning of a sentence.

Tokenization Finally, we employ PegasusTokenizer of the BigBirdPegasus model[17] and BertTokenizer of the SciBERT model[18] to tokenize sentences into words.

3.3 NER Model Training

One of the challenges of our curated dataset is that it does not include the position information of the curated entities, which makes the task of training a NER model more difficult. To train the NER model of BiomedCurator, a distantly supervised approach is taken into account to generate the training data. Given a set of entities, we retrieve all the sentences that are associated with the entities (with case-insensitive and a string matching threshold of 90%) and only use those as input data for training.

3.4 Implementation

We optimize all of our models using AdamW (Loshchilov and Hutter, 2019) with a learning rate of 3e-5. For curriculum learning, we trained our generative relation extraction models with 50 epochs and a total batch size of 32 on 8 GPUs (4 examples per GPU). We trained our NER models with 5 epochs and a batch size of 32 on a single GPU with half precision enabled. We conducted each experiment on a server with 8x NVIDIA A100 for NVLink 40GiB. For NER models, we set the max input length up to 512 tokens. For relation extraction models, we use the max length of 768 tokens for encoder input and 512 tokens for decoder output.

4 Results and Discussion

Table 2 shows the performance of 17 fields in terms of precision (P), recall (R), and F-score (F) over the PubMed dataset. In this table, most of the fields performance based on F-score performing well where some fields including `duration`, `grade`, `disease_name`, and `phenotype` are performing comparatively lower than other fields. For `disease_name`, the model is trained on a distantly supervised dataset, which is filtered on gold entity mentions. Since many disease names have multiple variant forms, many were left out by the strict match filtering of the noisy dataset, which led to a poor recall score.

In contrast, Table 3 shows the accuracy performance on six other fields on PubMed dataset. We compute the accuracy for evaluating the fields that have only one answer in an article. For example,

[15] `http://www.nactem.ac.uk/y-matsu/geniass/`

[16] `https://www.ncbi.nlm.nih.gov/pmc/`

[17] `https://huggingface.co/google/bigbird-pegasus-large-pubmed`

[18] `https://huggingface.co/allenai/scibert_scivocab_cased`

Dataset	Statistics					
	Split	#Docs	Avg. Tokens/Doc	Avg. Sec./Doc	Avg. Para./Doc
PubMed	Train	1542	3296.52	10.90	37.89
	Dev	514	3037.13	10.38	35.32
	Test	514	3277.14	10.87	36.96
ClinicalTrials.gov	Train	1421	1395.08	8.41	15.34
	Dev	475	1296.97	8.39	15.00
	Test	475	1343.81	8.43	15.07

Table 1: Statistics of curated dataset based on PubMed and ClinicalTrials.gov

Field Name	P	R	F (%)
associated_clinical trials	54.24	60.38	57.10
Relation of (drug/therapy-dose)	53.77	50.59	52.13
duration	4.91	38.57	8.71
Cell line/Model Name	44.07	41.67	42.83
study_type	85.80	82.43	84.08
ethnicity	27.72	73.29	40.23
grade	10.53	21.43	14.12
phase	18.07	82.86	29.67
disease_name	91.67	5.66	10.66
stage	44.34	70.19	54.35
association	97.00	97.00	97.00
phenotype	9.09	45.19	15.14
p_value	33.37	32.68	33.02
application	94.00	95.00	94.50
allocation	39.02	72.73	50.79
masking	37.50	46.15	41.38
authors	86.35	87.35	86.85

Table 2: Performance of extraction on PubMed dataset. The performances are based on F-score for evaluating fields that have multiple answers.

an article has only one published year information, and our system just needs to predict only one answer. So there are 2 possibilities: correct and incorrect. We compute the F-score for evaluating the fields that have multiple answers. For example, a certain document contains two gold answers and our system predicts one or more predictions.

In the ClinicalTrials.gov dataset, Tables 4 and 5 show the performance of different fields in terms of F-score and accuracy. In these tables, the results show the extraction performances over most of the fields are good except `duration`, `disease_sub_category`, and `BNAMIR` are relatively very poor. The low performance of the field `duration` can be explained by the fact that

Field Name	Accuracy (%)
type of alteration	87.44
phenotype_alteration	93.00
significance	99.95
author_conclusion	100.00
title	95.33
year	99.61

Table 3: Performance of extraction on PubMed Dataset. The performances are based on accuracy for evaluating fields that have single answer "correct" or "incorrect".

gold entities of the field `duration` are usually made up of 1-3 digits followed by a single word representing the unit of time (e.g. 24 hours, 120 days, 2 weeks, 3 months, etc.). As we use distant supervision to generate training examples, this results in the generation of many noisy sentences from which the entities were not actually curated. Training on this noisy data causes our model to ignore the context around entities. This explains why the model has low precision and high recall because the model tends to predict entities whenever it sees number-like tokens. Another major challenge that leads to poor scores in some fields: during manual data curation by domain experts, some information normalized or rephrased in different ways or collected in different ways which is hard to find in the article that leads to difficulty to evaluate.

5 Related Work

Several web-based tools exist that support the retrieval of biomedical information using text mining. Huang et al. (2021) addresses document-level entity-based extraction (EE), aiming at extracting entity-centric information such as entity types and entity relations, which is a key to automatic knowledge acquisition from text corpora for various domains. The authors propose a generative frame-

Field Name	P	R	F (%)
Relation of (drug/therapy-dose)	38.36	33.15	35.5
duration	2.53	81.82	4.90
disease_name	61.66	73.44	67.04
disease_sub_category	11.75	51.43	19.13
stage	23.44	85.80	36.82
BNAMIR	1.29	7.38	2.20
phenotype	22.43	51.03	31.16
total_sample_number	74.95	75.11	75.03
patient_number (case)	74.95	75.11	75.03
age(case)	87.77	87.96	87.86
gender(case)	99.37	100.00	99.68
ethnicity (case)	55.56	71.43	62.50
sponsor & collaborator	66.67	88.93	76.20
phase	97.31	97.97	97.64
inclusion_criteria	73.05	83.41	77.89
authors	95.61	94.37	94.99
intervention_model	96.25	96.48	96.37
masking	97.92	98.38	98.15
primary_purpose	98.84	99.07	98.96
association	98.00	98.00	98.00
application	99.00	99.00	99.00

Table 4: Performances on ClinicalTrials.gov Dataset over the 21 fields. BNAMIR indicates biomarker_name_as_mentioned_in_reference.

Field Name	Accuracy (%)
trial_status	56.21
title	93.89
year	86.11

Table 5: Performance of data extraction on ClinicalTrials.gov Dataset based on accuracy.

work for two document-level EE tasks: role-filler entity extraction (REE) and relation extraction (RE) to address the issue of long-term dependencies among entities at the document-level. In this work, the authors first formulate the task as a template generation problem, allowing models to efficiently capture cross-entity dependencies, exploit label semantics, and avoid the exponential computation complexity of identifying n-ary relations. Other works such as Christopoulou et al. (2019) and Jia et al. (2019) addressed the document-level relation extraction. Christopoulou et al. (2019) introduced constructing a document-level graph from sentence encoding, then extracting entity relations from edge representations in the graph. Where, Jia et al. (2019) proposed a layer classifiers-based pipeline architecture to obtain hierarchical representation of n-ary relations.

Li et al. (2022) proposed pubmedKB, a web server designed to extract and visualize semantic relationships between four biomedical entity types: variants, genes, diseases, and chemicals. pubmedKB uses state-of-the-art natural language processing techniques to extract semantic relations from the large number of PubMed abstracts. Wang et al. (2018) proposed a novel framework CPIE (Clause+Pattern-guided Information Extraction) that incorporates clause extraction and meta-pattern discovery to extract structured relation tuples. Deng et al. (2021) addressed an extraction of gene-disease association using a BERT-based language model. Xing et al. (2018) proposed a pipeline based approach to extract the relation between gene-phenotype from biomedical literature.

In contrast, our work is broader in the sense that it addresses entity and relation-based extraction along with entity linking based on external KB from PubMed and ClinicalTrials.gov datasets. We also introduce multi-class classification and pattern-based approaches for data curation.

6 Conclusion

We propose BiomedCurator based on several data curation approaches from biomedical literature. Our approach is distantly supervised based approach to create training data. Besides, it follows the state-of-the-art NLP techniques that extracts the information from PubMed and ClinicalTrials.gov articles and fill the 61 data fields. We also present an interactive web application of BiomedCurator to facilitate the biomedical research. Experimental results on two datasets show that BiomedCurator performs very well to extract the template fields information in terms of both F-score and accuracy. The BiomedCurator system is continually evolving; we will continue to improve the system as well as to implement new functions such as n-ary relation extraction to further facilitate BiomedCurator research.

Acknowledgements

This work is based on results obtained from a project commissioned by the Public/Private R&D Investment Strategic Expansion PrograM (PRISM). We appreciate insightful feedback from the anonymous reviewers.

References

Iz Beltagy, Kyle Lo, and Arman Cohan. 2019. SciBERT: A pretrained language model for scientific text. In *Proceedings of the 2019 Conference on Empirical Methods in Natural Language Processing and the 9th International Joint Conference on Natural Language Processing (EMNLP-IJCNLP)*, pages 3615–3620, Hong Kong, China. Association for Computational Linguistics.

Fenia Christopoulou, Makoto Miwa, and Sophia Ananiadou. 2019. Connecting the dots: Document-level neural relation extraction with edge-oriented graphs. In *Proceedings of the 2019 Conference on Empirical Methods in Natural Language Processing and the 9th International Joint Conference on Natural Language Processing (EMNLP-IJCNLP)*, pages 4925–4936, Hong Kong, China. Association for Computational Linguistics.

Chuan Deng, Jiahui Zou, Jingwen Deng, and Mingze Bai. 2021. Extraction of gene-disease association from literature using biobert. *The 2nd International Conference on Computing and Data Science*.

Jacob Devlin, Ming-Wei Chang, Kenton Lee, and Kristina Toutanova. 2019. BERT: Pre-training of deep bidirectional transformers for language understanding. In *Proceedings of the 2019 Conference of the North American Chapter of the Association for Computational Linguistics: Human Language Technologies, Volume 1 (Long and Short Papers)*, pages 4171–4186, Minneapolis, Minnesota. Association for Computational Linguistics.

Kung-Hsiang Huang, Sam Tang, and Nanyun Peng. 2021. Document-level entity-based extraction as template generation. In *Proceedings of the 2021 Conference on Empirical Methods in Natural Language Processing*, pages 5257–5269, Online and Punta Cana, Dominican Republic. Association for Computational Linguistics.

Robin Jia, Cliff Wong, and Hoifung Poon. 2019. Document-level n-ary relation extraction with multi-scale representation learning. In *Proceedings of the 2019 Conference of the North American Chapter of the Association for Computational Linguistics: Human Language Technologies, Volume 1 (Long and Short Papers)*, pages 3693–3704, Minneapolis, Minnesota. Association for Computational Linguistics.

Peng-Hsuan Li, Ting-Fu Chen, Jheng-Ying Yu, Shang-Hung Shih, Chan-Hung Su, Yin-Hung Lin, Huai-Kuang Tsai, Hsueh-Fen Juan, Chien-Yu Chen, and Jia-Hsin Huang. 2022. pubmedKB: an interactive web server for exploring biomedical entity relations in the biomedical literature. *Nucleic Acids Research*, 50(W1):W616–W622.

Ilya Loshchilov and Frank Hutter. 2019. Decoupled weight decay regularization. In *International Conference on Learning Representations, ICLR 2019, New Orleans, USA*.

Sameer S. Pradhan, Eduard Hovy, Mitch Marcus, Martha Palmer, Lance Ramshaw, and Ralph Weischedel. 2007. Ontonotes: A unified relational semantic representation. In *International Conference on Semantic Computing (ICSC 2007)*, pages 517–526.

Sampo Pyysalo, Tomoko Ohta, Rafal Rak, Andrew Rowley, Hong-Woo Chun, Sung-Jae Jung, Sung-Pil Choi, Jun'ichi Tsujii, and Sophia Ananiadou. 2015. Overview of the cancer genetics and pathway curation tasks of BioNLP shared task 2013. *BMC bioinformatics*, 16(10):1–19.

Robyn Speer. 2019. ftfy. Zenodo. Version 5.5.

Xuan Wang, Yu Zhang, Qi Li, Yinyin Chen, and Jiawei Han. 2018. Open information extraction with meta-pattern discovery in biomedical literature. *Proceedings of the 2018 ACM International Conference on Bioinformatics, Computational Biology, and Health Informatics*.

Wenhui Xing, Junsheng Qi, Xiaohui Yuan, Lin Li, Xiaoyu Zhang, Yuhua Fu, Shengwu Xiong, Lun Hu, and Jing Peng. 2018. A gene–phenotype relationship extraction pipeline from the biomedical literature using a representation learning approach. *Bioinformatics*, 34(13):i386–i394.

Manzil Zaheer, Guru Guruganesh, Avinava Dubey, Joshua Ainslie, Chris Alberti, Santiago Ontañón, Philip Pham, Anirudh Ravula, Qifan Wang, Li Yang, and Amr Ahmed. 2020. Big bird: Transformers for longer sequences. *CoRR*, abs/2007.14062.

A Curated Data Fields

The overview of categories, fields, related natural language processing techniques (NLPT), and descriptions are illustrated in Table 6. The first and second columns indicate category and its fields name. The third column stands for different NLP approaches applied in each field. In this column, PE, RE, EE, EL, and TC refer to pattern-based extraction, relation extraction, entity extraction, entity linking, and text classification-based approaches are applied for data curation. Besides, Fixed Value (FV) means a specific value in the curated data and NA means Not Available at the moment. Fields Descriptions are also added in column four.

Category	Field Name	NLPT	Description
Reference Information	reference_type	FV	Source of the article. Ex: PubMed or Clinical trial
	reference_id	PE	Unique Pubmed ID or Clinical trial id of the curated document
	associated_clinical trials	PE	Provides the associated clinicaltrial ids for which the results were published
	s_no	NA	Each assertion has given a unique number
Intervention Characteristics	drug/therapy	RE	Captured the list of authors focus drug/s of case group.
	reference_drug/therapy	RE	Captured the list of authors focus drug/s of reference group.
	treatment_details	NA	Detail description of the treatment, including but not limited to patient details, drug/therapy, dose/cycles, duration, route, schedule, analysis.
	dose	RE	It represents the concentration value of the drug used in the given reference
	route of administration	RE	The route through which the drug is administered.
	duration	EE+PE	Time period of the treatment.
	CAS id	EL	Chemical abstracts service registry number of the drug.
	ChEMBL	EL	Unique id as provided by ChEMBL.
	drug bank id	EL	Drug bank id for the given drug.
	approved_drug	NA	Name of the drug which is approved by any approval authority.
	approval_authority	NA	Name of the organization/institution has the authority to approve the respective drug. Ex: FDA.
Disease Characteristics	disease_name	EE+PE	Name of the focused indication for which the biomarker was studied.
	disease_sub_category	EE+PE	Represents the subtype or any state of the disease mentioned in the given reference.
	Stage	PE	Stages of the disease Eg: Stage I, II, III, IV, etc.
	Grade	PE	Grading of the disease Eg: Grade I, II, III, IV, etc.
	Histopathology	EE	Additional details of the disease mentioned in the article Ex: Stage, histopathology etc.
Biomarker Details	BNAMIR	EE	Complete name of the biomarker. Abbreviations are extended for ease of understanding.
	marker_type	EE	Represents the type of the biomarker based on the techniques used to measure the biomarker Eg: Biochemical, Genomic etc.
	marker_nature	EE	Represents the chemical nature of the biomarker based on the techniques used to measure the biomarker Eg: Protein, Gene, Lipid etc.
	Entrez id	EL	Unique ID as provided by the NCBI Entrez gene database for each gene.
	Uniprot id	EL	Protein accession number of UniprotKB database.
	type_of_variation	EL	Represents standard HGVS constructs unique for each variation.
	rs_id	EL	Represents the unique reference number for each SNP at a specific position. Taken from NCBI site – (dbSNP) Eg: rs763110.
	HGVS Name	EL	Field describes nucleotide/DNA (c.) change as per the HGVS format (the nucleotide/genomic numbering should be as in article only)
Biomarker association with outcomes	association	TC	Describes about the high level type/category of biomarker association with outcomes. Associations are of 5 types: Gene - drug relationships; Gene - gene interactions; Gene - pathway relationships; Gene - phenotype relationships; Gene - transcript information
	marker_alteration	EE	Represents the type of alteration or measurement done for biomarker Eg: Gene expression, Polymorphism, Biomarker level etc.
	type of alteration	PE	Represents the modification of the marker mentioned in the article i.e change of biomarker expression or levels. Eg: High; Low; Decreases; Association; Upregulation etc.
	phenotype	TC	Biomarker associates with any phenotype character, end point, outcome, any physiological process and other biomarkers of the study sample.
	phenotype_alteration	PE	Represents the state of change for the outcome variables which are associated with the studied biomarker.
	significance	PE	Represents the level of significance of P value between different groups Eg: Non-significant or Significant.
	p_value	PE	P value (Significance) between the different groups for comparison of biomarker result values or any other values related to biomarker. Ex: P=0.016
Utility	application	TC	Denotes the utility of the biomarker for a given condition in a specific reference (either clinical trial or pubmed article).
	author_conclusion	TC	Represents the utility of the biomarker from the author's perspective in the given reference. Yes indicates that author, in the reference, supports the application of the biomarker for the given indication. No indicates that author in the reference does not support the application of the biomarker for the given indication.
	evidence_statement	NA	Gives the structured description of the application text of the biomarker in a given condition specific to each reference and clinical status.
Study characteristics	study_type (Clinical/PreClinical)	PE	Represents the status of the clinical study Ex: Clinical, Preclinical etc.
	Cell line/ Model Name	EE	Represents the cell lines used in the preclinical model/It represents the preclinical model Eg: Mouse, rat etc.
	total_sample_number	PE	Denotes total number of participants from both study and reference sample group in a particular study.
	patient_number (case)	PE	To capture the study group sample size for the curated assertion from the article.
	patient_number (reference)	PE	To capture the reference group sample size for the curated assertion.
	age (case)	PE	Used to capture the study sample age from the article.
	gender (case)	PE	Used to capture the gender for studied samples from the article.
	ethnicity (case)	EE	This represents the nationality/ethnicity of the study group as stated in the article.
Trial level information	trial_status	PE	Current stage of a clinical study. Ex: Completed, Terminated etc.
	sponsor & collaborator	PE	Sponsors/collaborators of the clinical study.
	phase	PE	Represents the clinical phase of the trial. Ex: 0, I, II, III, IV.
	inclusion_criteria	PE	Description on the Inclusion criteria for the patients in the clinical study.
	exclusion_criteria	PE	Description on the Exclusion criteria for the patients in the clinical study.
Study design	allocation	PE	Assigning trial subjects to treatment or control groups. Ex: Non-randomized, Randomised.
	intervention_model	PE	Type of intervention model from the study. Ex: Single Group Design, Parallel Design, Crossover Design and Factorial Design.
	masking	PE	Types of Masking include None, Open Label, Single and Double Blind Masking.
	primary_purpose	PE	Represents purpose of the study primarily under taken for the research.
Additional details	pathway_name	EL+PE	Names of the pathways in which a biomarker has a role. Taken from KEGG database.
Reference details	Source	FV	whether the curated data is from full-text or abstract of the article or ClinicalTrials.
	Title	PE	Title of the article.
	Authors	PE	Authors of the article.
	Article/URL	PE	Name of the journal or specific links from which the information is captured
	Year	PE	Year in which the given article published Ex: Article published year. for Pubmed articles and First received year is considered for Clinicaltrials.

Table 6: An overview of category, field with corresponding description, and methodology.

Text Characterization Toolkit (TCT)

Daniel Simig[*], Tianlu Wang[*], Verna Dankers[*+], Peter Henderson[‡*], Khuyagbaatar Batsuren[†], Dieuwke Hupkes[*], Mona Diab[*]
[*]Meta AI, [+]University of Edinburgh, [†]National University of Mongolia, [‡]Stanford University
{danielsimig,dieuwkehupkes,mdiab}@meta.com

Abstract

We present a tool, *Text Characterization Toolkit (TCT)*, that researchers can use to study characteristics of large datasets. Furthermore, such properties can lead to understanding the influence of such attributes on models' behaviour. Traditionally, in most NLP research, models are usually evaluated by reporting single-number performance scores on a number of readily available benchmarks, without much deeper analysis. Here, we argue that – especially given the well-known fact that benchmarks often contain biases, artefacts, and spurious correlations – deeper results analysis should become the de-facto standard when presenting new models or benchmarks. TCT aims at filling this gap by facilitating such deeper analysis for datasets at scale, where datasets can be for training/development/evaluation. TCT includes both an easy-to-use tool, as well as off-the-shelf scripts that can be used for specific analyses. We also present use-cases from several different domains. TCT is used to predict difficult examples for given well-known trained models; TCT is also used to identify (potentially harmful) biases present in a dataset.

1 Introduction

NLP technology has progressed tremendously over the recent decades with significant advances in algorithms and modeling. Yet, by comparison, our understanding lags behind significantly for datasets (including all datasets types in the model life cycle: training, validation, evaluation) that contribute to model performance. This is mostly due to the lack of frameworks, methods, and tools to draw insights into datasets, especially at scale.

Most NLP models, to date, are evaluated using a relatively small number of readily available evaluation benchmarks, that are often created automatically, or via crowd-sourcing (e.g. Bowman et al., 2015; Wang et al., 2018; Williams et al., 2018; Zellers et al., 2018). It is well-known that most popular (evaluation) datasets are rife with biases, dataset artefacts and spurious correlations, and are prone to be solved with shortcuts (Gardner et al., 2021; Kiela et al., 2021). Presenting models with *adversarial examples* for which those biases or correlations do not hold, often results in stark performance drops (e.g. Linzen, 2020; McCoy et al., 2019; Jia and Liang, 2017; Chen et al., 2016; Tsuchiya, 2018; Belinkov et al., 2019). At best, using datasets with such known issues might result in overestimation of a models' capability on the task in question, which may not be reflective of how well they can execute this task in more realistic scenarios. More worrying, however, is that training or finetuning on datasets that contain biases and artefacts may result in models implementing undesired, biased behaviour (e.g. Rudinger et al., 2018; Blodgett et al., 2016).

Additionally, datasets are usually treated as homogeneous collections of text, performance for which is captured in a single number – even though there is often a substantial difference between the difficulty/complexity of different examples in a dataset (e.g. Sugawara et al., 2022). Research papers rarely report thorough analysis of performance broken down by characteristics of the data set examples ignoring underlying patterns performance numbers may reflect. The problem is exacerbated by the pervasiveness of benchmarks coupled with a leaderboard competitive culture, where what counts most is system rank.

In part, this may be due to the fact that deeper analysis of results – especially when a number of different datasets is involved – is complex and time-consuming, and there are no standard frameworks or protocols that practitioners can resort to. The problem is even more pervasive, where we curate datasets for development and evaluation. How we curate, create, select data plays a critical role in understanding our models. Many NLP models (even beyond text) require up/down sampling of specific

Proceedings of the 2nd Conference of the Asia-Pacific Chapter of the Association for Computational Linguistics and the 12th International Joint Conference on Natural Language Processing: System Demonstrations, pages 72–87
November 20–23, 2022.

types of data. These processes should rely on principled characterization of data for any given model.

To this end, we believe that the existence of a standard toolkit that provides an easy to use set of tools and metrics allowing researchers to analyze and systematically characterize datasets, *at scale*, involved in the model life cycle, while gaining insights into the relationship between model performance and data properties could become more common place.

In this paper, we introduce the *Text Characterization Toolkit*[1] (TCT), which aims to enable researchers to gain a detailed understanding of the datasets and models they create – with minimal effort. TCT is inspired by the Coh-Metrix toolkit (Graesser et al., 2004), a collection of over 100 diverse text characteristics intended for use for text analysis in various applications. TCT offers these capabilities at scale by design. While TCT can process a dataset of 20000 paragraphs in less than a minute on a MacBook Pro laptop, the very same library, for instance, can also be used as part of a distributed PySpark pipeline to compute text characteristics for a full snapshot of Common Crawl (3.1B web pages) in a matter of hours. While text characteristics in TCT are currently implemented for the English language only, the framework is designed to scale to any new language via configuration of new resource files and SpaCy backends.

In this paper we present:

1. A repository of text metrics that can help reveal (latent) patterns in datasets coupled with model performance on these datasets;
2. A set of off-the-shelf analysis tools that researchers can use in a simple notebook to study properties of the dataset and the influence of those properties on model behaviour;
3. A framework that enables the community to share, reuse and standardize metrics and analyses methods/tools;
4. Use cases that demonstrate the efficacy of TCT in practice covering Language Model prompting, Translation, and Bias Detection.

With these contributions, we aspire to help the NLP community in particular and the AI community at large improve how we assess NLP models, and get closer to a scenario where providing detailed results' analyses becomes the standard for NLP research. Equally important, we believe that

[1] https://github.com/facebookresearch/text_characterization_toolkit

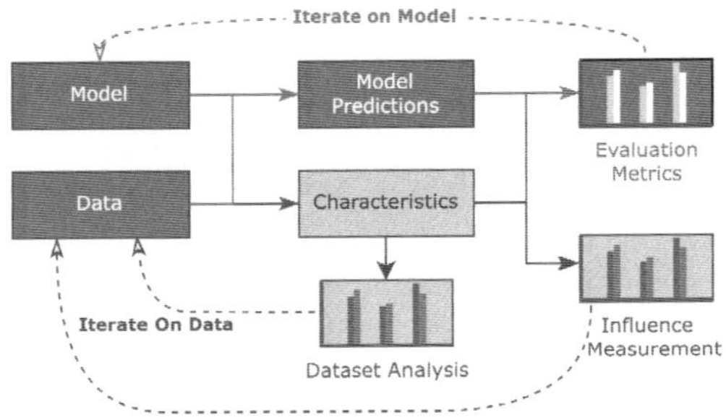

Figure 1: Text Characterization Toolkit extends model evaluation to provide insights about the role of data.

TCT could be an effective tool for data selection for both training and evaluation, in particular at scale.

2 [TCT] Text Characterization Toolkit

TCT consists of two main components:

- A framework for defining and computing text characteristics.
- A collection of analysis tools that help users interpret text characteristics and evaluate results with respect to these characteristics.

As illustrated by Figure 1, the workflow of extending a standard evaluation process with TCT is typically the following:

1. Given a dataset, extract text fragments from each data point into a file. For instance, a QA dataset comprising text fragments could be individual questions, whereas in document summarization, the text fragments would be the documents themselves.
2. Using the TCT command line tool, compute the characteristics of the text fragments and dump the results in a file. Furthermore, one might use the default characteristics already included in the framework or define their own specific metric in a new configuration file.
3. Create a Python notebook and include the TCT library. Using tools from this library load the computed characteristics and other evaluation specific data, then use some of the analysis tools provided by the framework: one might analyze the dataset itself (e.g. to identify spurious correlations or biases) or jointly analyze model evaluation metrics and text characteristics (e.g. through correlation analysis between TCT features and models' evaluation set accuracy).
4. Use the results of the analysis to improve the dataset, the model, or the evaluation protocol – for example by extending evaluation data

Category	Example Metrics
Descriptive	Word Count Sentence Length
Lexical Diversity	Type-Token Ratio MTLD
Complexity	Left Embeddedness # of NP modifiers
Incidence Scores	Different POS tags Types of connectives
Word Property	Age of Acquisition Concreteness

Table 1: Categories of characteristics currently implemented. See Appendix A for an exhaustive list.

with examples where a model is expected to perform poorly or focusing evaluation on a challenging subset of the test data.

Concrete examples of the workflow above are described in §3 and in Appendix B. The rest of this section provides more details on the two important components of the framework.

2.1 Text Characteristics

While the majority of the characteristics found in TCT is motivated by metric classes in Coh-Metrix (Graesser et al., 2004), we have included new data bases for existing metrics and added entirely new metrics. At the time of writing, there are 61 characteristics implemented in TCT. An overview of the main categories of currently implemented characteristics can be found in Table 1. The toolkit provides a standardized framework to implement, configure, and compute these metrics. Adding a new metric is as simple as implementing two Python functions: one that loads any required resource (such as a word database) and initializes computation, and one that computes the metric given these resources and an input text.

2.2 Analysis tools

To further decrease the effort required to carry out text characteristics based analysis, we provide an initial set of analysis tools that users can use out of the box. We encourage users to contribute their own implementations of TCT-based analyses to the toolkit, to allow for re-use in the future development of datasets and models. The current functionality of the toolkit includes:

1. Visualising distributions of different characteristics;
2. Visualising a pairwise correlation matrix for the characteristics, as illustrated in Figure 2;

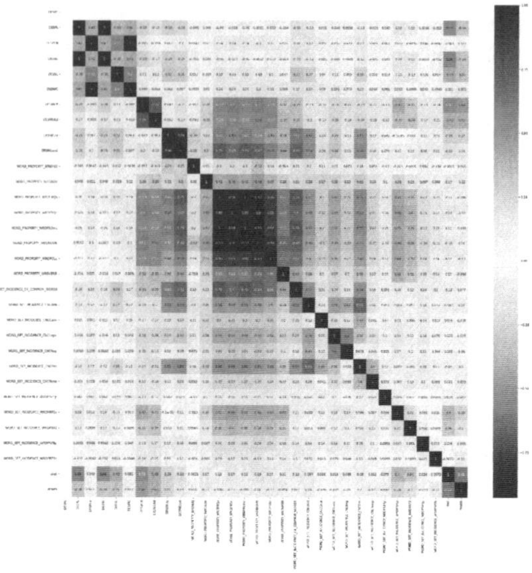

Figure 2: An illustration of a correlation plot from TCT. Users might find these plots valuable to find unexpected correlations or to interpret results of multi-variable regression models.

3. Visualising correlations between individual characteristics and outcomes (e.g., accuracy), as illustrated in Figure 4;
4. Fitting a model on all characteristics to outcomes (logistic regression and random forests are supported currently) and analyzing a model's predictive power and coefficients. This is illustrated in Figure 3.

3 Example Use Cases

In order to demonstrate the ability of TCT to produce meaningful and actionable insights, we provide 3 examples of its use on real world data. For each one of these use cases, a thorough description of the experimental setup and results is included in Appendix B and reference notebooks are provided in the `examples` directory of the TCT repository.

Predicting Accuracy of OPT Baselines Open Pre-trained Transformer Language Models (OPT, Zhang et al. 2022) are a sequence of publicly released LLMs that span model scales from 125M to 175B parameters. While scaling thees models lead to significant gains on numerous benchmarks, they still occasionally produce results that would seem trivially wrong to any human.

With the help of TCT, we attempted to better understand the robustness of these models quantitatively. We use the multi-variable logistic regression

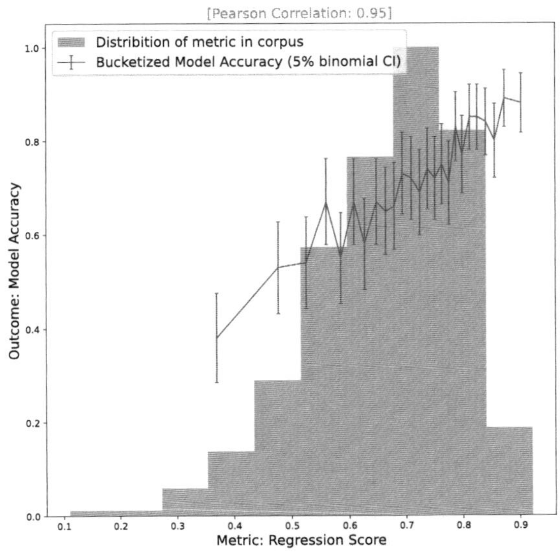

(a) Model accuracy versus the regression output variable. Using the multi-variable regression tool can surface larger variations in model performance.

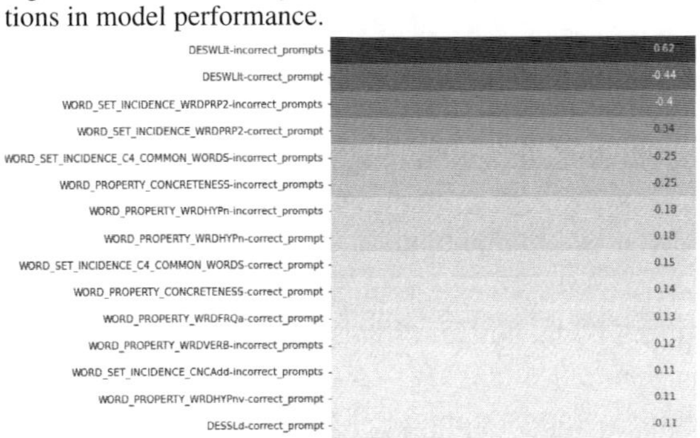

(b) TCT displays the most important feature coefficients to help users understand what characteristics contributed to the results shown in Figure 3a

Figure 3: Results from the TCT multi-variable regression analysis tool. Screenshots taken from the OPT analysis described in §3.

analysis tool to fit a model that predicts the accuracy of the 6.7B parameter OPT model on the HellaSwag common-sense inference task (Zellers et al., 2019) based on simple characteristics such as mean word length and concreteness. Using this model we can identify subsets of the test data with model accuracy as low as 40% and as high as 90% – shown on Figure 3.

Fluctuations in Translation Performance Using TCT we show how translation performance of the NLLB model (Costa-jussà et al., 2022) using the HuggingFace pipeline (Wolf et al., 2019) fluctuates as a function of sample characteristics, like the number of sentences - Figure 4 shows the output of TCT in this analysis. This performance

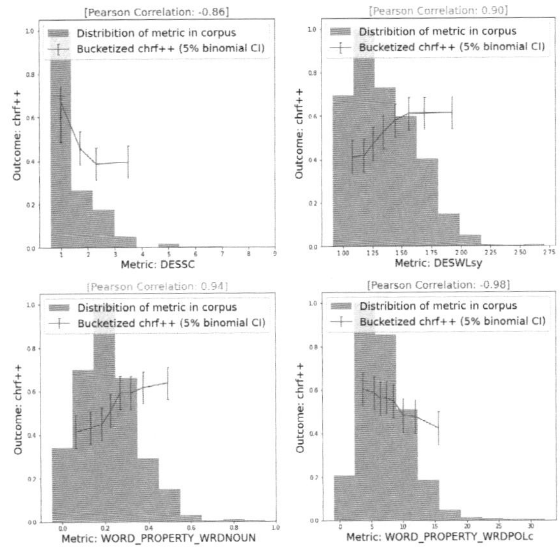

Figure 4: Model performance of a translation model in function of various characteristics of the text translated, produced by the TCT single-variable analysis tool. Appendix B.3 describes the experimental setup in detail.

heterogeneity can be fixed by segmenting sentences before using the pipeline, showing that TCT can help debug model pipelines even with many layers of abstraction.

Gender Bias in Co-reference Resolution By computing genderedness metrics on co-reference labels and using these metrics as inputs to the analysis tools, we reproduce the results of Zhao et al. (2018) showing that models perform much worse when the stereotypically associated gender of an occupation does not match the gender of the pronominal reference.

4 Related Work

There exist several tools that offer similar functionality to TCT in some specific respects. DataLab (Xiao et al., 2022) is a tool for detailed data analysis that, among other things, allows users to inspect datasets through the lens of a few text characteristics such as text length, lexical diversity and gender-related features. The *Know Your Data*[2] tool allows for inspection of image data, it surfaces spurious correlations, biases and imbalances in datasets. However, both tools do not connect model behavior to properties of datasets.

Collins et al. (2018) predicts overall hardness of classification datasets based on label statistics and a few text characteristics such as readability

[2]https://knowyourdata.withgoogle.com/

and lexical diversity. ExplainaBoard (Liu et al., 2021) focuses on model performance analysis and provides a model performance breakdown by simple attributes of data points such as text length, providing a functionality most similar to our work.

Our toolkit distinguishes itself by including a much wider variety of text characteristics. As a concrete example, ExplainaBoard does not provide features similar to WRDPRP2 (personal pronoun incidence), WRDPOLc (mean word polysemy) or DESSC (number of sentences per text), each playing an important role in our chosen use cases analyses described in §3. TCT also features a multi-variable analysis tool that can identify larger variations in model performance compared to simpler, single-variable analyses.

By packaging our toolkit as a simple Python library used in notebooks – in contrast to the previously described feature-rich systems – we also intend to minimize the effort needed to both use it as well as contribute to it (eg. crowd sourcing more functionality).

The Coh-Metrix tool (Graesser et al., 2004) collected the most diverse set of text characteristics to our knowledge, designed for various use cases in linguistics and pedagogy. However, the tool, developed in 2004, is slow as it is designed to process a single document at a time, relatively difficult to access, and the underlying word databases are outdated. Our toolkit aims to make a subset of the Coh-Metrix metrics easily accessible to the NLP community, while simultaneousy addressing the scale impediment noted in the original Coh-Metrix tool.

5 Future Work

As illustrated in §2 we envision TCT to be a framework and an associated tool that allows for community contributions, crowdsourcing even more functionality and use cases. Future work involves usage of the tool:

Firstly, we encourage creators of new datasets to use TCT as a data annotation tool, to extract a wide range of dataset statistics in a straightforward manner, and report about them in academic publications for transparency. Such statistics could be included in datasheets and data cards (Gebru et al., 2021), and they can aid in outlier detection during data (pre-)processing and cleaning.

We also prompt dataset creators to perform statistical analyses capturing which features are predictive of the gold targets *before* further training computational models, to ensure one is aware about potential shortcut learning opportunities due to biases in the dataset. Naturally, not all correlations are bad or avoidable – e.g. consider sentences containing the word 'fantastic' that are likely to have a positive label in sentiment analysis – but others are good to be aware of when working with a dataset – e.g. consider a natural language inference task where all sentences with the label 'entailed' have an atypical average word length. Such analyses could be included in a 'cautions' section with a dataset's release.

A third type of usage would be by owners of new models, that, on the one hand, use TCT to measure whether some dataset characteristics are predictive of success and failure by their model, and, on the other hand, provide performance on subclasses of samples. One may already know that model performance is lower for longer sentences, but what about performance on different readability classes, classes with varying amounts of causal connectives or different ratings for syntactic complexity (e.g. SYNLE)? TCT will help answer those questions. Understanding how the model performance fluctuates for different data subsets provides further understanding in model robustness, and can, in turn, improve datasets' quality if model owners report back on biases identified in datasets.

Limitations

Text Characteristics in our framework have varying levels of coverage depending on their type. Word property based characteristics, for example, are limited by the coverage of the word databases that back them – this can be limited even for English.

Despite covering a sizeable number of metrics in Coh-Metrix's original toolkit, we still don't cover all possible relevant metrics for text processing, especially at different levels of granularity (eg. document/paragraph/character levels).

We are mostly limited to the text modality which could cater to speech data however TCT lacks analysis tools and metrics for more speech oriented datasets such as prosody and syllables for instance.

While we plan to extend the framework to multiple languages in the near future, language coverage of backend word databases and NLP pipelines such as WordNet (Miller, 1995) or SpaCy (Honnibal et al., 2020) will affect the ability to scale the number of languages supported.

References

Yonatan Belinkov, Adam Poliak, Stuart Shieber, Benjamin Van Durme, and Alexander Rush. 2019. Don't take the premise for granted: Mitigating artifacts in natural language inference. In *Proceedings of the 57th Annual Meeting of the Association for Computational Linguistics*, pages 877–891, Florence, Italy. Association for Computational Linguistics.

Su Lin Blodgett, Lisa Green, and Brendan O'Connor. 2016. Demographic dialectal variation in social media: A case study of African-American English. In *Proceedings of the 2016 Conference on Empirical Methods in Natural Language Processing*, pages 1119–1130, Austin, Texas. Association for Computational Linguistics.

Samuel R. Bowman, Gabor Angeli, Christopher Potts, and Christopher D. Manning. 2015. A large annotated corpus for learning natural language inference. In *Proceedings of the 2015 Conference on Empirical Methods in Natural Language Processing*, pages 632–642, Lisbon, Portugal. Association for Computational Linguistics.

Marc Brysbaert, Paweł Mandera, Samantha F Mccormick, and Emmanuel Keuleers. Word prevalence norms for 62,000 English lemmas.

Marc Brysbaert, Amy Beth Warriner, and Victor Kuperman. 2014. Concreteness ratings for 40 thousand generally known English word lemmas. *Behavior Research Methods*, 46(3):904–911.

Danqi Chen, Jason Bolton, and Christopher D. Manning. 2016. A thorough examination of the CNN/Daily Mail reading comprehension task. In *Proceedings of the 54th Annual Meeting of the Association for Computational Linguistics (Volume 1: Long Papers)*, pages 2358–2367, Berlin, Germany. Association for Computational Linguistics.

Aakanksha Chowdhery, Sharan Narang, Jacob Devlin, Maarten Bosma, Gaurav Mishra, Adam Roberts, Paul Barham, Hyung Won Chung, Charles Sutton, Sebastian Gehrmann, et al. 2022. Palm: Scaling language modeling with pathways. *arXiv e-prints*, pages arXiv–2204.

Edward Collins, Nikolai Rozanov, and Bingbing Zhang. 2018. Evolutionary data measures: Understanding the difficulty of text classification tasks. In *Proceedings of the 22nd Conference on Computational Natural Language Learning*, pages 380–391, Brussels, Belgium. Association for Computational Linguistics.

Max Coltheart. 2018. The MRC Psycholinguistic Database:. *https://doi.org/10.1080/14640748108400805*, 33(4):497–505.

Marta R Costa-jussà, James Cross, Onur Çelebi, Maha Elbayad, Kenneth Heafield, Kevin Heffernan, Elahe Kalbassi, Janice Lam, Daniel Licht, Jean Maillard, et al. 2022. No language left behind: Scaling human-centered machine translation. *arXiv e-prints*, pages arXiv–2207.

Christiane Fellbaum. 2010. WordNet. *Theory and Applications of Ontology: Computer Applications*, pages 231–243.

Matt Gardner, William Merrill, Jesse Dodge, Matthew Peters, Alexis Ross, Sameer Singh, and Noah A. Smith. 2021. Competency problems: On finding and removing artifacts in language data. In *Proceedings of the 2021 Conference on Empirical Methods in Natural Language Processing*, pages 1801–1813, Online and Punta Cana, Dominican Republic. Association for Computational Linguistics.

Timnit Gebru, Jamie Morgenstern, Briana Vecchione, Jennifer Wortman Vaughan, Hanna Wallach, Hal Daumé Iii, and Kate Crawford. 2021. Datasheets for datasets. *Communications of the ACM*, 64(12):86–92.

Arthur C. Graesser, Danielle S. McNamara, Max M. Louwerse, and Zhiqiang Cai. 2004. Coh-Metrix: Analysis of text on cohesion and language. *Behavior Research Methods, Instruments, & Computers 2004 36:2*, 36(2):193–202.

Pengcheng He, Xiaodong Liu, Jianfeng Gao, and Weizhu Chen. 2020. DeBERTa: decoding-enhanced BERT with disentangled attention. In *International Conference on Learning Representations*.

Matthew Honnibal, Ines Montani, Sofie Van Landeghem, and Adriane Boyd. 2020. spaCy: Industrial-strength Natural Language Processing in Python.

Robin Jia and Percy Liang. 2017. Adversarial examples for evaluating reading comprehension systems. In *Proceedings of the 2017 Conference on Empirical Methods in Natural Language Processing*, pages 2021–2031, Copenhagen, Denmark. Association for Computational Linguistics.

Douwe Kiela, Max Bartolo, Yixin Nie, Divyansh Kaushik, Atticus Geiger, Zhengxuan Wu, Bertie Vidgen, Grusha Prasad, Amanpreet Singh, Pratik Ringshia, Zhiyi Ma, Tristan Thrush, Sebastian Riedel, Zeerak Waseem, Pontus Stenetorp, Robin Jia, Mohit Bansal, Christopher Potts, and Adina Williams. 2021. Dynabench: Rethinking benchmarking in NLP. In *Proceedings of the 2021 Conference of the North American Chapter of the Association for Computational Linguistics: Human Language Technologies*, pages 4110–4124, Online. Association for Computational Linguistics.

Victor Kuperman, Hans Stadthagen-Gonzalez, and Marc Brysbaert. Age-of-acquisition ratings for 30,000 English words.

Kenton Lee, Luheng He, Mike Lewis, and Luke Zettlemoyer. 2017. End-to-end neural coreference resolution. In *Proceedings of the 2017 Conference on Empirical Methods in Natural Language Processing*, pages 188–197, Copenhagen, Denmark. Association for Computational Linguistics.

Tal Linzen. 2020. How can we accelerate progress towards human-like linguistic generalization? In *Proceedings of the 58th Annual Meeting of the Association for Computational Linguistics*, pages 5210–5217, Online. Association for Computational Linguistics.

Pengfei Liu, Jinlan Fu, Yang Xiao, Weizhe Yuan, Shuaichen Chang, Junqi Dai, Yixin Liu, Zihuiwen Ye, and Graham Neubig. 2021. ExplainaBoard: An Explainable Leaderboard for NLP. *ACL-IJCNLP 2021 - 59th Annual Meeting of the Association for Computational Linguistics and the 11th International Joint Conference on Natural Language Processing, Proceedings of the System Demonstrations*, pages 280–289.

Tom McCoy, Ellie Pavlick, and Tal Linzen. 2019. Right for the wrong reasons: Diagnosing syntactic heuristics in natural language inference. In *Proceedings of the 57th Annual Meeting of the Association for Computational Linguistics*, pages 3428–3448, Florence, Italy. Association for Computational Linguistics.

George A. Miller. 1995. Wordnet: A lexical database for english. *Commun. ACM*, 38(11):39–41.

Kishore Papineni, Salim Roukos, Todd Ward, and Wei-Jing Zhu. 2002. Bleu: a method for automatic evaluation of machine translation. In *Proceedings of the 40th annual meeting of the Association for Computational Linguistics*, pages 311–318.

Kincaid Peter, Fishburne Jr Robert, L Rogers Richard, S Chissom Brad, and P J. Derivation Of New Readability Formulas (Automated Readability Index, Fog Count And Flesch Reading Ease Formula) For Navy Enlisted Personnel.

Maja Popović. 2017. chrf++: words helping character n-grams. In *Proceedings of the second conference on machine translation*, pages 612–618.

Rachel Rudinger, Jason Naradowsky, Brian Leonard, and Benjamin Van Durme. 2018. Gender bias in coreference resolution. In *Proceedings of the 2018 Conference of the North American Chapter of the Association for Computational Linguistics: Human Language Technologies, Volume 2 (Short Papers)*, pages 8–14, New Orleans, Louisiana. Association for Computational Linguistics.

Saku Sugawara, Nikita Nangia, Alex Warstadt, and Samuel Bowman. 2022. What makes reading comprehension questions difficult? In *Proceedings of the 60th Annual Meeting of the Association for Computational Linguistics (Volume 1: Long Papers)*, pages 6951–6971, Dublin, Ireland. Association for Computational Linguistics.

Masatoshi Tsuchiya. 2018. Performance impact caused by hidden bias of training data for recognizing textual entailment. In *Proceedings of the Eleventh International Conference on Language Resources and Evaluation (LREC 2018)*, Miyazaki, Japan. European Language Resources Association (ELRA).

Alex Wang, Amanpreet Singh, Julian Michael, Felix Hill, Omer Levy, and Samuel Bowman. 2018. GLUE: A multi-task benchmark and analysis platform for natural language understanding. In *Proceedings of the 2018 EMNLP Workshop BlackboxNLP: Analyzing and Interpreting Neural Networks for NLP*, pages 353–355, Brussels, Belgium. Association for Computational Linguistics.

Adina Williams, Nikita Nangia, and Samuel Bowman. 2018. A broad-coverage challenge corpus for sentence understanding through inference. In *Proceedings of the 2018 Conference of the North American Chapter of the Association for Computational Linguistics: Human Language Technologies, Volume 1 (Long Papers)*, pages 1112–1122, New Orleans, Louisiana. Association for Computational Linguistics.

Thomas Wolf, Lysandre Debut, Victor Sanh, Julien Chaumond, Clement Delangue, Anthony Moi, Pierric Cistac, Tim Rault, Rémi Louf, Morgan Funtowicz, et al. 2019. Huggingface's transformers: State-of-the-art natural language processing. *arXiv preprint arXiv:1910.03771*.

Yang Xiao, Jinlan Fu, Weizhe Yuan, Vijay Viswanathan, Zhoumianze Liu, Yixin Liu, Graham Neubig, and Pengfei Liu. 2022. DataLab: A Platform for Data Analysis and Intervention. pages 182–195.

Rowan Zellers, Yonatan Bisk, Roy Schwartz, and Yejin Choi. 2018. SWAG: A large-scale adversarial dataset for grounded commonsense inference. In *Proceedings of the 2018 Conference on Empirical Methods in Natural Language Processing*, pages 93–104, Brussels, Belgium. Association for Computational Linguistics.

Rowan Zellers, Ari Holtzman, Yonatan Bisk, Ali Farhadi, and Yejin Choi. 2019. HellaSwag: Can a Machine Really Finish Your Sentence? *ACL 2019 - 57th Annual Meeting of the Association for Computational Linguistics, Proceedings of the Conference*, pages 4791–4800.

Susan Zhang, Stephen Roller, Naman Goyal, Mikel Artetxe, Moya Chen, Shuohui Chen, Christopher Dewan, Mona Diab, Xian Li, Victoria Lin, Todor Mihaylov, Myle Ott, Sam Shleifer, Kurt Shuster, Daniel Simig, Singh Koura, Anjali Sridhar, Tianlu Wang, Luke Zettlemoyer, and Meta Ai. 2022. OPT: Open Pre-trained Transformer Language Models.

Jieyu Zhao, Tianlu Wang, Mark Yatskar, Vicente Ordonez, and Kai-Wei Chang. 2018. Gender bias in coreference resolution: Evaluation and debiasing methods. In *Proceedings of the 2018 Conference of the North American Chapter of the Association for Computational Linguistics: Human Language Technologies, Volume 2 (Short Papers)*, pages 15–20, New Orleans, Louisiana. Association for Computational Linguistics.

Category	Metric Key	Description
Descriptive	DESPC	Number of paragraphs
	DESSC	Number of sentences
	DESWC	Number of words
	DESPL	Average number of sentences per paragraph
	DESPLd	Standard deviation of paragraph lengths (in sentences)
	DESPLw	Average number of words per paragraph
	DESSL	Average number of words per sentence)
	DESSLd	Standard deviation of sentence lengths (in words)
	DESWLsy	Average word length (syllables)
	DESWLsyd	Standard Deviation of word lengths (in syllables)
	DESWLlt	Average word length (letters)
	DESWLltd	Standard Deviation of word lengths (in letters)
Lexical Diversity	LDTTRc	Type-Token Ratio (TTR) computed over content words
	LDTTRa	Type-Token Ratio (TTR) computed over all words
	LDMTLD	Measure of Textual Lexical Diversity (MTLD)
	LDHDD	HD-D lexical diversity index
Syntactic Complexity	SYNLE	Left embeddedness: average words before main verb
	SYNNP	Number of modifiers per noun phrase, mean
	SYNMEDpos	Average edit distance between POS tags of consecutive sentences
	SYNMEDwrd	Average edit distance between consecutive sentences
	SYNMEDlem	Average edit distance between consecutive sentences (lemmatized)
	SYNSTRUTa	Sentence syntax similarity, adjacent sentences, mean
	SYNSTRUTt	Sentence syntax similarity, all combinations, mean
Readability	RDFRE	Flesch Reading Ease (Peter et al.)
	READFKGL	Flesch-Kincaid Grade Level (Peter et al.)

Table 2: List of paragraph-level metrics currently supported by TCT

A List of Text Characteristics

Tables 2 and 3 list all currently implemented metrics along with a short description. For a large number of metrics the Coh-Metrix website[3] provides further details. For word property metrics we also document the source database in Table 3.

[3] http://cohmetrix.memphis.edu/cohmetrixhome

Category	Metric Key	Description
Incidence Scores	TOKEN_ATTRIBUTE_RATIO_ALHPA	Alphanumerical tokens
	TOKEN_ATTRIBUTE_RATIO_DIGIT	Tokens consisting of digits
	TOKEN_ATTRIBUTE_RATIO_PUNCT	Punctuation tokens
	TOKEN_ATTRIBUTE_RATIO_URL	URLs
	TOKEN_ATTRIBUTE_RATIO_EMAIL	E-mail addresses
	WORD_SET_INCIDENCE_WRDPRP1s	First person singular pronouns
	WORD_SET_INCIDENCE_WRDPRP1p	First person plural pronouns
	WORD_SET_INCIDENCE_WRDPRP2	Second person pronouns
	WORD_SET_INCIDENCE_WRDPRP3s	Third person singular pronouns
	WORD_SET_INCIDENCE_WRDPRP3p	Third person plural pronouns
	WORD_SET_INCIDENCE_CNCCaus	Causal connectives
	WORD_SET_INCIDENCE_CNCLogic	Logical connectives
	WORD_SET_INCIDENCE_CNCTemp	Temporal connectives
	WORD_SET_INCIDENCE_CNCAdd	Additive connectives
	WORD_SET_INCIDENCE_CNCPos	Positive connectives
	WORD_SET_INCIDENCE_CNCNeg	Negative connectives
	WORD_PROPERTY_WRDNOUN	Incidence score for POS tag 'PROPN', 'NOUN'
	WORD_PROPERTY_WRDVERB	Incidence score for POS tag 'VERB'
	WORD_PROPERTY_WRDADJ	Incidence score for POS tag 'ADJ'
	WORD_PROPERTY_WRDADV	Incidence score for POS tag 'ADV'
Word Property	WORD_PROPERTY_WRDFRQc	Mean Word frequency*, content words
	WORD_PROPERTY_WRDFRQa	Mean Word frequency*, all words
	WORD_PROPERTY_WRDFRQmc	Min Word frequency*
	WORD_PROPERTY_WRDFAMc	Mean Familiarity+, content words only
	WORD_PROPERTY_WRDCNCc	Mean Concreteness+, content words only
	WORD_PROPERTY_WRDIMGc	Mean Imagability+, content words only
	WORD_PROPERTY_WRDMEAc	Mean Meaningfulness+
	WORD_PROPERTY_WRDPOLc	Mean Polysemy†
	WORD_PROPERTY_WRDHYPn	Mean Hypernymy† (nouns)
	WORD_PROPERTY_WRDHYPv	Mean Hypernymy† (verbs)
	WORD_PROPERTY_WRDHYPnv	Mean Hypernymy† (verbs and nouns)
	WORD_PROPERTY_AOA	Mean Age of Acqusition (Kuperman et al.)
	WORD_PROPERTY_AOA_MAX	Max Age of Acqusition (Kuperman et al.)
	WORD_PROPERTY_CONCRETENESS	Mean Concreteness (Brysbaert et al., 2014)
	WORD_PROPERTY_PREVALENCE	Mean Prevalence (Brysbaert et al.)
	WORD_PROPERTY_PREVALENCE_MIN	Minimum Prevalence (Brysbaert et al.)

Table 3: List of word-level metrics currently supported by TCT. Common underlying word databases: *SpaCy (Honnibal et al., 2020) +MRC (Coltheart, 2018) † WordNet (Fellbaum, 2010)

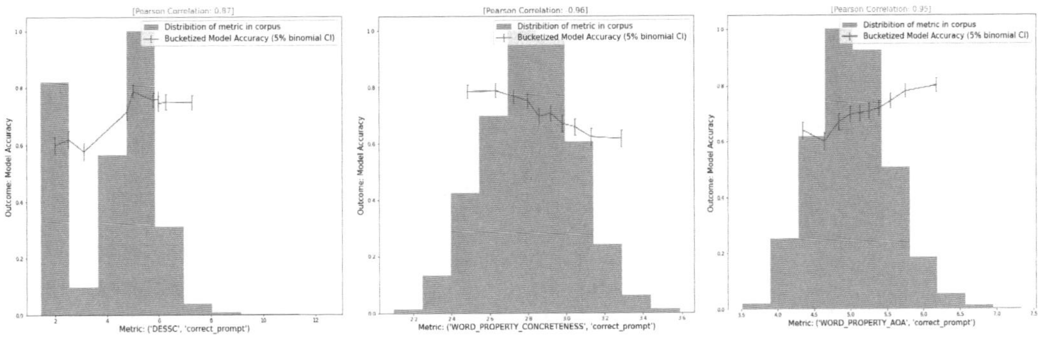

(a) Sentence Count (b) Concreteness (c) Age of Acquisition

Figure 5: Correlations between text characteristics and accuracy for OPT experiments,

B Sample Use Cases

In this section we demonstrate how users can gain actionable insights on existing evaluation data using TCT, with minimal amount of additional work. The examples provided below can be reproduced by Python notebooks we included in the examples folder of the TCT repository.

B.1 Predicting Accuracy of OPT Baselines

Despite the recent success of large pre-trained language models (LLM), there are still ongoing debates regarding how good they really are, and how to evaluate that. After all, LLMS such as PaLM (Chowdhery et al., 2022) or DeBERTa (He et al., 2020) have saturated the performance on benchmarks, even outperforming human scores at times, but, at the same time, there still exist a myriad of seemingly trivial scenarios in which they fail.

Experimental setup In this demonstration we offer an alternative approach: We take existing data from the evaluation of the 6.7B OPT baseline (Zhang et al., 2022) then attempt to use simple data characteristics to identify interpretable subsets of the dataset on which OPT's performance substantially differs from its overall high accuracy. We use the HellaSwag task (Zellers et al., 2019),[4] a common-sense inference task that is trivial to solve for humans but challenging for LLMs.

To evaluate OPT models on this task, prompts corresponding to different choices were scored with the LLMs and the answer with the lowest perplexity was considered to be the choice of the model. For each data point in the test set, we consider two text fragments: the prompt corresponding to the correct answer and the concatenation of all the prompts corresponding to incorrect answers (see Table 6 for an example). With a single command using the `command_line_tool.py` we compute characteristics for the extracted texts and load the results into a notebook. We also load the result of the model evaluation, which is a single binary variable per data point describing whether the model predicted the right answer.

Results First, we inspect correlations between individual metrics and model performance. This analysis tool orders data points with respect to a particular TCT metric, groups them into buckets of 100 data points and computes model accuracy for each bucket. We find several different data characteristics that show high correlation with model performance, for example number of sentences per prompt or average concreteness (Brysbaert et al., 2014) of words. A visualisation of these results is shown in Figure 5.

Secondly, we employ the TCT class named `PredictFromCharacteristicsAnalysis` to fit a logistic regression model using all characteristics to predict whether the model will yield a correct answer for a particular data point. The tool computes the regression scores on a held out part of the dataset and visualizes model accuracy with respect to this score per data bucket, as shown in Figure 3a. We find more variance between the best and worst performing buckets compared to the single variable analysis. On the bucket with the highest predicted score the OPT baselines yield a 0.9 accuracy, but in the lowest scoring

[4]We chose the HellaSwag task for this demo as it had sufficiently many examples in the test set and showed the most interesting correlations out of all tasks the model was evaluated on prior.

Correct Prompt	Roof shingle removal: A man is sitting on a roof. He starts pulling up roofing on a roof.
Incorrect Prompts	Roof shingle removal: A man is sitting on a roof. He is using wrap to wrap a pair of skis. Roof shingle removal: A man is sitting on a roof. He is ripping level tiles off. Roof shingle removal: A man is sitting on a roof. He is holding a rubik's cube.

Figure 6: Example of text features extracted from the HellaSwag evaluation of the OPT model

bucket the accuracy is below 0.4, which approaches the random baseline of 0.25. To interpret the fitted regression model, we inspect its coefficients,[5] illustrated in Figure 3b. Interestingly, coefficients for given characteristics often yield opposite signs associated with the correct and incorrect answers, indicating that they are in fact, on their own, predictive of the correctness of an answer. For instance, the *DESWLlt* metric (mean number of letters per word) has coefficients of -0.44 and 0.62 for the `correct_prompt` and `incorrect_prompts` features, respectively.

We argue that such analyses are useful from two perspectives: i) Analyses that uncover patterns in what characteristics make examples difficult help us improve our understanding of how well a model has in fact learned the task we intended it to. This, in turn, provides a better estimate of the wider applicability of a model. ii) If one knows which text characteristics lead to poor performance from LLMs, one could improve the dataset's coverage for characteristics associated with low model performance – e.g. one could curate data points including tokens with low concreteness scores.

Table 6, Figure 5 and Figure 3b illustrate the model analysis process described previously in this section.

B.2 Gender Bias in Co-reference Resolution Models

Second, we would like to illustrate how TCT can aid in identifying biases in NLP systems, by revealing gender bias in coreference resolution systems.

Experimental Setup We use a coreference resolution model proposed by Lee et al. (2017) and the WinoBias dataset (Zhao et al., 2018). The model is evaluated using exact match to compute accuracy. To capture gender statistics, we configure a new Word Property metric "genderedness" based on Labor Force Statistics[6] and compute it on two text fragments (the two spans of the ground truth co-reference). A higher genderedness score represents that the occupation is associated with a female stereotype and vice versa. For pronominal references, we assign 100 to female ones (e.g. "she", "her") and 0 to male ones (e.g. "he", "his"). We add the difference between the two characteristics as an additional feature for analysis.

Results The analysis obtained by the TCT toolkit is illustrated in Figure 7. There is a negative correlation between model accuracy and the genderness difference between the occupation and the pronominal reference. In other words, if a female stereotypical occupation and a male pronoun co-occur in a test example (e.g. "nurse" and "he") or a male stereotypical occupation and a female pronoun (e.g. "constructor" and "she") co-occurs, the model is more likely to make a wrong prediction.

B.3 NLLB: Interpretable Fluctuations of Translation Performance

A third example of a task that could benefit from using TCT in analyses is *Neural Machine Translation* (NMT). We apply TCT to source sentences to identify patterns in translation success for an off-the-shelf NMT system.

Experimental Setup To investigate performance heterogeneity in translation models, we use the No Language Left Behind 1.3B distilled model and the English-Russian validation split of the multi-domain dataset from the same work (Costa-jussà et al., 2022). We use the HuggingFace transformers translation pipeline for easy inference (Wolf et al., 2019). We extract translations using the pipeline, and employ the `chrf++` metric to measure success per individual data point (Popović, 2017).[7] Using the toolkit we characterize the English source data with default settings.

[5]Since inputs to the regression were scaled to unit variance, direct comparison of coefficients is meaningful

[6]`https://github.com/uclanlp/corefBias`

[7]Note: we use this as it has better per data point properties than other corpus statistics like BLEU (Papineni et al., 2002).

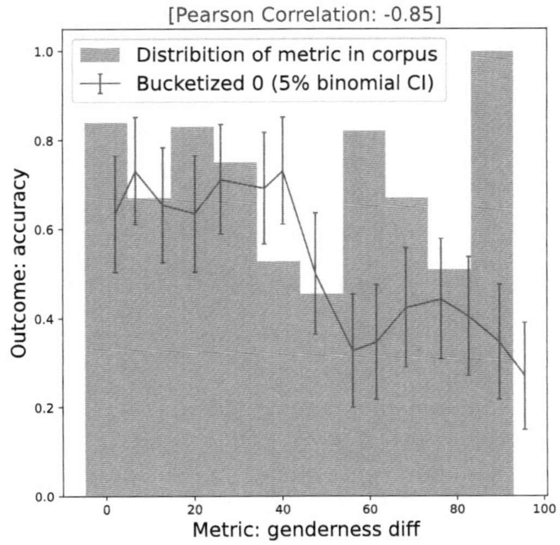

Figure 7: Genderness difference hurts the performance of a coreference resolution model.

Results Surprisingly, we find significant heterogeneity as seen in Figure 4. In particular, more sentences, more verbs, polysemy for content words, and chat-like messages lead to performance drops. Conversely, more nouns and words with more syllables correlate with better `chrf++` scores.

The driver of this heterogeneity may be deceptive. The HuggingFace translation pipeline does not keep track of the underlying model's training distribution. It would not know that the NLLB model was trained on sentence pairs and the evaluation data contains multi-sentence datapoints. An appropriate way to match the training distribution would instead be to split by sentences and translate individual sentences before re-concatenating. In fact, if we take this approach, we find that performance levels out with the biggest improvements coming from the largest sources of heterogeneity (Figure 10). This demonstration shows the power of TCT for debugging model workflows. With many layers of abstraction, it is easy to forget that underlying models are likely trained on a particular data distribution.

Additional Details Figure 8 shows the distribution of data-characterized performance for NLLB using the HuggingFace translate tool with no modification (other than increasing the maximum generated length to 512 tokens). Figure 9 shows the distribution of chrf++ scores for NLLB with sentence segmentation[8]. We pass each sentence in a batch to the segmentation pipeline before re-concatenating them by adding a space between sentences (since we only use English and Russian for this demonstration this is an appropriate concatenation method). Finally, Figure 10 shows the treatment effect. For each sentence we subtract the segmented NLLB chrf++ score from the unsegmented chrf++ score. Then we run the TCT toolkit on this outcome measure. We show that performance increases are such that they level out performance heterogeneity to some extent.

In Table 4 we demonstrate how the unsegmented NLLB model can drop out entire portions of the translation in multi-sentence validation datapoints. This is likely what leads to performance drops. The segmented version fixes this. As such, we suggest that TCT should be run at eval time even when using a known model that has been validated in the past. Different environmental setups can lead to failure modes such as this one that can be difficult to detect without data characterization.

[8] Sentence segmentation by SpaCy (Honnibal et al., 2020)

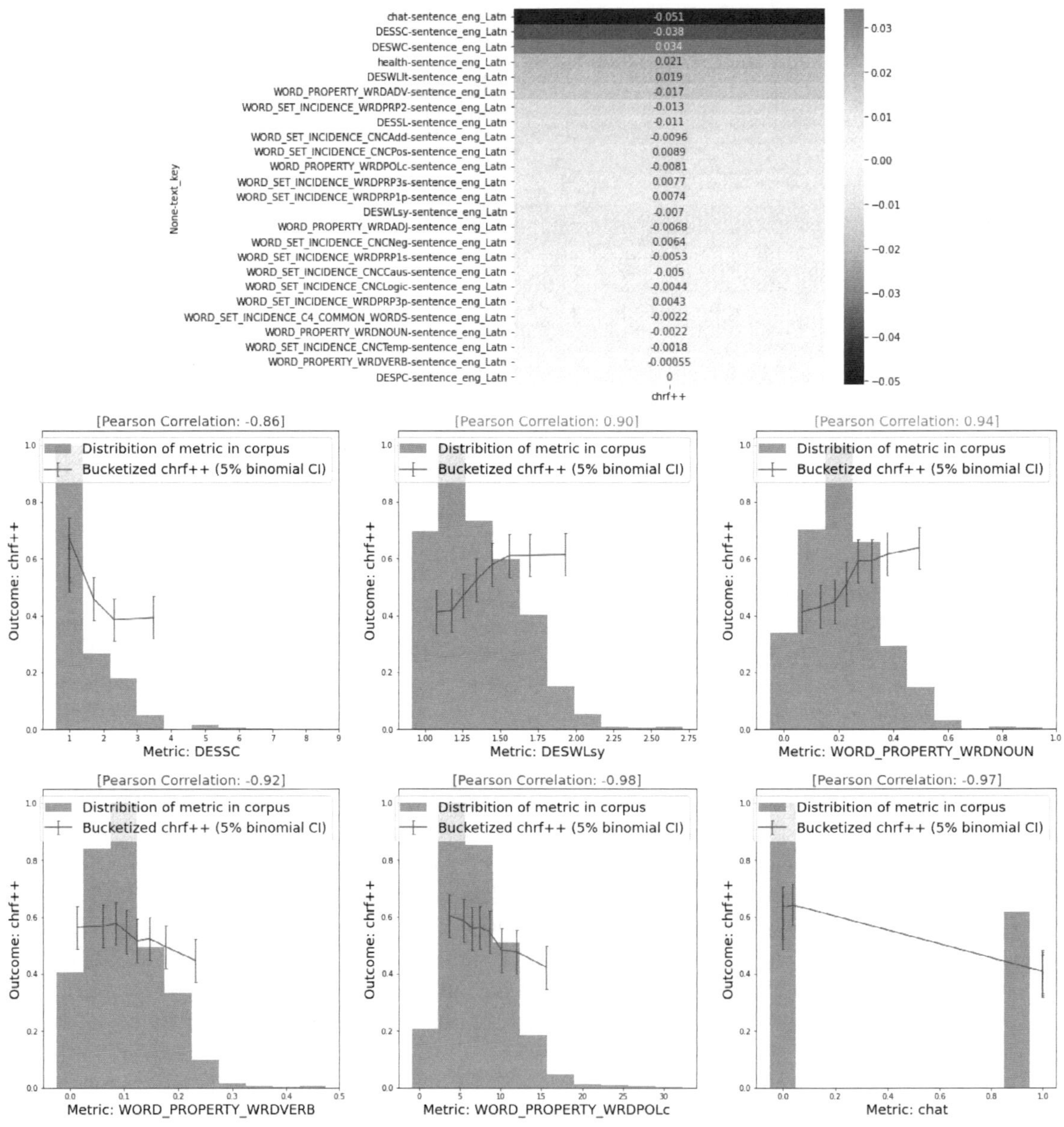

Figure 8: Top: A regression on the chrf++ score of a model pipeline using NLLB with no segmentation. Positive values indicate improved score, lower values indicate a negative correlation with score. Bottom: As can be seen there is even heterogeneity in treatment effects for several data characteristics.

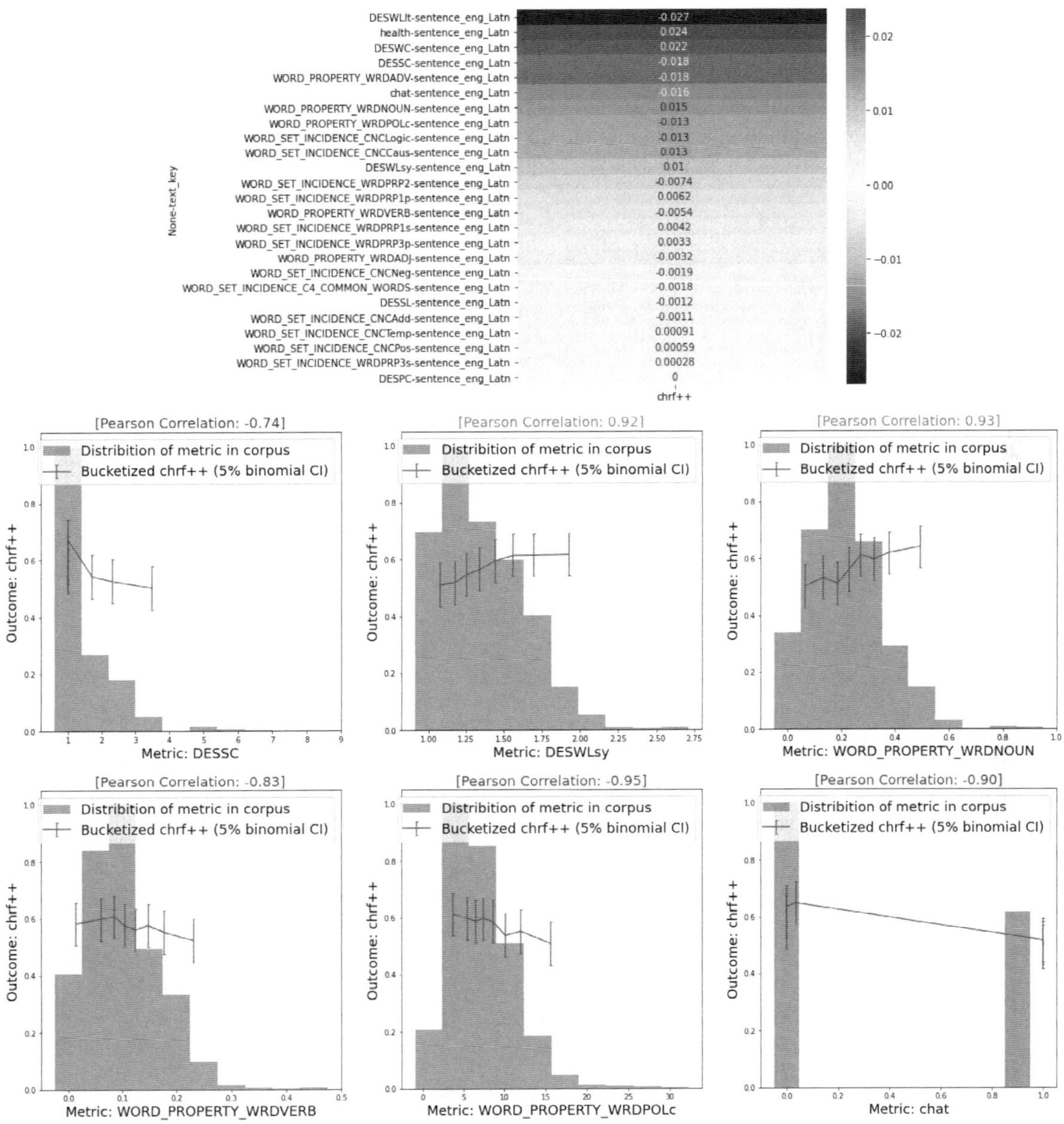

Figure 9: Top: A regression on the chrf++ score of a model pipeline using NLLB with segmentation. Positive values indicate improved score, lower values indicate a negative correlation with score. Bottom: As can be seen there is still some heterogeneity in treatment effects for several data characteristics but they have significantly flattened.

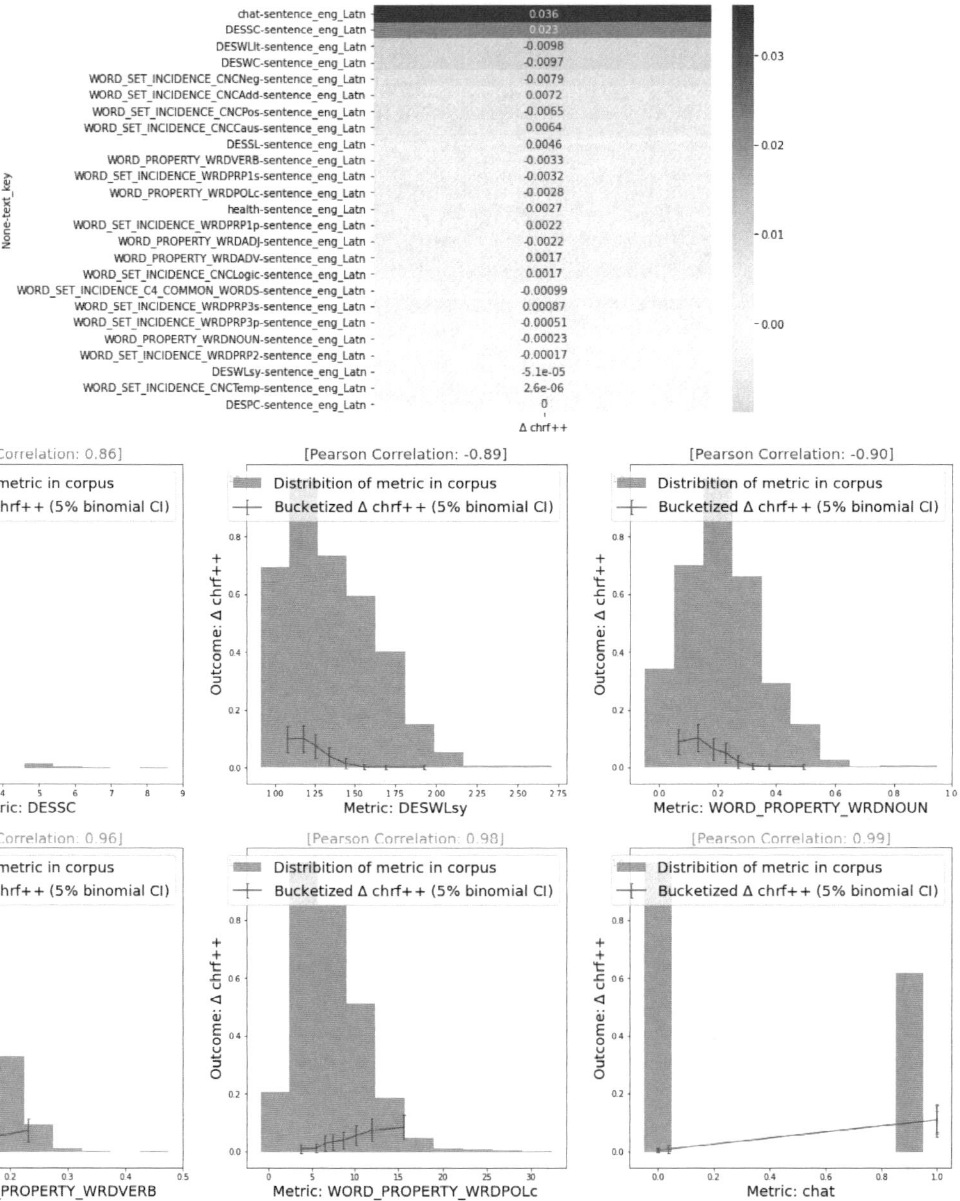

Figure 10: Top: A regression on the per-sentence treatment effect between a translation run through NLLB with and without sentence segmentation. Positive values indicate correlation with improved chrf++ from segmentation over the base model. Bottom: As can be seen there is even heterogeneity in treatment effects. Sentence splitting has the most positive effect correlation with the chat corpus and for the evaluation points with many sentences.

English	Yeah that would be so fun! It's really easy honestly, there's a bit of skill with steering but once you get the hang of it it feels super natural.
True	Да, было бы очень весело! Честно говоря, это очень просто, нужен небольшой навык руления, но как только вы поймете, ощущение будет очень естественным.
NLLB	Да, это было бы так весело! но как только ты научишься управлять, это будет очень естественно.
NLLB (seg)	Да, это было бы так весело! Это очень просто, честно говоря, требуется немного мастерства, но как только ты научишься управлять, это будет очень естественно.
English	That's right. How is your family? how many of you are there?
True	Точно. Как твоя семья? Сколько вас?
NLLB	Как ваша семья?
NLLB (seg)	- Да, это так. Как твоя семья? Сколько вас там?

Table 4: NLLB without proper segmentation misses entire portions of the context. For example, the red-highlighted portion is missing from the non-segmented NLLB text, but present elsewhere.

Meeting Decision Tracker: Making Meeting Minutes with De-Contextualized Utterances

Shumpei Inoue[1], **Hy Nguyen**[1], **Pham Viet Hoang**[1], **Tsungwei Liu**[1], **Minh-Tien Nguyen**[2,*]
[1]Cinnamon AI, 10th floor, Geleximco building, 36 Hoang Cau, Dong Da, Hanoi, Vietnam.
{sinoue, hy, hugo, tsungwei}@cinnamon.is
[2]Hung Yen University of Technology and Education, Hung Yen, Vietnam.
tiennm@utehy.edu.vn

Abstract

Meetings are a universal process to make decisions in business and project collaboration. The capability to automatically itemize the decisions in daily meetings allows for extensive tracking of past discussions. To that end, we developed Meeting Decision Tracker, a prototype system to construct decision items comprising decision utterance detector (DUD) and decision utterance rewriter (DUR). We show that DUR makes a sizable contribution to improving the user experience by dealing with utterance collapse in natural conversation. An introduction video of our system is also available at https://youtu.be/TG1pJJo0Iqo.

1 Introduction

Obtaining a brief description and salient contents of meetings is a functionality that can certainly help business operations. Although automatic speech recognition enables us to transcribe meeting records automatically, its transcription is possibly much more verbose, noisy, or collapsed, and is far from being utilized in its raw form. Previous research attempted to extract important information from dialogue, such as decision-making utterances, (Bak and Oh, 2018; Karan et al., 2021), extractive summaries of online forums (Tarnpradab et al., 2017; Khalman et al., 2021), or group chat threads (Wang et al., 2022). Another study, Lugini et al. (2020) presented a discussion tracker to facilitate collaborative argumentation in classroom discussion by visualizing discussion transcription.

However, extracted utterances are usually incomplete and difficult to understand due to ellipses and co-references in conversations (Su et al., 2019). Figure 1 (the right) shows an example of a partial dialogue ending with a decision-related utterance in our dataset. This shows that objects or indicatives in utterances in natural conversations are usually ambiguous, and the meaning of decision-related utterances has a strong dependency on context. Furthermore, especially in Japanese, the format of the spoken language is often far apart from the written language because of frank expressions and many filler phrases. This nature reduces user experience with the naive use of utterances extracted from dialogues. In response to this, Incomplete Utterance Restoration (IUR) (Pan et al., 2019; Su et al., 2019; Huang et al., 2021; Inoue et al., 2022) handles the problem where the model rewrites and restores incomplete utterances by considering the dialogue context with promising results. However, we have yet to see IUR models applied for practical use in actual business applications.

This paper presents *Meeting Decision Tracker (MDT)*, a system that automatically generates the itemized decision list from meeting transcription. Given the meeting transcription, MDT detects decision-making utterances and rewrites them to the *de-contextualized utterance*, i.e., the written form with omissions restoration and filler removal. Such a capability allows users to look back at the previous meeting contents quickly and have asynchronous communication with no effort from a minute taker. The system has three crucial characteristics.

- By combining modules for extracting and rewriting decision-related utterances, the system has a down-to-earth strategy to generate itemized decision lists from meeting transcription. The combination allows us to investigate the role of IUR in a bigger context with significant impact for real business applications.
- Besides the ordinary task of IUR, our rewriter handles the translation from the spoken language to written language by filtering filler phrases. It enables users to understand the decision item at a glance, which contributes to improving the user experience.
- Although our system is originally built for

*Corresponding Author.

Proceedings of the 2nd Conference of the Asia-Pacific Chapter of the Association for Computational Linguistics and the 12th International Joint Conference on Natural Language Processing: System Demonstrations, pages 88–94
November 20–23, 2022.

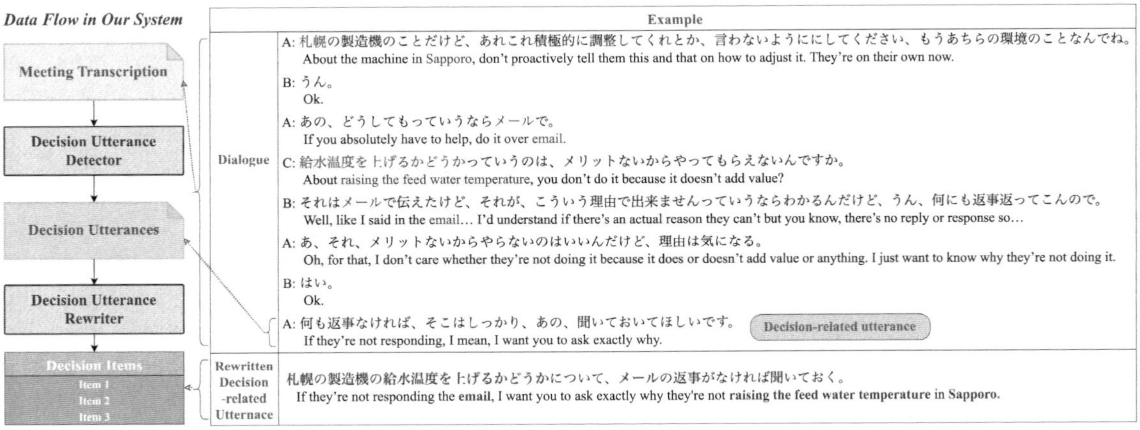

Figure 1: The data flow in our system and the conversation example. The red in the dialogue shows information omitted in the decision-related utterance. The blue shows information to be restored by Decision Utterance Rewriter.

decision utterance itemization, the proposed method can be applied as a general solution for information extraction from the dialogue.

2 System Design

The overall system architecture of Meeting Decision Tracker (MDT) is depicted in Figure 1 (the left). The main function of MDT is to generate decision items with de-contextualized representations from the transcription of daily business meetings. MDT comprises of two modules: Decision Utterance Detector (DUD) and Decision Utterance Rewriter (DUR). The detector extracts a decision list from meeting transcription and the rewriter translates (rewrites) the list to the written format. Figure 1 (the right) shows the example pair of the input and expected output for the system. The example indicates two points. First, the transcription contains decision-related utterances that can be used to summarize the content of the meeting. Second, the decision utterance itself is usually not self-consistent and comprehensible only after the utterance is restored by DUR. The next sections introduce the detector and rewriter.

2.1 Decision utterance detector

The first step of the detector is to detect decision-related utterances from transcription. We formulate the detection as a sequence labeling problem on the utterance level and describe the detector in two steps: input representation and classification.

Input representation The input uses the sequence of utterances $\{u_1, u_2, ..., u_w\}$ for the sequential classification, where w is the window size. Following Cohan et al. (2019), we used the input representation $\{[\text{CLS}], u_1, [\text{SEP}], u_2, [\text{SEP}], ..., u_w, [\text{SEP}]\}$, which contains the [CLS] token at the head of the whole input and [SEP] tokens at the tail for each utterance. Then the input was encoded by BERT (Devlin et al., 2019) for contextual representation. We set the window size as 5 empirically based on the observation of results.

Classification There are several studies have addressed the decision utterance detection as a classification. Fernández et al. (2008) defined the decision-making sub-dialogues as being composed of several dialogue act tags such as the introduction of issue, decision adopted/proposed/confirmed, agreement. Murray and Renals (2008) created abstract describing decisions, actions and problems of meeting and then associated the utterances used for abstract as the action item utterances. Chen and Hakkani-Tur (2016) classified action items in the token level following the semantic intent schema.

In this study, the task of decision-related utterance extraction was formulated as binary sequence labeling on the sentence level, different from Fernández et al. (2008). This is because we want to keep a simple setting to confirm the efficiency of IUR in actual cases. To take advantage of context, we followed Cohan et al. (2019) to jointly encode consecutive utterances. Preceding utterances leading to decision are essential because followed by Fernández et al. (2008), we hypothesize that the particular kinds of patterns of conversation co-occur with decision. Utterances following decision are also important since affirmative response by others supports the confidence of detection.

For sequence labeling, the model uses the encoding of [SEP] tokens corresponding to each utterance and predicts tags (decision or not) by a feedforward network. Different from Cohan et al. (2019), we used only the prediction for the second utterance from the back in the input and slide the window with the stride of 1 over conversation to obtain the predictions for all utterances.

2.2 Decision utterance rewriter

After extracting decision-related utterances, the rewriter translates the extracted utterances from the spoken to written language to improve user experience. We describe the rewriter in two steps: input representation and rewriting.

Input representation The input of DUR comprises of utterances $\{u_1, u_2, ..., u_n\}$ where $u_1, ..., u_{n-1}$ is contextual dialogue and the tail utterance u_n is the decision-related utterance. For input representation, we followed Inoue et al. (2022) to use three types of special tokens, $[X1]$, $[X2]$ and $<\backslash s>$. We inserted $[X1]$ after each utterance in contextual dialogue u_i for $i = 1, .., n-1$, $[X2]$ after decision-related utterance u_n, and $<\backslash s>$ at the tail of whole input as the EOS token. For inference, DUR rewrites only the decision utterances detected by DUD. For each decision utterance, we used preceding utterances, including up to 360 tokens by the T5's tokenizer as the contextual dialogue.

Rewriting JET (Inoue et al., 2022) was adopted and fine-tuned on our dataset for utterance rewriting. JET uses T5 (Raffel et al., 2020) for the picker and writer which were jointly trained for picking important tokens and text generation. The picker picks up important tokens from dialogue context which contribute to rewriting. The two components are jointly optimized by sharing parameters of the T5's encoder, which allows the model to restore omitted information while keeping the capability of abstractive text generation to translate from the spoken to written form with fillers removal.

3 Evaluation

In this section, we first show data annotation for the detector and rewriter, and then describe the settings used for experiments. We finally report the results and discussion of the detector and rewriter.

3.1 Dataset

Decision utterance detector Our Japanese dataset was constructed based on multi-party conversations with various users' intents and decisions in real-world business scenarios. We recorded client meetings in a variety of fields, including banking, finance, and insurance, and accurately transcribed all speeches including fillers.

For decision detection annotation, as stated in Section 2.1, we adopted the schema of binary to decide whether an utterance is a decision (labeled by TD) or not (non-TD). With this simple schema, we aimed to extract decision-related utterances with high coverage and relied on rewriter to restore the contextual information involving decision.

To do the annotation, we asked three annotators who have at least N2 Japanese skills to give a label for each utterance whether it is a decision utterance or not. N2 Japanese members are those who have ability to understand Japanese used in everyday situations and in a variety of circumstances to a certain degree.[1] We combined three annotators to create three groups in which each group has two annotators. To reduce resources and avoid specific bias, each group was assigned a small part of the dataset for annotation. To maintain label quality, annotators prepared a list of the specific expressions frequently used in decision utterances such as "I decided to...", "I have to..." and shared it between them. It comes from the observation that utterances containing the specific expression tend to be decision-related utterances. Each utterance was tagged by two annotators and if the tags differed, the final tag was determined after reconsideration. The Cohen Kappa agreement computed over the three groups is 0.672, showing that the agreement is moderate. It is understandable because transcription is quite noisy compared to common data types, e.g., news. The annotated data was divided into training, validation, and testing sets by meeting units and contains 27006, 3030, and 1425 utterances. The dataset is highly imbalanced where decisions only account for 6% of the entire data, creating challenges for classifiers.

Decision utterance rewriter We created the dataset for DUR based on the DUD dataset. We selected 1120 utterances tagged by **TD** and extracted their preceding utterances containing up to 360 tokens. Two native Japanese annotators created the rewritten version of decision utterances. Annotators re-wrote decision utterances with three requirements: (i) restore omitted information extracted from preceding utterances, (ii) remove fillers, and (iii) convert from the spoken form to written form.

[1] https://www.jlpt.jp/e/about/levelsummary.html

To prepare a consistent dataset, annotators reused the original words in contextual dialogue for rewriting as much as possible, rather than creating new phrases. Annotators also checked rewriting each other every 100 samples to align the quality.

3.2 Experimental settings

For the detector, we used pretrained BERT (Cohan et al., 2019) (cl-tohoku/bert-base-japanese) and fine-tuned MLP (dimensions $512, 400, 5$) by AdamW in 20 epochs with drop-out of 0.2, the batch size of 16, and the learning rate of $5e-5$. For rewriter, we trained JET with pretrained t5-base-japanese T5 by AdamW with weight decay of 0.01 in 70 epochs with the batch size of 6, the leaning rate of $2e-5$, and the beam size of 5. All models were trained on a single Tesla P100 GPU.

3.3 Results and discussion

Decision utterance detector We compared the BERT model with two different task formulations: sequential sentence labeling (SL) and sentence classification (SC). For sequence labeling, we used the same model described in Section 2.1. For sentence classification, we trained the model by using BERT to predict the tag of the second utterance from the back given the input utterances $\{u_1, u_2, ..., u_w\}$. It follows input representation in Section 2.1 and uses the [CLS] tokens for binary classification. To deal with the imbalanced dataset, we also tested the model with **back translation** (BT), a technique to augment the data by translating original text data into another language and then back into the original language. We augmented the positive samples[2] by seven times using seven languages.[3]

Table 1: Results of the Decision utterance detector.

Method	Precision	Recall	F1
BERT (SC)	0.32	**0.59**	0.42
BERT (SC) + BT	0.33	0.58	0.42
BERT (SL)	**0.48**	0.55	**0.51**
BERT (SL) + BT	0.44	0.55	0.49

Table 1 shows the performance comparison. As we can observe, sequence labeling (BERT (SL)) without using back translation is the best. BERT (SL) achieves better performance than BERT (SC) in general. This suggests that the knowledge of jointly predicting tags helps to better understand the dependencies between utterances. So it leads to improving the performance. Binary sentence classification does not show high F-scores even though the model uses context by using concatenation. It suggests more sophisticated combinations for improving the performance of binary sentence classification. Back translation does not help to improve the quality of the detector. This is because utterances are quite broken in terms of writing and contain fillers. It suggests other data augmentation methods for conversation.

Decision utterance rewriter For the writing part, we compared JET to T5 (Raffel et al., 2020) and s2s-ft (Bao et al., 2021) due to its efficiency for the IUR task. **T5** uses a text-to-text framework pretrained on data-rich tasks with transformer encoder-decoder. **s2s-ft** applies attention masks with fine-tuning methods for the generation task. We did not report the results of ProphetNet (Qi et al., 2020) and UniLM (Dong et al., 2019) due to no pre-trained models for Japanese; SARG (Huang et al., 2021) and RUN-BERT (Liu et al., 2020) due to its low accuracy for IUR (Inoue et al., 2022).

For evaluation, we followed Pan et al. (2019) to use ROUGE, BLEU and f-scores.[4] All methods used the beam width of 5. To obtain the reliable comparison, we also report the human evaluation by using **Text Flow** and **Understandability** (Kiyoumarsi, 2015). **Text Flow** shows how the rewritten utterance is correct grammatically and easy to understand. **Understandability** shows how much the prediction is similar to reference semantically. Three annotators (who are at least N2 Japanese skills) involved the judgement and each annotator gave a score (1: bad; 2: acceptable; 3: good) to each rewritten utterance. The three evaluators scored for each 190 testing samples and the final scores were calculated by the average of scores from the evaluators.

Results in Tables 2 and 3 show that JET is the best for both automatic and human evaluation. This is because the model was empowered by T5 and the picker, that picks up important tokens for rewriting. T5 is the second best due to the strong pre-trained model for Japanese. s2s-ft does not show competitive performance compared to model with text-to-text pre-training framework.

[2]positive sample refers the consecutive utterances $u_1, ..., u_w$ with the decision tags for u_{w-2}.

[3]We used Google Translate API with 7 languages, "vi", "en", "zh-CN", "zh-TW", "fr", "de", "ko"

[4]We used sumeval for ROUGE and BLEU scores (https://github.com/chakki-works/sumeval) and f-scores are based on n-grams with the MeCab tokenizer.

Table 2: Results of Decision utterance rewriter. RG is ROUGE and BL stands for BLEU.

Method	RG-1	RG-2	BL	f1	f2
JET	**56.71**	**36.60**	**25.97**	**36.81**	**21.52**
T5	54.91	35.10	24.48	36.61	21.42
s2s-ft	47.71	29.52	19.91	27.41	15.74

Table 3: Human Evaluation

Method	Text Flow	Understandability
JET	**2.53**	**1.90**
T5	2.41	1.79
s2s-ft	2.16	1.55

Effectiveness of utterance rewriter A human evaluation was conducted to see how the rewriter contributes to improving the quality of decision items. A good rewriter requires (i) to keep the original contents before writing and (ii) to enrich the content by supplementing omitted information. Given the pair of the original decision utterance (ODU) and the rewritten decision utterance (RDU), we defined the scoring criteria in the range of 1 to 5 as the following.

1. RDU completely lost meaning of ODU.
2. RDU somewhat lost meaning of ODU.
3. RDU keep meaning of ODU but no additional information.
4. RDU keep meaning of ODU with a few additional information.
5. RDU keep meaning of ODU with sufficient additional information.

As far as the RDU lost the meaning of ODU, the score would be 1 or 2 even there was any additional information. In accordance with this criteria, we collected the scores from the three evaluators by using the utterances before and after the rewriting on test data from the DUR dataset. These three evaluators are annotators who also worked to construct the RDU dataset (Section 3.1).

Table 4: Effectiveness evaluation.

score	1	2	3	4	5
ratio	3.76%	7.04%	20.7%	27.7%	40.8%

Table 4 shows the result of evaluation with the ratio of each score. It indicates 10.8% of samples decrease in quality (score $\leq$ 2) while 68.5% of samples increase in quality (score $\geq$ 4). The average score from the evaluators was 3.948, higher than 3, showing that the quality of decision items increases by our rewriter in general. These results show our rewriter certainly contributes to better user experience when displaying decision items (Figure 2b).

4 Demonstration Scenario

We provide a UI[5] that allows users to look back at decision-making items in past meetings at a glance. Especially in business settings, the accumulation of daily meetings can be compactly stored as itemized decisions to be accessed easily and support project progress management and sharing.

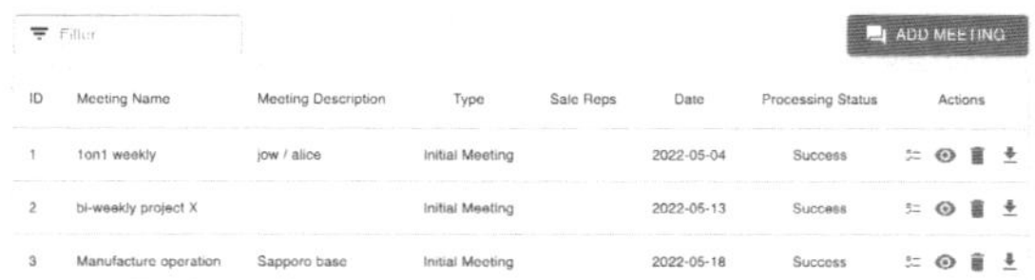

(a) The uploaded meeting list.

(b) The decision items.

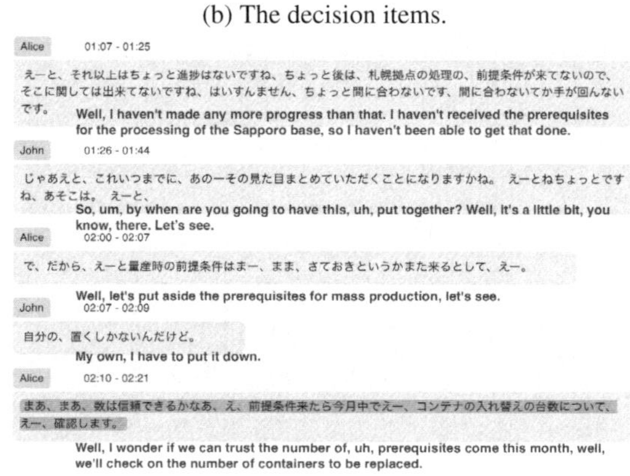

(c) The original transcription.

Figure 2: The screenshots from the system.

Figure 2 shows an example processed by our system. The original decision-related utterance is highlighted in blue in Figure 2c. Its content *"Well, I wonder if we can trust the number of, uh, prerequisites come this month, well, we'll check on the number of containers to be replaced."* is rewritten and displayed in the first line of the decision list in Figure 2b as the de-contextualized form, *"Once the prerequisites for processing at the Sapporo site*

[5]The system: https://bit.ly/3sH6193; user and pwd are `Guest123@MDT.com`. Please skip verification when login.

arrive, the number of containers to be replaced should be confirmed..".

The view of the first run is the list of the meetings uploaded (Figure 2a). When users click on the meeting from the list they intend to go back, so decision items for corresponding meeting are unfolded (Figure 2b). Here we display *de-contextualized* decision by DUR instead of original decision-related utterances. Since the DUR module makes decision-related utterances self-contained in the written language format, displayed decision items are straightforward and user-friendly to quickly understand them. To allow users to see the context of the discussion, users can click on the decision item and view the original transcription with a scrolling position where the corresponding decision-related utterance is at the bottom (Figure 2c).

5 Conclusion and Future Work

In this paper, we presented *Meeting Decision Tracker*, a system to automatically itemise the decision-making in daily meetings as well as the tracking of past discussions. We showed the effective adaptation of IUR for decision-item tracking in the context of actual business scenarios. MDT not only displays itemized decision-utterances with an easy-to-understand format, but also allows users to go back and review the contextual dialogue deriving for the decision. Future work will firstly improve the quality of the detector and rewriter. Other potential directions will incorporate ASR into MDT to create an end-to-end system and add functions to remind users of detected decisions and to search for past meetings.

Acknowledgement

We would like to thank Nguyen Duy Anh for the discussion and support of the decision utterance detector. We also thank anonymous reviewers who gave constructive comments on our paper.

References

JinYeong Bak and Alice Oh. 2018. Conversational decision-making model for predicting the king's decision in the annals of the joseon dynasty. In *Proceedings of the 2018 Conference on Empirical Methods in Natural Language Processing*, pages 956–961.

Hangbo Bao, Li Dong, Wenhui Wang, Nan Yang, and Furu Wei. 2021. s2s-ft: Fine-tuning pretrained transformer encoders for sequence-to-sequence learning. *arXiv preprint arXiv:2110.13640*.

Yun-Nung Chen and Dilek Hakkani-Tur. 2016. Aimu: Actionable items for meeting understanding. In *Proceedings of the Tenth International Conference on Language Resources and Evaluation (LREC'16)*, pages 739–743.

Arman Cohan, Iz Beltagy, Daniel King, Bhavana Dalvi, and Daniel S Weld. 2019. Pretrained language models for sequential sentence classification. *arXiv preprint arXiv:1909.04054*.

Jacob Devlin, Ming-Wei Chang, Kenton Lee, and Kristina Toutanova. 2019. Bert: Pre-training of deep bidirectional transformers for language understanding. In *Proceedings of the 2019 Conference of the North American Chapter of the Association for Computational Linguistics: Human Language Technologies, Volume 1*, pages 4171–4186.

Li Dong, Nan Yang, Wenhui Wang, Furu Wei, Xiaodong Liu, Yu Wang, Jianfeng Gao, Ming Zhou, and Hsiao-Wuen Hon. 2019. Unified language model pre-training for natural language understanding and generation. *Advances in Neural Information Processing Systems*, 32.

Raquel Fernández, Matthew Frampton, Patrick Ehlen, Matthew Purver, and Stanley Peters. 2008. Modelling and detecting decisions in multi-party dialogue. In *Proceedings of the 9th SIGdial Workshop on Discourse and Dialogue*, pages 156–163, Columbus, Ohio. Association for Computational Linguistics.

Mengzuo Huang, Feng Li, Wuhe Zou, and Weidong Zhang. 2021. Sarg: A novel semi autoregressive generator for multi-turn incomplete utterance restoration. In *Proceedings of the AAAI Conference on Artificial Intelligence, vol. 35, no. 14, pp. 13055-13063*.

Shumpei Inoue, Tsungwei Liu, Nguyen Hong Son, and Minh-Tien Nguyen. 2022. Enhance incomplete utterance restoration by joint learning token extraction and text generation. In *Proceedings of the 2022 Conference of the North American Chapter of the Association for Computational Linguistics: Human Language Technologies*, pages 3149–3158.

Mladen Karan, Prashant Khare, Patrick Healey, and Matthew Purver. 2021. Mitigating topic bias when detecting decisions in dialogue. In *Proceedings of the 22nd Annual Meeting of the Special Interest Group on Discourse and Dialogue*, pages 542–547.

Misha Khalman, Yao Zhao, and Mohammad Saleh. 2021. Forumsum: A multi-speaker conversation summarization dataset. In *Findings of the Association for Computational Linguistics: EMNLP 2021*, pages 4592–4599.

Farshad Kiyoumarsi. 2015. Evaluation of automatic text summarizations based on human summaries. *Procedia - Social and Behavioral Sciences*, 192:83–91.

Qian Liu, Bei Chen, Jian-Guang Lou, Bin Zhou, and Dongmei Zhang. 2020. Incomplete utterance rewriting as semantic segmentation. In *Proceedings of the*

2020 Conference on Empirical Methods in Natural Language Processing, pp. 2846–2857.

Luca Lugini, Christopher Olshefski, Ravneet Singh, Diane Litman, and Amanda Godley. 2020. Discussion tracker: Supporting teacher learning about students' collaborative argumentation in high school classrooms. In *Conference Proceedings of the 28th International Conference on Computational Linguistics.*

Gabriel Murray and Steve Renals. 2008. Detecting action items in meetings. In *International Workshop on Machine Learning for Multimodal Interaction*, pages 208–213. Springer.

Zhufeng Pan, Kun Bai, Yan Wang, Lianqiang Zhou, and Xiaojiang Liu. 2019. Improving open-domain dialogue systems via multi-turn incomplete utterance restoration. In *Proceedings of the 2019 Conference on Empirical Methods in Natural Language Processing and the 9th International Joint Conference on Natural Language Processing (EMNLP-IJCNLP), pp. 1824-1833.*

Weizhen Qi, Yu Yan, Yeyun Gong, Dayiheng Liu, Nan Duan, Jiusheng Chen, Ruofei Zhang, and Ming Zhou. 2020. Prophetnet: Predicting future n-gram for sequence-to-sequence pre-training. *arXiv preprint arXiv:2001.04063.*

Colin Raffel, Noam Shazeer, Adam Roberts, Katherine Lee, Sharan Narang, Michael Matena, Yanqi Zhou, Wei Li, Peter J Liu, et al. 2020. Exploring the limits of transfer learning with a unified text-to-text transformer. *J. Mach. Learn. Res.*, 21(140):1–67.

Hui Su, Xiaoyu Shen, Rongzhi Zhang, Fei Sun, Pengwei Hu, Cheng Niu, and Jie Zhou. 2019. Improving multi-turn dialogue modelling with utterance rewriter. In *Proceedings of the 57th Annual Meeting of the Association for Computational Linguistics*, pages 22–31.

Sansiri Tarnpradab, Fei Liu, and Kien A Hua. 2017. Toward extractive summarization of online forum discussions via hierarchical attention networks. In *The Thirtieth International Flairs Conference.*

Dakuo Wang, Ming Tan, Chuang Gan, and Haoyu Wang. 2022. Summarization of group chat threads. US Patent 11,238,236.

Author Index

Association for Computational Linguistics
209 N. Eighth Street
Stroudsburg, Pennsylvania 18360

ISBN 978-1-7138-6311-3

9 781713 863113

CURRAN ASSOCIATES INC.
proceedings.com